knowledge café

for

INTELLECTUAL PRODUCT
AND
INTELLECTUAL CAPITAL

Warsaw 2001

knowledge café

for

INTELLECTUAL PRODUCT
AND
INTELLECTUAL CAPITAL

editors

STEFAN KWIATKOWSKI
CHARLES STOWE

Published by: Leon Koźmiński
Academy of Entrepreneurship and Management
Jagiellońska Street 59, 00-987 Warsaw
Poland
Warsaw 2001

Production editor: *Marek B. Kamiński*
Cover design: *Paweł Rosołek*

ISBN 83-86846-65-8

Typesetting by: "Polico-Art", Warsaw, Borowskiego Street 2
Printed by: Z.P. "Hera", Warsaw, Golędzinowska Street 10

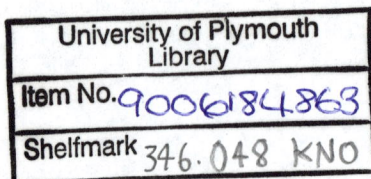

CONTENTS

Stefan Kwiatkowski

JOIN US FOR THE KNOWLEDGE CAFÉ ON INTELLECTUAL ENTREPRENEURSHIP FOR SUSTAINABLE DEVELOPMENT...

Abstract

The study of entrepreneurship is the study of individuals, systems, environmental factors that result in human activity that creates wealth through satisfaction of human needs in a voluntary market-based economy. Such understanding of entre preneurship encourages research on those factors that enhance standard of living, promote employment and provide ongoing, legitimate business and income that support sustainable development. Entrepreneurship, in this light, is not the removal of wealth from one party to another, but the creation of new wealth that arises from social and economic synergy. It is not a primitive, early capitalism throat to throat competition of zero sum game character, but a cooperative game for better living against the ever changing and ever smarter Nature. Entre preneurship understood this way is what we consider intelle ctual entrepreneurship.

This knowledge café involves a diversified group of people from different countries working in different organizations. They have conducted research both independently of this knowledge café and specifically for this publication. Through an intense pre-seminar dialog and through the very event itself we will have tremendously enriched our knowledge of intellectual entrepreneurship.

THE ONE AND MANY WORLDS

We all live in one world, and are often reminded of that through global disasters caused by Nature, by Mankind, or by both of them joining forces for destruction. The majority of us tend to perceive this world as fragmented, separated by natural and artificial boundaries, and not easily accessible by all. In addition to the purely physical, economic and political reasons that constraint our holistic understanding of the world, we impose our own mental barriers to global understanding. We build our own road-maps to give us orientation and direction but our maps reflect our cultural biases. We hear there is a developed world, and an under-developed one. There even exists the misdeveloped world. Are their boundaries clearly defined? Are they not overlapping? We often hear about growing connectivity, growing speed, continuous change, discontinuities, blur, chaos ... All these phenomena can be neither neglected nor overlooked by those studying contemporary social, political and economic systems. They render categorization and systematization difficult, if not totally impossible. Yet we need some categories just to orient ourselves. At least to start with, or to depart from.

As figure 1 is intended to illustrate, there is just one world, non-categorized and difficult to comprehend. But still, there is a need to develop some categories to use while attempting to grasp and comprehend what we try to study and understand. We should recognize that the non-categorized world (the world which really exists) is multidimensional, and permanently changing. This is what makes it so difficult to comprehend. The categorized world (the world which we assume as some distant approximation of the real one) is not unchangeable, not stable. It also changes, but it is just assumed to have less dimensions and elements. Assumed, since it is constructed with mere purpose of better understanding of real processes taking place in the real world.

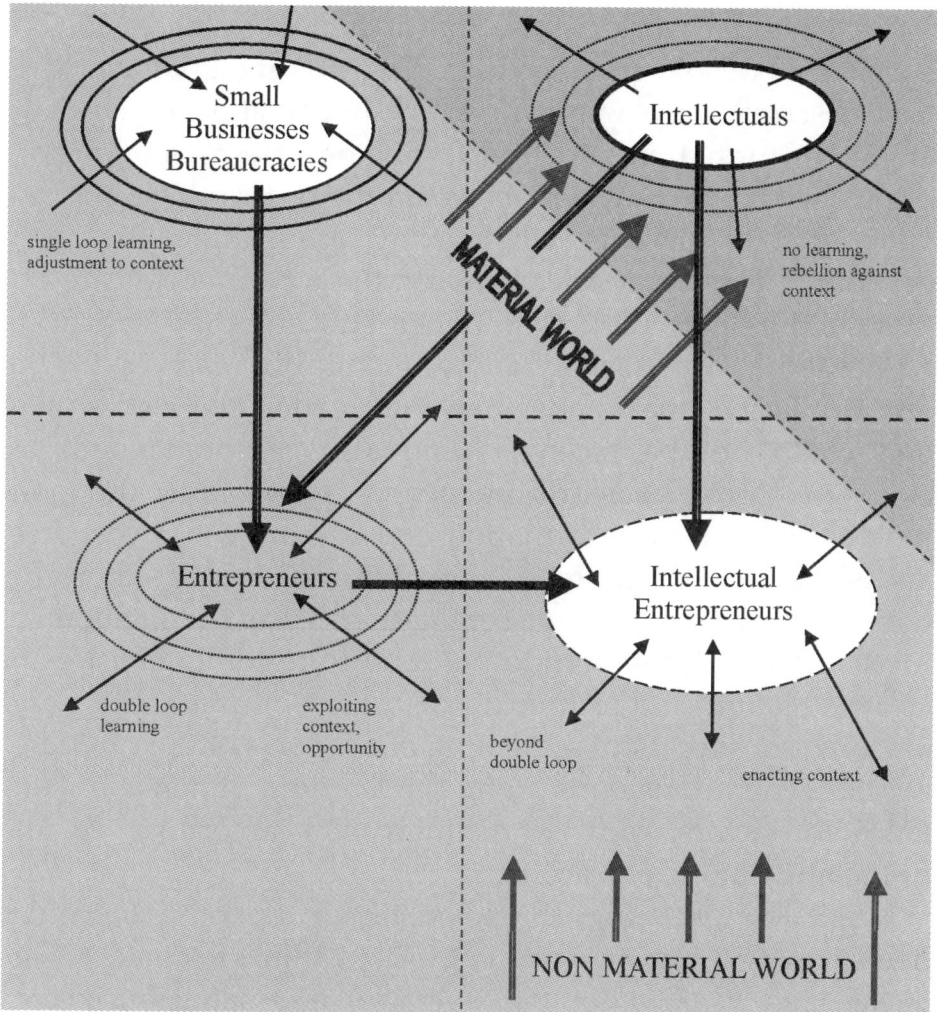

Figure 1

Within the simplistic approximation of the real world which figure 1 is intended to illustrate there are two main divides worth highlighting.

The first division is between the old XIX and early XX century MATERIAL WORLD that could be characterized as fabricating the fabric of the wealth of nations in the fabric, and the one in which we already live, NON-MATERIAL WORLD, in which information is the main factor of formation and transformation.

The material world is one that is bound by necessities of survival: food, shelter, security. The non-material world is best described as a world in which information is the main engine of formation and transformation of economic factors of production. Somewhere, between the past and present, we have shifted towards what many are calling the 'new economy'. The boundaries between these two worlds are not that solid as they used to be when education (at least at its higher levels) was socially and economically reserved for the few privileged ones, and when information traveled slowly and could not be received (and also comprehended) by everyone. Material world is deeply penetrating the non-material one, since information and ideas are not cost free, and since there needs to be some material infrastructure for their development and dissemination. Also the creators of ideas and of information do not tend to reside in cloisters of knowledge, but rather quickly discover both necessities and amenities of successful marketing of products of their minds.

The second division is along the learning dimension. Four kinds of actors can be distinguished according to the dominating mode of learning.

Single loop learning, characteristic for repetitive behavior, helps the organization or individuals to adjust to context. This is the kind of behavior bureaucracies and small businesses encourage. Where there is no change, such behavior can facilitate survival at individual level. So it is characteristic for a stable and consistent world. But there is very limited, if any, space here for individual growth, for self-actualization, for becoming. It is seemingly reserved for another actor – the intellectual. In this petrified world, intellectual has limited opportunities to interact with other actors, however. He would rather teach them. But since his teaching will be probably not comprehended, he might be deprived of the feedback from his potential listeners. Thus he does not learn. He can only preach and rebel against the social, political, or economic context. Needless to say, these two kinds of actors can coexist in categorized, petrified environment where they are led by completely differing values – material ones (small businesses and bureaucracies), and non-material ones (intellectuals). The main facilitator of this co-existence, or rather parallel existence, is visibility of social, economic and political barriers between people and institutions. Another words, it is the very essence of social, political and economic divisions that exist in the categorized world.

These divisions fade with entrepreneur's entrance. His behavior is based on questioning rather than accepting the prevailing norms of social and economic conduct. Hence double loop learning and innovation which is naturally contingent on it. Led by opportunity, the entrepreneur tries not to adjust to the context (by doing what others do), but rather to exploit it (by doing it differently). This demiurge of social and economic change still operates in the material world, but with all technological changes accelerating at tremendous speed the entrepreneur quickly realizes that the boundaries between that world and the other one of non-material character are meaningless and not relevant for business success or mere survival. So he gradually moves where pursuit of opportunity leads him. He moves to a different kind of behavior based on still another learning mode – the one I coined "beyond double loop". And here he meets a stranger, an actor from completely different theater, an inhabitant of a different world, a person speaking completely different language – an intellectual either tempted to enter the world of business, or forced to do it by biological and economic necessities. This is how intellectual entrepreneurship originates. Its beginnings are not easy to comprehend, not simple to follow and study. But results are amazing and dramatic. They are convincing and mesmerizing.

UNDERLYING PROCESSES

At least in the developed world two phenomena are radically changing the social and economic architecture of the market. The first one is expansion and diversification of both formal and non-formal education, and the second one – a gradual shift of market composition of products and services away from prevailingly material towards intellectual ones. Also intellectual content of tangible products increases dramatically. These phenomena are closely interrelated and affected by changes in broadly understood information and telecommunication technologies (ICT).

The growing role of intellectual products is visible on both consumer and industrial markets. On both these markets almost purely intellectual products, often devoid of their material supplement, successfully compete with those which clearly dominated several years ago. Thus, in manufacturing we witness expansion of technical consultancy – a purely intellectual and marketable component contributing to value creation in a client organization through technology development. In tourism or finance the same role is played by consultancy offered by various advisors. The Internet is competing with traditional printed media, often rendering material "wrapping" of intellectual product obsolete. Similar changes are observable in medicine, arts, and education itself. The intellectual component is substantially increasing in all products and services. From agriculture to steel manufacturing new processes of production have radically changed all major industries. The intellectual component of production of crops now involves satellite technology to map precisely the application of fertilizers and water, and to monitor environmental and climatic changes. The production of steel is much more than the application of energy and raw materials by brute manpower. It involves sophisticated continuous mill furnaces. While productivity has increased in most industries resulting in less direct labor to produce more goods, this productivity increase is backed by a new generation of computer programmers, computer engineers, process control experts, environmental experts, etc. In short, even in heavy industry, the intellectual component has dramatically increased during the past years.

Growing educational achievement levels and standards contribute towards further diversification of social needs on one hand and to bigger supply of potentially new entrepreneurs on the other. Intellectual products need new intellectual entrepreneurs. And with growing commercialization of all spheres of human life there are more instances of intellectuals turned entrepreneurs. Intellectuals also move towards entrepreneurship in non-intellectual, traditional businesses. There are countless examples of glaring business success of people with academic education and high standing in sociology, physics, mathematics or philosophy. Entering business world, they offer not new products only, but also new perceptions, procedures and – as a consequence – new kinds of management processes. All of this is especially visible in the countries under social, economic and political transformation where government support for intellectual life dramatically decreases and market gradually replaces central regulation. The implications for these countries themselves, and for the world community at large are rather obvious. Unless the intellectuals are certain they can create wealth and/or play socially acceptable roles, they will likely use their capabilities and talents in other directions - the non-productive, the non-constructive, and even destructive ones.

The phenomenon of intellectual entrepreneurship is not confined to the countries under economic and social transformation, however. Social and market demand on one hand, and growing education and sophistication of entrepreneurs on the other result in intellectualization of all spheres of economic life. This is a ubiquitous process that might be more visible in countries under transformation. Still it is probably more profound in the developed ones, simply because of the already achieved levels of education, and of consumption of other non-material products. But this process is also present and increasingly important in developing countries. Increasingly important because of both negative consequences of lack of opportunity and challenge to productively utilize intellectual capabilities, and of positive ones, resulting from possible enhancement of endogenous capacities for sustainable development.

Intellectual entrepreneurship is not only one possible kind of entrepreneurship, but an aspect of any successful entrepreneuring as well. A study of it involves not only research on entrepreneu-ring intellectuals but also on intellectual features of any successful entrepreneurship. Through studying intellectual entrepreneurs we detect thee features of entrepreneurship which are contemporarily necessary for, or at least facilitating, entrepreneurial success. We also get an opportunity to better understand the growing intellectual content of economic activity of individual entrepreneurs and of their companies. As we explore the nature of intellectual entrepreneurship, we unravel its potential for improving standard of living and for contributing to sustainable development at both the individual and societal level.

POSSIBLE APPROACHES TO MANAGEMENT

Entrepreneurship is part of management theory and practice. It is most often defined as approach to, part of, or even dimension of management. Management is an art and science of resource handling. The more resources we have, the more important is their efficient use, their administration. Administration is about already created resources, about accumulated wealth. Entrepreneurship is about resource creation, creation of wealth. Both approaches to resource handling are always present in management. But from the macro (and regional or specific sector) development perspective the very crucial question is which prevails - wealth administration or wealth creation.

The study of entrepreneurship is the study of individuals, systems, environmental factors that result in human activity that creates wealth through satisfaction of human needs in a voluntary market-based economy. This definition of entrepreneurship encourages research on those factors that enhance standard of living, promote employment and provide ongoing, legitimate business and income that support sustainable development. Entrepreneurship, in this light, is not the removal of wealth from one party to another, but the creation of new wealth that arises from social and economic synergy. It is not a primitive, early capitalism throat to throat competition of zero sum game character, but a cooperative game for better living against the ever changing and ever smarter (if not even vicious) Nature.

Most literature on entrepreneurship comes from America, so far the only truly entrepreneurial society of the world. Entrepreneurship was for long time defined in that country as "creation of something of value from nothing", or – to make this definition more acceptable – "... from practically nothing". The initial study of intellectual entrepreneurship indicates that this very "nothing" becomes the quintessence of new kind of entrepreneurship.

Both managers and "traditional" entrepreneurs have always dealt with material resources. They administer them and create them; create and administer. For intellectual entrepreneurs, it is not visible material capital, but invisible intellectual one that they start with. The resources they use and leverage are personal (often tacit) knowledge and personal networks. They rather embrace business challenge (sometimes out of sheer curiosity) than seize or tap opportunities, which is typical of vintage entrepreneur.

Entrepreneurship is often incidental for them, just an instance of reaction to environment change. But once enacted, concrete venture breeds new challenges, fascination, and both physical and emotional involvement. Intellectual entrepreneurs learn that the best way to predict the future is to create it. And while doing this, they discover the joy of creating a win-win type of personal business relationships. Thus they do not only leverage and further develop their personal human capital, but they also create conditions for development of organizational, structural and customer capital.

NEW KIND OF ENTREPRENEURSHIP

As intellectual entrepreneurs join the business world, they face same standards and tests other business actors do. But due to their already achieved social status (they are usually welcome in many places, welcome to perform varied jobs and functions), their familiarity with criticism, and their readiness to experience the unknown, they seem to have less risk aversion than traditional entrepreneurs. Their learning mode is also different. They neither adjust to existing context (single loop learning), nor exploit it (double loop learning). They see what and where others do not see, and have both competence and courage to enact what becomes a new context. All of this allows them to accept instability, and to incorporate change into the very systems they design to deal with reality. They have not only sensibility to but also comprehension of chaos. While anchoring themselves to their own business, they not only continue seemingly chaotic behavior but also encourage chaos and teach their partners not to fight it but rather to deal with it.

In any growing and developing venture most tensions are generated by unavoidable conflicts between requirements imposed by resource creation (the very essence of entrepreneurship) and by resource handling (the very essence of administration). Successful intellectual entrepreneurs do not resemble traditional Schumpeterian creative destructors. They are neither neces-sarily destructive in their creation process, nor are they necessarily to be destroyed by their potential successors. They are not "one season winners". They start and continue their business adventure as chaos tamers. Unlike Schumpeterian heroes, they combine social roles and functions of innovators, inventors and capitalists (intellectual capitalists!). Thus, without any doubt, they face personal risk of failure. And, once successful, they learn how to combine the administrative function of resource handling with requirements imposed by the need for continuous innovation. They learn a need of constant change. They seldom destruct and seldom tame people. They manage chaos and thrive on opportunities it opens to the knowledgeable and the courageous.

PRELIMINARY RESEARCH AND ITS FUTURE DIRECTIONS

The systematic study of phenomenon of intellectual entre-preneurship is only beginning. The term was used in 1996 independently by Robert Chia (University of Essex), and by Thomas Dandridge (Grand Valley State University, Michigan), Bengt Johannisson (Växjö University) & Stefan Kwiatkowski (Leon Koźmiński Academy of Entrepreneurship and Management). During the same year some empirical cases of successful intellectual entrepreneurship were identified by Dandridge in the USA, Johannisson in Sweden and Kwiatkowski in Poland. A more intensive and better-structured study of intellectual entrepreneurship was carried out in Poland from 1997 to 1999 under the grant of Polish Committee of Scientific Research. Although still exploratory in nature, the research was conducted to clarify several hypotheses generated during the very initial stage of empirical study. The underlying assumption was that economic growth, social change, development, and sustainability at the level of the firm, sector or society, require new managerial skills, new kinds of organizational learning, new resources and new ways of dissemination and application of scientific and technological advances. In May of 1998, UNESCO/EOLSS[1] Chair in Intellectual Entrepreneurship for Sustainable Development in the World of Work and Higher Education was founded at the Leon Koźmiński Academy of Entrepreneurship and Management in Warsaw with the goal of researching the issues related to intellectual entrepreneurship and sustainable development.

The idea is getting popular. In 1997, a professional development program in Intellectual Entrepreneurship was established at the University of Texas at Austin. Its mission is "... to help students realize the value of their expertise, discover their disciplinary identity, and become successful academic professio-nals"[2]

Within the UNESCO/EOLSS Chair the research is conducted in three societal sectors, at three levels:
- industry – the level of the firm and of its manager/ /entrepreneur,
- academe – the level of knowledge creator and disseminator,
- school – the student level.

All this research is based on intensive interviews and surveys. Longitudinal studies of individual ventures/ /enterprises have also been initiated.

Research conducted in the industry clearly indicates a broadly perceived need for new managerial skills and for new modes of organizational learning. It also illustrates

---

[1] EOLSS is Encyclopedia of Life Support Systems

[2] Developing Intellectual Entrepreneurship, 2001, The Scientist, March 5, page 32

growing product diversification and intellectualization on both industrial and consumer markets. Furthermore, it has revealed that people with non-business education have enjoyed great business success. One serious question requiring both longitudinal and cross-cultural studies is to what degree the phenomena that are observed in Poland and some other post-socialist countries are typical throughout the world. Are they not simply resulting from deregulation and decentralization, representing a clear example of deferred entrepreneurship, impossible under central planning regimes?

In the academe, leading scientists representing natural and management sciences are asked about the content and goals of their teaching, about the reasons of evident business success of non-business graduates, and about the skills and structures needed for application of scientific advances to successful business ventures. The initial results suggest that in so moderately developed countries as Poland or Latvia natural science education constitutes a very solid base for both understanding development of science and technology, and for practical application of their results to varied businesses. Professors of natural sciences seem to be emphasizing the "Paradigm-shifting mentality", claimed to be necessary for sustained success in contemporary changing world, much more often than management professors. This is probably caused by the fact that contemporary experimental research itself becomes an entrepreneurial and managerial venture requiring orchestration of intellectual and material resources. The very participation in it might then be a good preparation for eventual business ventures.

Our research conducted in tertiary and secondary level schools has been so far less conclusive. It is still in the preliminary stage and definitely requires both longitudinal and comparative (cross-cultural) perspective. The basic assumption here is that young people in secondary and tertiary level schools have some orientations, or attitudes towards entrepreneurship and management, and that these approaches can (should?) evolve as a result of formal and informal education, and of social maturation.

SUSTAINABILITY AT SOCIETAL LEVEL AND AT NEW BUSINESS LEVEL

Our empirically conceived of research does not aim yet at macroeconomic conclusions. But at least the most obvious ones should be signaled.

♦ Regardless of achieved level of technological development, each nation needs different kinds of research, including the basic one, necessary to develop some new technologies, but above all – to facilitate communication with the world community in its future only common language – the language of science and technology. The most important element of this two-way communication is technology assessment necessary to understand possible applications and limitations of generic technologies (such as those on which broadly understood systems of ICT are based). The ability to successfully evaluate research encourages nations to participate in the global community. Natural science and engineering education will be always necessary in any country. These are all quite well known truths repeated at hundreds of high level international conferences addressing questions of sustainability of nations under conditions of ever growing cost of basic research and high class education, and of their alarmingly growing concentration in a few developed countries. Empirical data on educational background of successful new business founders could shed some fresh light on this problem. There is a need for much broader and deeper research to provide a thorough analysis of this phenomenon.

- Sustainability at the national level is no doubt directly dependent on growth of a viable business sector. And here our initial stage analytical study of new Polish businesses started by intellectual and non-intellectual entrepreneurs reveals a startling reality. The first ones grow faster, bring more profit and employment, need less outside financial capital, become unquestionable business leaders. The latter, although originally often also amazingly successful, seem to be much more vulnerable to market competition, and not seldom disappear unable to withstand the 'winds of creative destruction'. It would be quite naive to attribute this difference to just personal characteristics of the entrepreneur, although, through his/her human capital accumulation they certainly play significant role. Much more important seems to be the nature of innovation on which new venture is based.

  Intelligent enterprising requires a global business perspective. Business success might be more volatile than perceived in a local context. Successful business navigation is impossible without the ability to perceive both the immediate and remote environments. But mere perception will not suffice. True, it could save money and effort while facilitating safe exit. By no means, however, will it guarantee business success. Success seems to be contingent on the nature of innovation.

For the purpose of brevity let us distinguish two types of innovations – original and imitative ones. For closed systems and highly regulated markets both types of innovation might bring similar effects. This is why Richard Cantillon's XVIII century definition of entrepreneur as market equilibrator through buying low and selling high is appealing to contemporary critics of Schumpeterian idea of innovation as a force of creative destruction. Globalization of the world requires very careful approach to the repeated platitude of context specificity of innovation. In our contemporary globalized world, innovation is context-specific only if it contains some new elements specific for this and only this context. If it is merely repetition, however, of the same product or same process introduced somewhere else (a typical 'me to' behavior) the seemingly context specific innovator is quite vulnerable to fierce competition. While the initial risk of introducing an innovation transferred from another place is limited, the entrepreneur faces an unlimited potential for competition since the barriers for others is so low.

In discussing features of entrepreneurship we arrived at classical considerations of free competitive market. Such market seems to exist in small business realm only. Real entrepreneurship is impossible without original (certainly also context specific) innovation temporarily reducing competitive forces of the market. Here, intellectual entrepreneurs play a vital role as economic and social agents of change. Through participation in different environments, through their openness and criticism, but above all due to the nature of their learning process (beyond double loop), they become contemporary heroes of entrepreneurship. Their behavior pattern is neither Cantillonian nor Schumpeterian. It is difficult to comprehend and explain within a traditional perspective and with the use of traditional tools of research and reasoning. But it is certainly attractive and worthwhile to study!

*

*   *

This knowledge café involves a diversified group of people from different countries working in different organizations. They have conducted research both independently of this knowledge café and specifically for it. Through intense pre-seminar dialog and through the very event itself we will have tremendously enriched our knowledge of intellectual entrepreneurship, intellectual capital and intellectual product.

This publication represents a sharing of some of the inputs we see as the most important and vital at this stage. But we have still much to explore on the nature of intellectual entrepreneurship and its relevance for promoting sustainable development. To this end, we will devote much more time and lots of coffee... Please join us!

Jan Kozłowski

INTELLECTUAL CAPITAL, KNOWLEDGE MANAGEMENT AND INTELLIGENT PRODUCTS IN THE LIGHT OF CATALOGUE AND ABSTRACT DATA BASIS

Abstract

In mid 1990. a new area in management sciences around terms "intellectual capital"(IC) and "knowledge management" (KM) has crystallized. In a few years a new IC/KM definitions and taxonomies, measurement techniques, empirical observations and recommendations were built. This new knowledge was immediately used for constructing managerial methods, as well in forecasting and economics. New professions arose around IC/KM. In the same time IC/KM gave rise or re-defined the whole group of cognate terms, like e.g. human resources, intangible resources, intellectual assets, intellectual capital, intellectual capitalism, knowledge assets, knowledge capital, knowledge capitalism, organizational capital, relational capital, structural capital, tacit knowledge. A new language, new research in managerial practices, and a new ways of thinking have been born.

On the foundation of data basis (OCLC data bank) and document delivery systems (ProQuest) paper shows birth and growth of literature on three topics mentioned in the title. For many reasons intellectual capital, knowledge management and intelligent products seem to deserve our attention. All three are different expressions of the same deep changes occurring in the contemporary societies and economies – discovering *intangible resource* as an important kind of *capital*, drift towards "knowledge society", and "knowledge economy". Analysis of them show how we conceptualize changes and what intellectual tools we invent and use to grasp and influence these changes.

A. O. Lovejoy's[1] book on the history of ideas led to many books and papers discussing the typical phases of ideas' life. "There is often one period when a new idea is *conceivable*, as evidenced by the printed word; another when it becomes *topical*, as shown by multiple discussions; and sometimes another when it becomes manifestly *effective* – stated Lancelot Law Whyte. Moreover ideas may undergo cycles of influence, and may be temporarily inhibited, and consciously, transformed. (...) Ideas are not discovered once and for all and passed on like museum object. They are part of the life though and must come to life, be kept alive, and be made productive in the process of human minds and the activities of individuals."[2]

The concept of the history of ideas might be of great interest not only for historian, but also for other social and human scientists. It is also interesting to describe not only ideas with long history (like e.g. classical Lovejoy's "chain of being" or Whyte's "unconsciousness"), but also ideas relatively new ones and emerging.

New electronic bibliographical techniques allow us to show birth and growth of literature on certain topics. Description of new emerging topics might be of use not only for scholars, but also practitioners.

For many reasons intellectual capital, knowledge management and intelligent products seem to deserve our attention. All three are different expressions of the same deep changes

---

[1] Arthur O. Lovejoy, The Great Chain of Being. A Study of History of Idea, Harvard University Press, 1936.

[2] Lancelot Law Whyte, The Unconscious before Freud, Tavistock Publications, 1962, p. 15.

occurring in the contemporary societies and economies – discovering *intangible resource* as an important kind of *capital*, drift towards "knowledge society" and "knowledge economy". Analysis of them show how we conceptualize changes and what intellectual tools we invent and use to grasp and influence these changes.

This paper is based on using computer access reference services to find abstracts and information on books and articles containing English terms of "intellectual capital", "knowledge management" and "intelligent products" in their titles and/or key words. Information was collected from data basis accessible through one of the most popular and used OCLC data bank. OCLC WorldCat, ArticleFirst, Social Sciences Abstracts, WilsonSelectPlus, Business and Management Practices were the electronic reference services consulted for this review. WorldCat – the biggest book on-line catalogue in the world contains 41,000,000 records describing written sources from the beginning of written materials kept in library stocks up to present time. ArticleFirst covers over 12,000 journals and contains over 9,277,000 records from 1990 to present. Social Science Abstracts consists of over 550 journals, over 600 000 records, from 1983 to present. WilsonSelectPlus indexes over 1300 sources, over 320,000 records 1994 to present. Business and Management Practices lists over 795 sources, over 130,000 records, from 1995 to present. Additionally, the ProQuest data basis accessible through Higher School of Business – NLU at Nowy Sącz was used.

BRIEF HISTORY OF THREE CONCEPTS

The intellectual interest for three above-mentioned concepts is not equal. During the past century up to the end of 2000 year there were 435 books that used the expressions "knowledge management", 80 for "intellectual capital" and only 1 for "intelligent products" in their titles. The meanings of the "intellectual capital" and "intelligent products" were much more homogenous than "knowledge management". However, these proportions between materials concerning these concepts and other sources of information (especially in Internet) might be different.[3]

Word co-occurrence with "intellectual capital" (IC) and "knowledge management" (KM) are as follows: books with "intellectual capital" in titles the most frequently contain also terms "success in business" and "human capital" (26%) and "creative abilities in business" (20%) in their bibliographical descriptions; 8% of the books with "knowledge management" contain terms "expert systems" and "database management".[4] However, one should remember that usually word co-occurrence changes in time.

Both concepts of "intellectual capital" and "knowledge management" had started before the name has been found and its meaning has stabilized and, on other hand, the names - "intellectual capital" and "knowledge management" – were previously used in different meanings.

The expression "intellectual capital" (as recorded in WorldCat) was first used in 1975 by George F. Feiwell in the book entitled *The Intellectual Capital of Michal Kalecki: A Study in Economic Theory and Policy* (Knoxville : University of Tennessee Press). This comprehensive 583 pages monograph is registered in 500 libraries registered by OCLC system. However in 1981 in Spanish translation: *Michal Kalecki: contribucio-*

---

[3] OCLC WorldCat.
[4] OCLC WorldCat.

nes a la teoría de la política económica term "intellectual capital" was omitted.

The next time IC was used in book title just in 1990.: in Christine D. Keen M.A. thesis *Business Ethics and Intellectual Capital Complications for an Information Economy* (George Washington University, 1992) and in the book by William J. Hudson *Intellectual Capital: How to Build It, Enhance It, Use It* (New York : J. Wiley, 1993). In 1993 and 1994 term was used 3 times each, in 1996 – 5 times, in 1997 – 15, in 1998 and 1999 – 17 each, and in 2000 – 15 (esp. this last number might increase). In mid 1995, the term's meaning seemed to stablize (see e.g. Zucker, Lynne G.; Darby, Michael R.; Armstrong, Jeff., and others, *Intellectual Capital and the Firm: The Technology of Geographically Localized Knowledge Spillovers*, 1994; *Managing, Measuring & Valuing your Company's Intellectual Capital*, 1995, or Annie Brooking, *Intellectual Capital*, 1996).

The history of "knowledge management" – now used often as equivalent or supplement to "intellectual capital" – is slightly different. The first time term "knowledge management" was used was in 1966 in the context of information management and retrieval systems by Hungarian author Pal Tomcsanyi (A kutatói ismeretgazdálkodás és kézi lyukkártya technikája, English title on page facing *Knowledge Management in Research Work and Hand-Sorted Punch Card Techniques*, Budapest). Chida and Apté's book, *Expert Knowledge Management for Multi-level Modelling: With an Application to Well-log Analysis* was published 18 years later (New Brunswick, N. J.: Dept. of Computer Science, Rutgers University, 1984). Apte's book initiated the use the term KM in the information technology context. For many years KM was used in book titles treating with topics referring to the electronic and traditional data management (management and artificial intelligence, decision support systems, data base management system, computer programs, design knowledge management system, data processing, information resources management, information services, indexing, and the like).

Around 1993, Karl M. Wiig introduced a new and broader meaning of knowledge management in *Knowledge Management Foundations: Thinking about Thinking : How People and Organizations Create, Represent, and Use Knowledge*, 1993; *Knowledge Management: The Central Management Focus for Intelligent-acting Organizations*, 1994, *Knowledge Management Methods: Practical Approaches to Managing Knowledge*, 1995, all three published by Arlington, Tex. Schema Press). Since that time a new broader meaning slowly pushed out the old ones. The number of books with KM in their titles increased steadily (7 in 1992, 1993 and 1994 each; 14 – 1996; 29 – 1997; 56 – 1998; 102 – 1999; 81 – 2000; esp. the last number might increase).

"Intelligent products" has not become a comparable *schlagwort* (only one book and only five uses in journals registered in Article One. The first one was titled "Development of An Intelligent Product Design System: Integration Strategies," Roy, Utpal; Bharadwaj, Balaji; Sarathy, Sriprakash, and others, *Applied artificial intelligence AAI*. vol. 9 no. 6 1995).[5]

Summing up, it is significant that exactly in the same time in mid 1990, three important concepts stabilized their meaning and gained momentum.

In the subsequent parts of this chapter, the main thesis of the articles on IC, KM and intelligent product are summarized on the basis of data base abstracts. Using abstracts from the data bases, provides insight on how those concepts were developed. The abstracts allow for a quick exploration of what kind of definitions were formulated, the taxonomies proposed, measurement techniques, rules and observations described, and how these concepts were used as a "crystallization" points of managerial techniques.

---

[5] WorldCat; ArticleFirst.

INTELLECTUAL CAPITAL AND SURROUNDINGS: DEFINITIONS AND TAXONOMIES

A common theme in the literature is that wealth will ultimately move from natural resources owners to those who
control ideas and knowledge. Intellectual capital is almost
impossible to measure, but its returns can be nearly infinite.[6]
The global marketplace of the 21st century will reward firms
that value entrepreneurial risk-taking, invest heavily in developing their IC, promote individual growth, and adopt
policies that are environmentally friendly.[7] It is often said that
the value of a company is based more on IC – organizational
culture, customer loyalty, and brand equity than on traditional financial measures (like price/earnings ratios, revenue
and market share).[8] IC can help to convert tacit knowledge
into an explicit, usable resources. IC is based on the conviction that intangible assets and external relationships with
customers/suppliers are often more valuable and critical to
success than tangible assets.[9] IC managing is sharing-
cooperative culture (instead of individualistic, competitive
business culture).[10]

Intangible resources include: human, organizational, relational and technological capital.[11] Intangibles might be broken

[6] Thomas A. Stewart, Now capital means brains, not just bucks (intellectual capitalism, ideas for 1991), *Fortune* v. 93 1991 p. 31-31.

[7] Shaker A. Zahra, The changing rule of global competitiveness in the 21 st
century, *Academy of Management Executive* v. 13 no. 1 1999 p. 36-42.

[8] Noah P. Barsky, Garry Marchant, The most valuable resource: measuring
and managing intellectual capital, *Strategic Finance Magazine*, v. 81 no. 8
2000 p. 58–62.

[9] Daniel L. Knight, Performance measures for increasing intellectual capital, *Strategy and Leadership* v. 27 no. 2 1999 p. 22–27.

[10] Bernadette E. Lynn, Intellectual capital: unearthing hidden value by
managing intellectual assets, *Ivey Business Journal* v. 64 no 3 2000 p. 48–52.

[11] Esteban Fernandez, Jose M. Montes, Camilo J. Vasques, Typology and
strategy analysis of intangible resources: A resource-based approach, *Tech-
novation* vol. 20, no. 2, 2000 p. 81–92.

down into four categories: market assets, such as brands and franchises; intellectual property, such as copyright; human-centered assets, including the knowledge of staff; and infrastructure assets, which concerns a company`s strength, corporate culture, and relationship with financial community.[12] Intangible liabilities encompass unrecorded and unrecognized and recorded and recognized ones.[13]

Intellectual assets could be divided into human capital, innovation, brand equity and network of relations.[14]

Knowledge creates continuum; from structured and codified to the unstructured and uncodified.[15] Knowing is defined as: distinction making, caring (keeping close attention), languaging, shaping the future.[16] Information theory should be considered as the basis for understanding knowledge and its transfer. Analogy compute/information and brain/knowledge is dangerous. E.g. it omits "tacit knowledge" and "tradition".[17] Knowledge confers advantage by enhancing one's ability to take action. Knowledge Capital (KC) depends on people to create it, but also for a management process to harness it in some value-creating way.[18]

[12] Sue Beenstock, The calculation IT can't make (Impact of information technology on business) *management Today* June 1998 p. 72–74.

[13] Michael G. Harvey, Robert F. Lusch, Balancing the intellectual capital books: Intangible liabilities, *European Management Journal* vol. 17 no 1 1999 p. 85–92.

[14] Thomas A. Stewart, Taking risk to the marketplace (intellectual asset risk management for knowledge companies) *Fortune* v. 141 no 5 2000 p. 424.

[15] Ted Gautschi, The knowledge continuum, *Design News*, vol. 54 (i.e. 55) no 12 1999 p. 170.

[16] Georg Van Krogh, Johan Roos, Five claims on knowing, *European Management Journal*, v.14 1996 p. 423–426.

[17] Karl-Erik Sveiby, Transfer of knowledge and the information processing professions, *European Management Journal* vol. 14 August 1996 p. 379––388.1

[18] J.P. Donlon, Harnessing knowledge, *Chief Executive* no 142 March 1999 p. 52-59.

Intellectual capital defined as conversion of brainpower into something that has value[19] consists of: human and structural,[20] human, structural and customer,[21] human, innovation, process and capital,[22] structural, relational and human,[23] human, structural, intellectual property,[24] human, renewal, structural, relationship.[25] There are different kinds of assets: market, intellectual property, human-centered and infrastructure,[26] human (all skills and capabilities of the people who work in an organization), relational (organizational connections: customers and clients), structural (organizational tone and capabilities),[27] human (the abilities of the individuals needed to provide solutions to customers), customer (the penetration, coverage, loyalty and profitability of customers), structural (the ability of the firm to satisfy market needs). Intellectual capital might also be divided into tacit (including beliefs and values) and explicit,[28] sum and synergy of a company's knowledge, experience, relationships, processes, discoveries, innovations,

---

[19] See footnote 5.

[20] John Roos, Exploring the concept of intellectual capital, *Long Range Planning*, vol. 31, no 1, 1998, p. 150–153. Human capital refers to the knowledge, skills and experience of employees. Structural capital refers to the extension and manifestation of human capital into innovations, business processes and relationships with dealers and others.

[21] Benedict Rogers, Are you capitalizing on your intellectual assets? *China Staff*, vol. V no. 8, p. 12–15.

[22] Mark E. Van Buren, A Yardstick for Knowledge Management, *Training & Development*, vol. 53, no. 5, 1999 p. 71–78.

[23] Andrew Wileman, A capital idea, *Management Today*, April 1999, p. 97.

[24] Steven D. Hyden, Michael J. Mard, R. Wade Wetherington, Identifying, protecting and valuing intellectual property, *Journal of Asset Protection*, vol. 3 no. 6 July/August 1998 p. 32–38.

[25] William Miller, Building the ultimate resource, *Management Review* vol. 88 no. 1 1999 p. 42–45.

[26] Timo Nyberg, Sami Saru, Aspects on high technology transfer, *International Journal of Technology Management*, vol. 18, no. 5, 1999, p. 604–609.

[27] See footnote 5.

[28] Hubert Saint-Onge, Tacit knowledge: the key to the strategic alignment of intellectual capital, *Strategy and Leadership*, v. 24 March/April 1996 p. 10–14.

market presence and community influence.[29] Market value equals book value + IC.[30] Intellectual entrepreneurship integrates many of the concepts of intellectual capital into the paradigm of the creation of high growth, entrepreneurial firms.[31]

Components of **organizational capital** include: external orientation, professional orientation, employee orientation and remaining organizational processes.[32] Organizational learning occur within team learning, cross-team learning and market learning.[33]

Structural capital is defined as the knowledge network allowing a firm to arrange, store, and provide access to the collective knowledge of all its employees and it offers pointers and access to learning resources. One of the main components of resources is repository, usually a database of knowledge and experience specific to a particular company.[34]

The idea of the **learning organization** was made popular after the publication of Peter Senge's book *The Fifth Discipline – the Art and Practice of the Learning Organization*.[35] Distin-

---

[29] See footnote 20. See also Johnson, William H. A., An integrative taxonomy of intellectual capital: Measuring the stock and flow of intellectual capital components in the firm, *"International journal of technology management"*, Volume 18, Number 5, pp. 562, 1999.

[30] See footnote 4.

[31] Kwiatkowski Stefan, Edvinsson Leif, Knowledge Cafe for Intellectual Entrepreneurship, Warsaw, 1999, and Kwiatkowski Stefan, Przedsiebiorczosc intelektualna, Warsaw, 2000

[32] Ursula Glunk, Celeste Wilderom, Predictors of organizational performance in small and medium-sized professional service firms, *International Journal of Technology Management*, vol. 16, no. 1/2/3 1998 p. 23–36.

[33] Gary S. Lynn, New product team learning: Developing and profiting from your knowledge capital, *California Management Review* v. 40 no 4 1998 p. 74–93.

[34] Daniel R. Tobin, Networking your knowledge (employee access to the company's collective information) *Management* Review, vol. 87 no. 4 April 1998, p. 46–48. See also Thomas A. Stewart, The case for managing structural capital, *Health Forum Journal*, v. 42 no. 3 1999 p. 30–33.

[35] Sultan Kermally, The learning organization, *European Management Journal* v. 15 April 1997 p. 208.

guishing characteristics of mutual learning is that people learn together and from each other. Mutual learning allows senior executives and employees at every level to: increase their ability, to work together effectively, to speed up organizational learning, to avoid duplicating mistakes.[36]

Three elements of the **knowledge capital** are: people, processes and technology.[37]

There is a significant overlap between knowledge management (KM), intellectual capital (IC) and learning organization concepts.[38] Elements of knowledge management/intellectual capital that foster real wisdom are: extensive education and training program; creativity as a vocational skill; counterintuitive thinking; searching for the essence; quality for the leadership; quality of though; a true understanding of values.[39]

R&D is considered as an investment that produces firm's long-term intellectual capital. There are connections between long-term R&D and innovation (in most technologies), recruitment, guaranteed entry into research networks that can give firms access to newly discovered technologies.[40]

Social capital is a new metric that gauges how the intellectual, civic and social well-being of a company contributes

[36] Stephen P. Kelner, Lois Slavin, The competitive strategy of mutual learning, *Training and Development* vol. 52 no 6 June 1998 p. 72-75.

[37] Mike Vollmer, Tessy Phillips, Growing intellectual capital: how it relates to the bottom line, *Offshore*, vol. 60 no. 3, 2000, p. 74, 100.

[38] Gearge Benson, Battle of the buzzwords (intellectual capital, knowledge management, and the learning organizations), *Training and* Development, vol. 51 July 1997 p. 51–52; Karl M. Wiig, Integrating intellectual capital and knowledge management, *Long Range Planning* vol. 30 June 1997 p. 399–405.

[39] Robert Galvin, Managing knowledge towards wisdom, *European Management Journal* vol. 14 August 1996 p. 374–378.

[40] Diana Hicks, Six reasons to do long-term research, *Research Technology Management*, vol. 42 no 4 1999 p. 8–11. Technology management: see Elias G. Careyannis, Jeffrey Alexander, The wealth of knowledge: converting intellectual property to intellectual capital in co-operative research and technology management settings, *International Journal of Technology Management*, vol. 18 no ¾, 1999, p. 326–352.

to the economic health of a country.[41] It is defined as an organization's emotional and spiritual resources that are critical to competitiveness and strategic efforts.[42]

There are also presented concepts of **knowledge capitalism**[43] and **intellectual capitalism**[44].

IC/KM MANAGERIAL TECHNIQUES

IC is a new management paradigm and a new accounting and management model. ICM supports corporate knowledge by building a new framework for growing, extracting, and measuring corporate value.[45]

The process of knowledge creation consists of a three stages. Stage one involves inquiring about causes, effects, relationships, and results; and then inferring the implications. Stage two entails inventing creative solutions focused on explicit and implicit issues and then inspiring others with a compelling case for change. Stage three is installing and testing solutions in partnership with clients and inspecting over the long term to see what is wrong and what is not.[46]

Particular methods and techniques. Management's inherited tendency is over-dependence on financial measures of performance. It partly stems from the difficulty of measuring

[41] David Stamps, Social capital, *Training*, vol. 35 no 11 1998 p. 44–46.

[42] Lovemore Mbigi, Managing Social Capital, *Training & Development*, vol. 54, no 1, 2000, p. 36–39.

[43] Burton-Jones, Alan, Knowledge capitalism: business, work, and learning in the new economy, Oxford [England]; New York, 1999, VIII, 248 p.: ill.

[44] Swanborg, Rick; Reck, Bob, Grow Your Own Consultants - INTELLECTUAL CAPITALISM Using in-house consultants helps retain all the intellectual capital a project generates. But beware: Many of these efforts fail, *CIO*, vol. 12, no 13/2 1999, p. 76.

[45] Ramona Dzinkowski, Mining intellectual capital, *Strategic Finance Magazin*, vol. 81 no 4 1999 p. 42–46.

[46] Stephen L. Cohen, Nena K. Backer, Making and mining intellectual capital: method or madness? *Training and Development*, vol. 53 no 9 1999 p. 46–50.

IC.[47] The aim of many tools is to map IC and to decant it into organizational networks and structures.[48] The new strategic focus in human resources management is return-on-employee investment. That goes along with the attitude shift of employers, who now view their workforce as IC – a complex body of individual talents and backgrounds that should be analyzed carefully and deployed for maximum benefit. The Ayers Group has following suggestions for maximizing return-on-employee investment: train employees; coach supervisors to build a leader image, improve work relationships, and strengthen teams; have senior managers fine-tune their management styles and delegate more work to lower-level managers; have managers to monitor the skills of staff-members and match those skills to current and future company needs.[49] Techniques to develop IC encompass increased training and expanded communication to other employees, customers and vendors.[50] IC may be protected by diversifying the ownership of essential knowledge through the promotion of teamwork, introducing learning programs to combat obsolescence, and administering golden handcuffs to retain key people.[51] Other strategies of managing IC include: participative development of systems supporting the management of skills (learning systems), information (information systems), experience (experience systems) and attitudes (compensation, selection, career development systems).[52] Mentoring relationship programs develop the skills, knowledge, and leadership abilities of new and seasoned professionals and strengthen

---

[47] See footnote 24.

[48] Keith Bradley, *Business Strategy Review*, vol. 8, no 1, 1997, p. 53–62

[49] No author, Trend Watch, *Training and Development*, vol. 52, no. 5, 1998, p. 12.

[50] Tom Brown, Ringing up, *Management Review*, vol. 87 1998 p. 47–49.

[51] See footnote 9.

[52] Vasilis Masoulas, Organizational requirements definition for intellectual capital management, *International Journal of Technology Management*, vol. 16 no 1–3 1998 p. 126–143.

employee commitment.[53] A firm's web site aims to increase the productivity, innovation, and creativity of natural work groups and cross-functional teams by synchronizing IC, imagination, and critical thinking skills within a pro-active problem solving framework.[54]

Leif Edvinsson presented an overview of the managerial techniques used in business.[55] Other examples included: Xerox Corp. which pioneered KM with a technique based on aligning knowledge sharing with business goals.[56] IBM uses own Intellectual Capital Management program.[57] Similarly, Sun Microsystems has its own internal system.[58] KM in Henkel company incorporates both "asking systems" and "answering systems" which are connected by the market research interface.[59] Apart from benchmarking the current processes of knowledge management, Henkel considered the creation of a transnational warehouse – the process of creating competitive knowledge by generating integrated (i.e. across sources) and international (i.e. across countries) insights as key tool.[60] Xerox is a pioneer of 'R&D in KM', a technique based on aligning knowledge sharing

[53] Max Messmer, Mentoring: building your company's intellectual capital, *HR Focus*, vol. 75 no 9 September 1998 p. 811–812.

[54] Greg Roberts, How to ensure your Web site is solving the right problems, *Marketing*, vol. 105 no 10 March 13 2000 p. 21.

[55] Leiff Edvinsson, Patrick Sullivan, Developing a model for managing intellectual capital, *European Management Journal*, vol. 14 August 1996 p. 356–364.

[56] Michael Hickins, Xerox shares its knowledge, *Management Review,* vol. 88 no. 8 September 1999 p. 40–45.

[57] K.-T. Huang, Capitalizing on intellectual assets, *IBM Systems Journal*, vol. 37 no 4 p. 570–383.

[58] James Brian Quinn, Strategic outsourcing: leveraging knowledge capabilities, *Sloan Management Review* vol. 40 no 4 Summer 1999 p. 9–21.

[59] Hans-Willi Schroiff, The Henkel Case: Creating Competitive Intellectual Capital, *Marketing & Research Today* vol. 27, no 4 1998 p. 148–155.

[60] Hans-Willi Schroiff, Esomar awards – Creating competitive intellectual capital – The Henkel case, Marketing and research today: the journal of the European Society for Opinion and Marketing Research, Volume 26, Number 4, pp. 148, 1998.

with business goals that allows workplace habits to drive the process.

Xerox aligns its KM practice with its business plan, and its overarching KM strategy is to create added value by capturing and leveraging knowledge. Xerox examined how social dynamics shaped the pattern of knowledge sharing to produce technologies that reflects such factors as work habits, the perceived benefits of sharing, and the context in which sharing is natural.[61] As a KM technique a *quiz* might be used.[62] Other technique is called *storytelling*. It can be combined with various recording methods that both spread the knowledge and capture the knowledge around certain events or projects. Both storytelling and *communities of practice* are organic means of growing knowledge. Storytelling requires a company culture that is tolerant of watching and recording. Communities of practice need the company infrastructure to find and reward moderators.[63] New tools for KM include tools to better control and reduce patent costs and tools to help the company to turn its knowledge into profitable products more quickly.[64] It also is suggested that companies can leverage the content of their accumulated knowledge by building collaborative communities[65].

Because employees like to be recognized for the contributions they made and because they prefer to work in an environment in which they feel valued and get real satisfaction from their work, it is important for managers to be more

[61] See footnote 50.

[62] Thomas A. Stewart, Grab a pencil – it's a knowledge quiz, *Fortune* v. 136 1997 p. 241–242.

[63] See footnote 31.

[64] Germeraad, 35/36.

[65] Havens, Charnell; Knapp, Ellen, Easing into knowledge management, *Strategy & leadership* Volume 27, Number 2, pp. 4, 1999.

pragmatic, and to practice openness in communicating their expectations to the workers.[66]

Mapping knowledge in a company in an important knowledge management tool for chief information officers in implementing KM in their organizations. Knowledge mapping is defined as the process of associating items of information or knowledge, preferably visually, in such a way that the mapping itself also creates additional knowledge. The mapping process often creates intellectual capital value through creation of new knowledge from discovering previously unknown relationships or gaps in expected ones. Knowledge maps are visual, intuitive, and accessible by huge numbers of workers. These maps show the relationships between the key components of business and IT, facilitating faster and more complete understanding, alignment, and communicating at all organizational levels. The knowledge maps also allow responsive "what-if" change to affect analysis. Users can immediately trace potential effect of changes of proposed processes or organizational structures on the corresponding IT systems and applications, or vice versa. IT users can extend the power of the map by integrating it with their own knowledge resources. An efficient knowledge map must evolve through use to remain up-to-date and accurate.[67]

A special method of upgrading social capital is based on African rituals. Such a technique can be utilized as a tool for auditing the dominant spirits and cultural values of an organization in a live, collective, and participative way. It can also be utilized as a framework for managing and transforming organization's social capital. In South Africa, big business and state organizations organize workshops integrating music, drumming, and dancing. Two common ritualistic elements of the workshops are storytel-

---

[66] No author, When intellectual capital starts heading for the door, *Management Today*, 1999 p. 9, 10.

[67] Edmond F. Vail, Knowledge Mapping: Getting Started With Knowledge Management, *Information Systems* management, vol. 16, no. 4 1999 p. 16––23. See footnote 39, and See footnote 42.

ling, and organizational myths and spirits. There are several spirits of management: the destructive spirit, the powerless spirit, the innovative spirit, the family spirit, the personal spirit, the spirit of truth, the restless spirit, and the relational spirit.[68]

Another aspect of KM consists of intellectual property management.[69]

OBSERVATIONS, RULES, SUGGESTIONS, RECOMMENDATIONS

Knowledge. Basic characteristics: messy; seeks community; travels via langue; is self-organizing; does not grow forever; will take care of itself in a supportive environment; and must be supported at multiple levels in a variety of ways; no one person can take responsibility for collective knowledge; too much rigidity and formality regarding knowledge results in the stultification of creativity; some knowledge systems more effective; the best approach to managing is not set in stone; the way in which knowledge is defined determines how it is managed.[70]

IC management. Market value equals book value plus intellectual capital, with book value usually only at the tip of the iceberg of wealth. The real value of the organization is below the visible surface, in its intellectual capital. Investments made in human capital, more competent and capable people developing better structural capital, result in leading to the development of more productive external capital, resulting in better financial performance.[71] A critical task for any

---

[68] See footnote 36.

[69] See Kerri Walsh, Taking Stock of Intellectual Capital, *Chemical Specialities*, vol. 1 no 5 1999 p. 46–49; Elias G. Carayannis, Alexander Jeffrey, *International Journal of Technology Management*, vol. 18, no 3–4 1999 p. 326–352; Justin Hibbard, *Information Week*, 1999 p. 50–61.

[70] Verna Alee, 12 Principles of Knowledge Management, *Training and Development*, vol. 51 November 1997 p. 71–74.

[71] See footnote 4.

organization is to turn the core competencies of few smart into core competencies of the whole organization.[72] A critical factor in the successful implementation of IC management strategy is to have supportive corporate culture that encourages cooperation, communication and creativity[73] or world-class and visionary executive teams. IC is method of both making and mining it.[74] IC management consists of gathering and warehousing the tacit knowledge of employees.[75] IC is a product of competence plus commitment; neither is sufficient by itself to provide a useful resource for company.[76] The task of employees is to invest, renew and leverage core capabilities. Thanks to core capabilities, employees are able to offer leading-edge value to their company and its customers: expanding intelligence, promoting creativity and innovation, and exercising integrity in relations.[77] IC can be evaluated by employing a cross-sectional team of managers and workers to 1) identify the knowledge that gives the organization a competitive advantage, 2) compiling all of the accrued knowledge into a succinct format.[78] Many managers still equate leadership with autocracy. However, today competitiveness is dependent on the leader's capacity to harness and nurture IC in such a way as to create outcomes that the marketplace defines as a bold and dramatic.[79] IC should be managed in such a manner that excess

[72] Kjell Nordstrom,Pick your brains, *People Management*, vol. 5 no 14 July 15 1999 p. 29.

[73] B.E. Lynn, Culture and intellectual capital management: a key factor in successful ICM implementation, *International Journal of Technology Management*, v. 18 no 5 1999 p. 590–603.

[74] See footnote 40.

[75] Eliezer Geisler, Harnessing the value of experience in the knowledge-driven firms, *Business Horizons*, vol. 42 no 3 May/June 1999 p. 18–26.

[76] Ted Gautschi, Develop your intellectual capital, *Design News*, vol. 53 (i.e. 54) July 20 1998 p. 170.

[77] William C. Miller, Fostering intellectual capital, *HR Focus*, vol. 75 January 1998 p. 9–10.

[78] See footnote 44.

[79] Oren Harari, Leadership vs. autocracy: they just don't get it! *Management Review*, vol. 85 August 1996 p. 42–45.

knowledge can be exploited by licensing technology to others, and deficiencies addressed by licensing from others.[80] IC is also a tool for resolving problems connected with the firm's growth.[81] Companies looking to manage intellectual assets must form networks of knowledge workers who are linked by IT to experts in the firm responsible for routing and maintaining incoming information. In addition, firms have to develop processes built around the effective use of information from around the world.[82] The real power of modern networked communication lies in its ability to make distance irrelevant. With this ability, electronic communication tools should address not only how companies communicate with customers and other external stakeholders but also how companies can enhance communication among employees and partners.[83]

Knowledge capital. For the full utilization of knowledge capital the integration of KC into strategic management processes is needed.[84] Information value-added is not the same as KC. For the utilization of KC – conceptualization and measurement of KC are needed.[85]

Knowledge management. KM aims: to make employees more productive; to break down the traditional organizational hierarchy on its plant floors. KM is the way to maximize innovation, to increase profits, reduce costs, enhance competitiveness, and develop new markets.[86] Overall corporate KM system

[80] See footnote 21.

[81] See footnote 53.

[82] Rick Mullin, Intellectual assets: know-how management systems, *Chemical Week*, vol. 158 December 11 1996 p. 26–27.

[83] Carol M. Stephenson, Knowledge: the critical capital, *Ivey Business Quarterly* vol. 63 no 1 Autumn 1998 p. 22–23.

[84] Grant Miles, Raymond E. Miles, Vincenzo Perrone, Leif Edvinsson, *California Management Review* vol. 40 no 3 Spring 1998 p. 181–188.

[85] Paul A. Strassmann, Taking the measures of knowledge assets, *Computerworld*, vol. 32 no 14 April 6 1998 p. 74.

[86] Laton McCartney, Getting smart about knowledge management, *Industry Week*, vol. 247 no 9 p. 30.

with a built-in set of incentives for managers will (probably) not work. Techniques of debriefing and mentoring (which will ensure that the knowledge of experienced managers is passed on to less experienced juniors) are recommended.[87] A company that is considering implementing a KM system needs to ensure that its management style, work environment, and culture are fostering an environment of sharing and openness.[88] KM barrier: the lack of understanding between training KM managers and IT departments.[89] An effective KM program includes interactive learning to encourage workers to continuously share knowledge. Interactive learning occurs either through work experience or communication with co-practitioners. A KM program requires the creation of a new culture, planning, leadership, motivated participants, measures of results, employees who are natural leaders and teachers and (at a certain point of its development) support of senior management.[90]

KM is establishing human and technological networks that are capable of harnessing a company's collective expertise. In the past, KM meant constantly pushing data, information, and knowledge up the ladder to top executives. The system became overloaded with useless information. KM in the future means that anyone within the organization could have access to the knowledge as needed.[91]

The following conditions are required for successful KM. The firm needs to ensure that there is a focus around which knowledge can be organized. Guiding principles and strategies to expand knowledge must be communicated to employ-

---

[87] See footnote 69.

[88] Michael A. Verspej, Knowledge management: system or culture? *Industry Week*, vol. 248. no 15 August 16 1999 p. 20.

[89] Jack Gordon, Intellectual capital and YOU, *Training*, vol. 36 no 9 September 1999 p. 30–36.

[90] Louisa Wah, Making knowledge stick, *Management Review*, vol. 88 no 5 May 1999 p. 24–29.

[91] Samuel Greengard, Storing, shaping and sharing collective wisdom (knowledge management), *Workforce*, vol. 77 no 10 Ocober 1998 p. 82–84.

ees. Management must create an environment and culture that supports continuous learning. The ways of building knowledge across multiple performances must be planned. Management must have vehicles that can support knowledge exploration and feedback and measurement must be used.[92]

To increase IC it is necessary to expand intelligence, encourage innovation, and to exercise integrity (3 core IC competencies).[93]

Crucial KM success factors include: creating a "knowledge culture" that values knowledge where needed, democratizing knowledge, valuing diversity, having a subversive effect on traditional management hierarchies, and always having the eye on the "knowledge grid" – which examines the various classes of knowledge that the firm knows or does not know. KM also involves individual learning, team learning, organizational learning, and customer learning.[94] The five principles of KM in knowledge-based organization are: 1) conceptualize the business, 2) create high-value know-how, 3) organize around information, 4) productively manage knowledge workers, 5) transform work using IT.[95] Two basic KM strategies are codification and personalization.[96] Real success usually comes to those who know what to do with the knowledge, how to interpret it, how to use the intuition, and how to experience it.[97] Successful KM needs forecasting input.[98] KM could

---

[92] See footnote 69.

[93] See footnote 20.

[94] Michele S. Darling, Building the knowledge organization, *Business Quarterly* vol. 61 Winter 1996 p. 61–66.

[95] William H. Read, Managing the Knowledge-Based Organization: Five Principles Every Manager Can Use, *Technology Analysis and Strategic Management*, vol. 8 no 3 September 1996 p. 223–232.

[96] See footnote 73.

[97] See footnote 13.

[98] See footnote 133.

be treated as "movement". In American industry KM movement "gained its momentum" in 1996.[99]

Human resources. To be successful, HR must develop and implement a change – management strategy of total organizational re-learning and re-envisioning and such change will not happen without learning and development programs. HR plan should take into account future performance capabilities, firm's values and culture, its learning and system thinking, a desire to improve partnering and collaborating, communication and commitment.[100]

Organizational Capital. There are five C's of organizational capital: consciousness of system and self, congruence of purpose, charity of commitment, capacity for connection, and coordination of action.[101] There are different aspects of the organizational capital: OC and Leibenstein's x-efficiency theory[102]. OC and the choice between specialization and diversification.[103] From the organizational point of view, employees efforts are typically sub-optimal because they make efforts on behalf of their own interest. Employees efforts are optimal when they make efforts on behalf of organizational interest. The difference is that organizational capital is formed during the joining-up or in preparation for it.[104]

[99] Debora M. Amidon Rogers, Knowledge management gains momentum in industry, *Research Technology Management*, vol. 39 May/June 1996 p. 5–7.

[100] Doug Treen, Strategic human resources, *Ivey Business Journal*, vol. 64 no 3 January/February 2000 p. 62–67.

[101] Diane Russ, Jeri Darling, Building Relationship Capital, *Human Resource Professional*, vol. 12 no 4 1999 p. 28–32.

[102] John F. Torner, Organizational capital: The path to higher productivity and well-being, Greenwood Press, Praeger, 1987, pp. XVI, 188.

[103] Michael Gort, Henry Grabowski, Robert McGuckin, Organizational Capital and the Choice between Specialization and Diversification, *Managerial and Decision Economics*, vol. 6 no 1 March 1985 p. 2–10.

[104] John F. Torner, Organizational capital and joining-up: Linking the individual to the organization and to society, *Human Relations*, vol. 51 no 6 June 1988 p. 825–846.

Structural capital. Managing SC can result in rapid knowledge sharing, collective knowledge growth, shortened lead time, profits, and more productive people.[105]

Relational Capital. Value-added relational capital is a business asset. Value-added capital is defined as relationships with employees, customers, suppliers, stakeholders, larger community.[106]

Knowledge assets. KA are created when 'knowledge ' is applied and becomes an asset. KA has three critical characteristics: 1) the product or service provided formally captures the knowledge asset in many forms – the product itself, marketing, distribution, support, and other related activities, 2) the product communicates the knowledge asset to the consumer, 3) the consumer values the KA.[107]

Tacit knowledge. Training professionals can cultivate the sharing of tacit knowledge among employees in their organization by observing what people do and how they do it; creating an environment of trust, respect, and commitment; allowing people to learn by doing; and assigning time for reflection and interpersonal exchange during training exercise.[108]

IC/KM institutions. There are numerous new institutions created to foster IC/KM: e.g. KCI Knowledge Capital International, Institute for Intellectual Capital Research Inc. (IICR), Intellectual Capital A.C.T., KNOWCORP, @BRINT Institute,

---

[105] See footnote 4.

[106] Diane Russ, Jeri Darling, *Human Resource Professional*, vol. 12 no 4 1999 p. 28–32.

[107] John W. Hebler, Doris C. Van Doren, Unfettered leverage: the ascendancy of knowledge-rich products and processes, *Business Horizons*, vol. 40 July/August 1997 p. 2–10.

[108] Bonnie Durrance, Some explicit thoughts on tacit learning, *Training and Development*, vol. 52 no 15 December 1998 p. 24–29. See also Ross, John A, A Comment on Explicit Versus Tacit Knowledge: Student Achievement in Laboratory Investigations, *Journal of research in science teaching*, Volume 32, Number 9, pp. 997, 1995; Toh, Kok-Aun; Woolnough, Brian E., Explicit Versus Tacit Knowledge in Laboratory Investigations: A Reply to Ross, *Journal of research in science teaching*. Volume 32, Number 9, pp. 999, 1995.

Community Intelligence Labs[109], KPMG Knowledge Management, the Netherlands[110].

IC/KM functions and roles. There are some new roles, functions or professions, like e.g. the chief learning or knowledge officer[111]

Intellectual nomad. Nancy Pollak describes herself as an intellectual nomad (interests in healthcare, interactive television, training industry, digital literacy program, the portfolio management system for IC, and the Web site of Leovision, etc).[112]

Other. A new way of thinking regards employee not assets but investors. Employees invest time, energy, and intelligence. Employees investments + firm's intangible assets + financial assets combine together to form the corporate stock of human capital.[113] In the area of breakthrough discoveries organizational boundaries act as information envelopes. The more valuable the information produced, the more its dissemination is limited. In geographic areas where a higher proportion of co-author pairs

---

[109] CoIL is an incubator of co-creative projects at the center of a business ecosystem comprised of our clients, partners and allies. A firm providing a wide range of services in consulting, research, development and facilitation of virtual teams and communities, we thrive on a vast network of mutually supportive professional relationship.

[110] KPMG Knowledge Management, The Netherlands provides information on value based knowledge management, offers two on-line assessments, one concerning your company's ability to turn knowledge into value, the other tests which learning style you personally possess. KPMG site also contains information about our package KPMG knowledge management, value-based knowledge management, strategic knowledge management, operational knowledge management, knowledge economy, knowledge value, the 21st century company, quantum economy, meaningful knowledge, knowledge intensive, knowledge professional, value-based self-management, competency-based team management, knowledge tools, knowledge environment, intellectual capital, knowledge creating company.

[111] Stuller Jay, Chief of Corporate Smarts – As companies struggle to capture, organize and apply their intellectual capital, a new breed of executive- the chief learning or knowledge officer-can be either a trendy cipher or a vital fulcrum. *Training*, Volume 35, Number 4 pp. 28, 1998.

[112] Jennifer J. Salopek, Intellectual Nomad, *Training and Development*, vol. 53 no 5 1999 p. 48–49.

[113] Thomas A. Stewart, New way of thinking about employees, *Fortune* v. 137 no. 7 1998 p. 169–170.

come from the same organization, diffusion of new collaborators is retarded.[114] The predictors of stakeholders performance in mid-sized computer service firms are the inspiration provided by the top management, managerial and entrepreneurial capital, and communication between the management and the employees.[115]

MEASUREMENT OF IC, KM AND INNOVATION

The majority of managers evaluate their firm's performance using financial measures. Although such measures might be appropriate in a stable environment, they are insufficient in today's fast-moving environment in which IC is becoming the dominant wealth creator. In order to leverage its IC, a company must become a knowledge-based organization and revise its performance measures accordingly.[116] Good measurement is central to effective management. Measurements are tools for alignment. Measurement indicators and trends are as significant as value targets. A small number of meaningful measures direct the organization to act is a fundamental design principle of all measurement systems and particularly important principle when measuring the value contributions of intellectual assets.[117] Despite of the fact that intellectual assets are not visible, they can be measured and managed.[118] The measurement and management of IC (or non-financial assets) has become a major strategic objective in

---

[114] Lynne G. Zucker et al., Collaboration Structure and Information Dilemas in Biotechnology: Organization Boundaries As Trust Production, *National Bureau of Economic Research Working Paper* 5119 July 1995 p. 19.

[115] See footnote 20.

[116] See footnote 4.

[117] Wendi R. Bukowitz, Gordon P. Petrash, Visualizing, measuring and managing knowledge, *Research Technology Management*, vol. 40 July/August 1997 p. 24–31.

[118] See footnote 3.

a number of industries.[119] If academics truly wish to develop a broad theory of knowledge and if managers are serious about enhancing their knowledge assets, then it is time for all parties to seriously establish reliable and valid measures of knowledge. Measuring knowledge involves measuring the knower, and therefore it is vital to examine the capabilities of an organism as an information processor and learner.[120] The American Society for Training and Development (ASTD), in collaboration with several firms, established a foundation of standards used for measuring and managing IC. Among the areas measured are the stocks of IC, the KM process, and the economic value generated by IC.[121] Among the ways that firms can measure IC are benchmarking, competency models, business process auditing, micro-lending, and colorized reporting.[122] In the Balance Performance Measurement System, four factors combine to create the virtuous cycle that leads to increased market value. These four factors are human capital, structural capital, external capital and financial performance.[123] IC Management Model includes two sets of measures. 1) A core set of measures to enumerate the IC are stocks, 2) A set of key measures of financial performance to evaluate effectiveness.[124] Measures of IC include: activity-based costing, intangible assets monitor, business navigator.[125] Two Skandia's approaches to measuring IC: the Skandia Value Scheme

---

[119] See footnote 76.

[120] Rashi Glazer, Measuring the knower: towards a theory of knowledge equity, *California management Review*, vol. 40 no 3 Spring 1998 p. 175–194.

[121] See footnote 17.

[122] Haidee E. Allerton, A dozen capital ideas, *Training and Development*, vol. 51 no 9 p. 9–10.

[123] See footnote 4.

[124] See footnote 17.

[125] See footnote 3.

and the Skandia Navigator.[126] The new accounting is based on such intangibles as the knowledge of employees, current R&D activities, and the time and money that firms invest in creating efficient manufacturing and service processes and in information technology (IT).[127] Skandia uses both Balance Sheet Approach and Profit and Loss Approach to measure Intellectual Capital.[128] Other approach consists in producing two-by-two matrices, multiple regression analyses, conceptual equations, etc.[129] The Value Added Intellectual Potential Method and Value Added Chain Matrix (VAIP/VAIC) represent a new methods of managing intangible assets.[130]

Knowledge Assets. Baruch Lev and Marc Bothwell prepared the Knowledge Capital Scorecard, a measurement tool (with trademark rights).[131] They contend that it is hard to tell if KM and IC are useful measures of company's performance. They argue that a true measure is output.[132] In general, the most often used measures of knowledge capital stress input, but new measure designed by Baruch Lev suggests methods of estimating the earnings impact of knowledge-based activity, how much knowledge assets contribute to the results.[133]

Innovation. The "National Innovation Index" was built for understanding of innovation by looking at the quality of in-

---

[126] Leif Edvinsson, Developing intellectual capita at Skandia, *Long Range Planning* vol. 30 June 1997 p. 366–373. See also no author, *The Economist* vol. 347 no June 6 1998 p. 64.

[127] See footnote 76.

[128] Goran Roos, Johan Roos, Measuring your company's intellectual performance, *Long Range Planning*, vol. 30 1997 p. 413–426.

[129] Geoffrey Colvin, How to get your head around measuring minds, *Fortune* vol. 140 no 12 December 20 1999 p. 334.

[130] Manfred Bornemann, Potential of value systems according to the VAIC method, *International Journal of Technology Management*, vol. 18 no 5–8 1999 p. 463–475.

[131] Karen Kroll, Calculating knowledge assets, *Industry Week*, vol 248 no 13 July 5 1999 p. 20.

[132] Strassman, NL 7.

[133] Anne Graham, Boost your magazine's intellectual capital, *Magazine for Magazine Management*, vol 28 no 8 July 1 1999 p. 27–28. See footnote 125.

ventions, not just quantity. It measures international patents filed, R&D spending, share of GDP spent on higher education, etc.[134]

Few smart. The aim of IC management is to transform the skills of a few supersmart employees into organization's core competencies. Those core competencies make the products and services unique. They are vital because either they are extremely smart themselves, or they know who is smart, where these people are located, and how to get them to cooperate.[135] The retention and motivation of valuable employees requires an evaluation from the employers of the situation and work environment of such personnel. Employee turnover is expensive with the cost of exit interviews, severance pay, hiring costs, and lost productivity. In addition, there are the less obvious costs that come with the loss of IC, decreased morale, increased stress, and the adverse effect on a company's reputation.[136] Losing their intangible assets is the great fear of most companies. Foremost to this is losing their brilliant and prized employees to the competition. The best way to retain staff is to offer them more incentives. Employees like to be recognized for the contributions they made and they prefer to work in an environment in which they feel valued and get real satisfaction from their work. The best way to protect such intangible assets is to be more pragmatic, meaning, and to practice openness in communicating their expectation to the workers.[137]

---

[134] Robert Buderi, In search of innovation, *Technology Review,* vol. 102 no 6 1999 p. 42–47.

[135] See footnote 66.

[136] Robin Thompson, Secrets to keeping good employees, *Business Credit,* vol. 102 no 1 2000 p. 68–69. See also Anthony L. Velocci, Loss of intellectual capital challenges company ingenuity, *Aviation Week & Space Technology* vol. 152 no 17 2000 p. 26.

[137] No author, When intellectual capital starts heading for the door, *Management Today* 1999 p. 9, 10. SmartSkills, The Centre For High Performance-SmartSkills, 1999, text/html http://www.smartskills.com/testsite/index.html; Loss of intellectual capital challenges company ingenuity. Some companies mount vigorous campaigns to attract and retain smartest engineers they can find, *Aviation week and space technology* vol. 152 no 17 2000 p. 26.

IC/KM IN BRANCHES AND SECTORS

IC/KM tools and techniques are being developed at universities[138], in banks[139] and pension funds[140] in aerospace industry[141], for "smart products production"[142], in biotechnology industry[143], IT industry[144], electronics industry[145], chemical industry[146], recreation industry[147], textile industry[148], design in-

[138] Colin Coulson-Thomas, Carry on campus, *People Management* vol 6 no 4 February 17 2000 p. 33. Corporate learning centers are missing opportunities to share knowledge and resources with traditional universities, are internally focused and generalist, and are ignoring such areas as entrepreneurship, developing knowledge, and creating IC.

[139] Patricia Galagan, The workplace in 2020: three scenarios, *Training and Development*, vol. 50 1996 p. 50–52; Ramona Dzinkowski, Managing the brain trust, *CMA Management* vol. 73 no 8 1999 p. 14–18; Arvind Singh, Deutsche Can Become a Leader – or a Dinosaur, *American Banker*, vol. 164, no 23 1999 p. 24.

[140] Terry Williams, NY pension fund loses intellectual capital, *Crains New York Business,* vol. 14 no 2 p. 20.

[141] Velocci, See footnote 130.

[142] See footnote 88.

[143] L.G. Zucker; M.R. Darby; M.B. Brewer, Intellectual Capital and the Birth of U.S. Biotechnology Enterprises, Working paper series, Number 4653, 1994; Lynne G. Zucker, Michael R. Darby, Marylinn B. Brewer, Intellectual human capital and the birth of US biotechnology enterprises, *The American Economic Review*, vol. 88 no 1 March 1998 p. 290-306; See footnote 46. See also Oliver, Amalya L; Liebeskind, Julia Porter, Three Levels of Networking for Sourcing Intellectual Capital in Biotechnology Implications for Studying Interorganizational Networks, *International studies of management & organization,* Volume 27, Number 4, pp. 76, 1997.

[144] Susan S. Hanley, A Culture Built On Sharing, *Information Week* 1999 p. 16. See footnote 46.

[145] Peter C. Grindley, Licensing and cross-licensing in electronics: managing intellectual capital for design freedom and wealth creation, Berkeley, 1996, 49 p.; Peter C. Grindley; David J. Teece, Managing Intellectual Capital: Licensing and Cross-Licensing in Semiconductors and Electronics, *California Management Review*, Volume 39, Number 2, pp. 8, 1997.

[146] Rick Mullin, Knowledge management: a cultural evolution, *Journal of Business Strategy*, vol. 17 September/October 1996 p. 56–59.

[147] See footnote 127: steps to shift mind-sets and practices among magazine staffs toward the importance of capturing and harnessing information and knowledge.

[148] Rodolfo C. Celis, FROM THE FRONT LINES - Fruit of the Loom - Intellectual capital is a textile designer's most valuable asset. Often it takes technology to realize its, *Inc.* vol. 20, no 13, pp. 27 1998.

dustry[149], as well as in international alliances[150], multinationals[151], silicon valley[152], health service[153], venture capitalists,[154] or in public sector[155].

E.g. it is said, that in multinational firms, because they face competition globally, innovation is fostered throughout the organization, rather than being limited to the home country. A key implication for multinationals is that they can create their IC by fostering and harnessing the specialized knowledge that is embedded in all their functional and geographic areas, and not just the R&D department in-house. Specifically, firms need to cultivate specialist networks to innovate and spread the innovations.[156] Silicon Valley, in the light of the socio-ecological approach, is more than a random gathering of high-tech firms

---

[149] See footnote 70.

[150] Christpher C. Baughn, John H. Stevens, Johannes G. Denekamp, Protecting intellectual capital in international alliances, *Journal of World Business*, vol. 32 Summer 1997 p. 103–117. Successful alliance management involves process of designing, staffing, and monitoring the collaborative interface to balance the requirements for learning and information sharing with protecting of IC.

[151] James H. Tiessen, Developing intellectual capital globally: an epistemic community perspective, *International Journal of Technology Management*, vol. 18 no 5 1999 p. 720–730.

[152] Homa Bahrami, Stuart Evans, Flexible re-cycling and high-technology entrepreneurship (in Silicon Valley), *California Management Review*, vol. 37 Spring 1995 p. 62–89.

[153] Grantham, 61. See also Robinson, James C, Financial Capital And Intellectual Capital In Physician Practice Management, Health affairs. Volume 17, Number 4, pp. 53, 1998; Stewart, T. A., The Case for Managing Structural Capital, *The Healthcare Forum journal*, Volume 42, Number 3, 30, 1999.

[154] Stowe, Charles R. B. „Intellectual Capital – Implications for Venture Capitalists" Kwiatkowski Stefan, Edvinsson Leif, *Knowledge Cafe for Intellectual Entrepreneurship* , Warsaw, 1999, pp 75–94.

[155] Milner, Eileen, Managing information and knowledge in the public sector, London, Routledge, 2000, 224 p.; Weston H. Agor, The Measurement, Use and Development of Intellectual Capital to Increase Public Sector Productivity, *Public personnel management* vol. 26, no 2 1997 p. 175; Daniel D. Barron, Staffing Rural Public Libraries: The Need to Invest in Intellectual Capital, *Library Trends*, vol. 44 no 1 1995, p. 77.

[156] See footnote 145.

in a well-defined locale. Like a natural ecosystem, the Silicon Valley's growth and success can be attributed to the continuous formation of a diversified multitude of specialized entities that both are fed and feed one another.

Components of the ecosystem include venture capitalists, high-tech talents, universities and research institutions, an advanced service infrastructure, and large numbers of customers, lead users, and early adopters of new technologies. The Silicon Valley's ecosystem is nourished and renewed by a process of "flexible recycling" in which the IC and other resources of enterprises that fail or reach the end of their life cycles are continually reabsorbed and re-channeled.[157] As concerns corporate universities, they differ from training schemes because they allow participants to take a major role in the organization's IC (unlike training, where pro-active response is limited).[158] Business schools are important producers of IC, the continuous development of new insights and models and the discovery of today's best management practices.[159] Business professors advise and have equity stakes in e-commerce start-ups.[160] Many universities are creating their own venture capital funds in order to generate more income.[161] Other strategies for business schools to create "intellectual capitalists" involve the use of adult learning techniques, the addition of courses requiring creativity, in-

[157] See footnote 146.

[158] See footnote 73.

[159] Lawrence G. Tapp, Management education in Canada: a wake-up call, *Ivey Business Quarterly*, vol. 62 no 3 1998 p. 7–9. See also Clifford M. Gross, The new idea factory: expanding technology companies with university intellectual capital, Columbus, Ohio, Battelle Press, 2000; NEXUS – Intellectual Capital – The Most Strategic Asset, *Planning for higher education*, vol. 28 no 3 2000, p. 45.

[160] David Whitford, The intellectual capitalist. (Business school professors who trade their intellect for stakes in e-commerce start-ups), *Fortune*, vol. 141 no 8 2000 p. 553–556.

[161] Antonio Regaldo, Intellectual capital, *Technology Review*, vol. 102 no1 1999 p. 25.

corporation of travel into the curriculum, and teaching faculty how to improve their teaching.[162]

Intellectual Entrepreneurship. Arising from Warsaw, but encompassing concepts and activities world-wide, is the concept of "intellectual entrepreneurship." In March 1999, a group of scholars, and entrepreneurs were assembled at historic Nieborow Palace to contemplate the implications of intellectual entrepreneurship on both management scholarship and for entrepreneurs and venture capitalists. Routes to intellectual capital Formation, the nature of intellectual product, the development of the term and its implications to date were explored by participants and published.[163] This book represents a continuation of the effort to stimulate intellectual inquiry into intellectual capital and its related terms by its initiator, Stefan Kwiatkowski of Warsaw University and Leon Kozminski Academy of Entrepreneurship and Management.

IC/KM FORECASTING

The challenges confronting company's management are shifting away from the administrative and toward the entrepreneurial.[164] The shift from "hard-asset" management to that based on IC requires an integration of technical and business perspectives presenting an intellectual management model with particular characteristics.[165] Successful competitiveness

---

162 Stowe, Charles R. B. „On Developing Intellectual Capitalists" *Knowledge Cafe for Intellectual Entrepreneurship,* Kwiatkowski & Edvinsson, Warsaw, 1999, pp. 129–140.

163 Kwiatkowski Stefan, Edvinsson Leif, *Knowledge Cafe for Intellectual Entrepreneurship* , Warsaw, 1999.

164 David J. Teece, Capturing value from knowledge assts: the new economy, markets for know-how, and intangible assets, *California Management Review,* vol. 40, no 3 1998 p. 55–79.

165 Charles E. Grantham, Larry D. Nichols, A framework for the management of intellectual capital in the health care industry, *Journal of Health Care Finance,* vol. 23 Spring 1997 p. 1–19.

in the 21st century will demand the use of visionary and dedicated leadership, a balanced scorecard that improves corporate accountability, and sustained investment in creating dynamic capabilities. Globalization will continue to escalate, transferring technologies, bringing cultures and societies closer, and fostering cooperation among nations.[166] The meltdown of traditional boundaries is altering how business is conducted. In the new "blurred" economy boundaries are eradicated. The lines between buyer and seller, product and service, employee and entrepreneur are also blurred. Blur is defined as speed multiplied by connectivity multiplied by intangibles.[167] Scenarios on how smart products, interconnected workers and IC will influence each other has been built.[168] The effect on current trends on the future of training professionals has been described.[169] Although many variables will influence the future of the workplace, a critical few are likely to have or make-or-break consequences for the work of training and development professionals in 2020. These variables are smart products, whereby microelectronics technology makes it possible to place information services in products and in distribution channels for products and services; connectivity, which refers to the ability of various technologies to connect – and by extension, the ability of people to connect with one another by using those technologies; and IC and hard capital, IC's ability to attract hard capital for investment and development influencing the future of many industries.[170] Technology will play a role in the reform of the university, but it will never be a glamorous one. For instance, more courseware will be designed, and uses of multimedia and the Internet will increase. Technology will

---

[166] Zahra, see footnote 2.
[167] Stacy Ven der Wall, Adapting to a Blurred Economy, *HR Magazine*, vol. 43 no 13 1998 p. 139–140.
[168] See footnote 133.
[169] Curtis E. Plott, Lohn Humphrey, Preparing for 2020, *Training and Development*, vol. 50 November 1996 p. 46–49.
[170] Zahra, see footnote 2.

enable new organizational forms. Techology creates new communication paths, and connections with the global IC. Distance learning will become commonplace as will networked and virtual universities. Technology permits the customization of educational products and technology will permit just-in-time learning. However, these are all technological applications, none of which alone can radically transform the university. The challenge of transformation for universities is basically intellectual rather than technological.[171]

The control of wealth is shifting away from institutions and corporations, and into the hands of individuals. There are some forces behind this shift.[172] It is identified that successful companies of the future will be those that will exploit the advances in technology for product specialization and superior distribution. These advances, especially the convergence of telecommunications and computers, bring about a world wherein products are becoming digital, markets are becoming electronic and connected, and a corporation's key assets are increasingly IC and ingenuity.[173]

INTELLIGENT PRODUCT

Today sensors can be found almost everywhere in industry, from conveyors and boilers to process lines and air handlers. Thanks to advances and innovation in such areas as microprocessor technology, new, more intelligent products offer greater performance capabilities. Regardless of sensor type,

---

[171] Gerry Gingrich, The role of technology in the transformation of the university, *Journal of End User Computing*, vol. 8 Spring 1996 p. 32–33. See also Stowe, Charles R. B. "On Developing Intellectual Capitalists" in Knowledge Café for Intellectual Entrepreneurship, Kwiatkowski and Edvinsson, Warsaw 1999, pp. 129–140.

[172] Gina Fraone, Employees for sale? *Electronic Business* vol. 26 no 3 2000 p. 117.

[173] Khail Barsoum, The technology revolution and how it will change our approach to business, *CMA Magazine*, vol. 70 no 5 1996 p. 4.

functionality can be increased with the integration of intelligence into device.[174] Sony hopes to parlay a new PlayStation-on-steroids into a central role in the digital home entertainment system of the future. Sony President Nobuyuki Idei hopes the new player will evolve into family of other intelligent products.[175] As demand increases for bandwidth-intensive applications, so does demand services and applications, network service providers need flexible, standards-based infrastructure solutions that scale to thousands of subscribers and integrate seamlessly with existing equipment. Subscriber management systems are a new class of high-density, highly intelligent product that can configure, deploy and manage a large number of broadband access subscribers.[176] Through cyclic intelligent product systems, visionary companies can reduce waste and conserve resources by designing products for use, return, remanufacturing, and redistribution, with the ultimate goal being industrial sustainability. The goals of this new approach are to: increase a firm's eco-efficiency, enhance industry competitiveness, and promote innovative environment management approaches. The benefits of intelligent product systems include minimal environmental impact, optimization of natural resource use, increased customer loyalty, an enhanced public image, and economic advantage over other competitors who do not employ proactive approaches.[177]

---

[174] Jeanine Katzel, Sensors: Smart Devices, Smarter Solutions, *Plant engineering,* vol. 53 no 8 August 1999 p. 61–69.

[175] Benjamin Fulford, Killer sequel, *Forbes,* vol. 163 no 7 April 5 1999 p. 52–53.

[176] Larry Blair, Enabling broadband services with subscriber management systems, *Telecommunications,* vol. 33 no 2 February 1999 p. 47.

[177] Katherine Blue, Nicholas E. Davidson, Eriko Kobayashi, The 'intelligent product' system, *Business & Economic Review,* vol. 45 no 2 January-March 1999 p. 15–20.

IC/KM/R&D ECONOMIC IMPACT

The study of risk management applied to R&D expenditures, innovation and IC found that as currently measured, the returns are highly skewed, so that a few inventions earn high returns and most earn low or no returns. It is possible to generate distribution of returns that is concave when plotted against Pareto-Levy space.[178] Knowledge capital stocks are obtained by cumulating R&D expenditure. Results show that competitiveness is determined not only by the R&D activity of the representative firm, but also by total R&D in the domestic industry as well as economy-wide stocks of knowledge, indicating the presence of local externalities. Competitiveness is also affected by factor prices and resource endowments as well as scale economies and learning by doing. Economies of scale is important in R&D internal to the firm, of the degree of openness for the capacity to utilize global spillovers and of investment for introduction of embodied technical progress. The R&D impact is higher in high-and-medium than in low-tech industries.[179] There is empirical correlation between balance sheet data and expenditure for the intellectual potential.[180] Not only are forward-thinking companies tapping the intellectual capital of employees, they are developing structured systems that support and measure the return on knowledge-sharing investments.[181] Organizational capital seems to be good explanation for firm behavior and productivity, especially how productivity is related to inter-

---

[178] Derek Bosworth, Gregory Jobome, The measurement and management of risk in R&D and innovation, *International Journal of Technology Management,* vol. 18 no 5 1999 p. 476–499.

[179] Patrik Gustavsson, Par Hansson, Lars Lundberg, Technology, resource endowments and international competitiveness, *European Economic Review* vol. 43 no 8 August 1999 p. 1501–1530.

[180] See footnote 124.

[181] Martinez, Michelle Neely, The Collective Power Of Employee Knowledge – *HRMagazine* vol. 43, no 2 1998 p. 88.

organizational behavior.[182] Public structural capital is a source of endogenous growth.

There are two contrary growth models: endogenous and exogenous. In exogenous growth economies temporary innovations in policy variables lead only to temporary changes in GNP levels. In endogenous growth economies, innovation can lead to permanent changes in GNP levels. Structural components of public structural capital contribute significantly to and have a statistically and economically important effect upon long-run GNP levels.[183] Preliminary research involving a cross-industry survey of over 500 organizations in the US shows that companies that investment in IC by training results in a strategic edge. There is a link between investment in IC and organizational measures of performance, including market-to-book value. The market itself and stakeholders also recognize the value that they generate.[184] A survey of 423 enterprises, each with revenues of over $270 million per year, reveals that large companies understand the value of fully implemented knowledge management program, but they are losing out in terms of realizing full benefits.[185] CHI Research developed data linking a company's patent impact and science linkage with financial returns. Francis Narin and Baruch Lev's study shows a 10–25% higher return for companies with strong patents and science linkage.[186]

---

[182] See footnote 96.

[183] Narayana Kocherlokata, Yi Kei-Mu, A simple Time Series Test of Endogenous vs. Exogenous Growth Models: An Application to the United States, *Review of Economics and Statistics,* vol. 78 no 1 February 1996 p. 126–134.

[184] Laurie Bassi, Mark E. Van Buren, Valuing investments in intellectual capital, *International Journal of Technology Management,* vol. 18 no 5 1999 p. 414–432.

[185] No author, Clearing obstacles to true knowledge management, *KMWorld* vol 9 no 3.

[186] No author, Patents As Corporate Assets, *Chemical & Engineering News,* vol. 76 no 36.

The latest data show that hi-tech leaders poured record amounts into new technology development to stay ahead of the market.[187]

BEA has prepared a satellite account that is designed to facilitate analysis of the role of research and development (R&D) in the U.S. economy. In the R&D satellite account, R&D expenditures are treated as a form of investment, and the resulting investment flows are used to estimate stocks of R&D fixed intangible capital. The stock of R&D capital grew rapidly during 1953-70, slowed sharply during 1970-81, and then grew somewhat more rapidly. Adding the constant-cost net stock of R&D fixed capital to the NIPA constant-cost net stock of fixed reproducible tangible capital would have raised the net wealth of government and business by nearly 9 percent in 1992.[188]

---

[187] No author, Research and Development – High-Tech Leaders Pour Record Amounts Into New Technology Development to Stay Ahead of the Market, *Computer Reseller News*, p. 134.. See also: Jeffrye Ian Bernstein, Rates of return on physical and R&D capital and structure of production process: cross section and time series evidence, Cambridge, National Bureau of Economic Research, 1988, 32 p.; Adams, James D. (James Dutton), Endogenous R&D spillovers and industrial research productivity, Cambridge, MA: National Bureau of Economic Research, 2000, 50 p.; Nerdrum, Lars, The economics of human capital: a theoretical analysis illustrated empirically by Norwegian data, Oslo, Scandinavian University Press, 1999, xiv, 274 p. Thesis (Ph. D.)-University of Fribourg (Switzerland).

[188] A Satellite Account for Research and Development. *Survey of current business*, vol. 74, no 11 37, November, 1994; White, J., R&D – a centre for profit, not cost: Some of the factors behind changing routes to the acquisition of intellectual capital, *IEE Review* vol. 42 no 3 1996 p. 103; M. Ishaq Nadiri, Ingmar R. Prucha, Estimation of the Depreciation Rate of Physical and R&D Capital in the U.S. Total Manufacturing Sector, *Economic Inquiry* vol. 34 no 1 1996 p. 43.

CONCLUSIONS

In mid 1990s a new area in management sciences crystallized around terms "intellectual capital" and "knowledge management." In just a few years, new IC/KM definitions, taxonomies, measurement techniques, empirical observations and recommendations were built. This new knowledge was immediately used for constructing managerial methods, forecasting and in economics. A new cadre of professionals have developed embracing the concepts of intellectual capital and knowledge management. During the same time IC/KM gave rise or re-defined a whole group of cognate terms including: human resources, intangible resources, intellectual assets, intellectual capital, intellectual capitalism, knowledge, knowledge assets, knowledge capital, knowledge capitalism, learning organization, organizational capital, relational capital, social capital, structural capital, tacit knowledge, and many others. A new language, new research and managerial practices, and a new ways of thinking has been born.

Charles R. B. Stowe

INTELLECTUAL ENTREPRENEURSHIP – THE CONVERSION OF INTELLECTUAL CAPITAL INTO FINANCIAL CAPITAL

Abstract

Much of the research on intellectual capital and knowledge management has dealt with the topics of definition, measurement, and management of knowledge as applied to large organizations. The intellectual entrepreneur must be concerned with the conversion of intellectual capital into financial capital. Converting intellectual capital to financial capital means: (1) increasing intellectual capital through creating large networks both professional and personal, (2) taking the time to do a really detailed self-assessment, (3) developing industry expertise, (4) understanding that business means providing cost-effective, practical solutions to problems, (5) understanding the important difference between creating wealth and income, and (6) continuing to look over the horizon at future challenges posed by advancing technology.

INTRODUCTION

This chapter explores some of the research on intellectual capital and recent economic developments to better define intellectual entrepreneurship and to offer specific advice to prospective intellectual entrepreneurs. While much of the existing literature focuses on large organizations and their need to measure and manage intellectual capital, this chapter defines intellectual entrepreneurs and the special challenges they face in creating new organizations. Finally, if the world is to achieve sustainable development, there are specific societal conditions necessary to foster intellectual entrepreneurship that will create an age of intellectual entrepreneurship.

The real issue facing intellectual entrepreneurs and their organizations is not one of measurement of intellectual capital but one of understanding the process of converting intellectual into financial capital or profit. Drawing on selected writings on the subject by journalists, business leaders, and academicians, this chapter explores the concepts of intellectual capital and intellectual entrepreneurship. Whereas Kozlowski's chapter presents a review of hundreds of abstracts of articles and books to present a static view of major issues and concepts, this chapter presents an analysis of literature on intellectual capital and knowledge management relevant to the problem of conversion of intellectual capital into financial capital.

There are some fundamental economic realities that affect even intellectual entrepreneurs. The experience of the 1990's where companies with almost no tangible assets, no management, no intellectual property protection and little in the way of a marketing program commanded attention from venture capitalists and other investors has come to a halt. The NASDAQ stock exchange where so many dot.com companies went public is down over 40 percent. The IPO market, referring to any company that is attempting to raise money from the sale of its shares from the public, has been quieted by the decline in investor interest in high technology stocks. What was unique about the recent cycle of frenetic investing is that venture capital companies committed large sums of money to companies that were start-ups. Normally, venture capital companies prefer to invest in companies that have a financial history and track record, and a market for their products that is fairly well established.

The real issue facing society, scholars and intellectual entrepreneurs is to advance the understanding of the conversion process of intellectual capital into financial capital. Although not a focus of this article, a similar concept applies to non-profit organizations including governments. The fullest realization of the potential benefits of the intellectual capital paradigm lies in harnessing individual and organizational talents and systems to best incite, harness, access and convert creativity to greater product or service value and higher profits.

FROM MEASUREMENT TO MANAGEMENT TO CREATION

There has been a certain progression of thinking on intellectual capital. From an analysis of this progression of thinking, there are important lessons to be observed. First, knowledge grows exponentially and not in a linear progression. Second, the growth of knowledge is proportional to the numbers of people and personal networks they form. The more individuals research a subject and the more these individuals interact with each other, the more momentum builds as more 'disassociated' concepts are brought into the subject. Third, at a certain critical point, the amount of knowledge on a particular subject becomes so pervasive and diverse that a system to access and deploy that knowledge becomes as valuable as the information itself. Fourth, intellectual capital or knowledge can only develop commercial value if it can be used to solve a problem. Each of these lessons deserves discussion in the context of past research.

The first writings on the subject dealt with the problem of defining intellectual capital and the issue of measurement of the intangible assets of a firm. The next phase of publications shifted focus from measurement to the issue of 'managing' intellectual capital. A third phase of intellectual inquiry deals with strategies organizations can use to foster the creation of intellectual capital. The emerging field of intellectual capital or knowledge management and its relevance to intellectual entrepreneurship lies in the fourth phase. This fourth phase lies in developing a better understanding of the conversion process from intellectual capital to financial return.

Kozlowski traces the term 'intellectual capital' to literature first published some twenty years ago. Other chapters attribute the term to a variety of authors. However, the term 'intellectual capital' in its current context can be traced to two sources: Leif Edvinsson, the first Corporate Director of Intellectual Capital for Skandia Financial Services, and Thomas A. Stewart, an American journalist (Edvinsson, Stewart).

Stewart was writing for *Fortune* magazine when he was assigned the task of writing about the brain and why companies were selling at valuations that defied logic. His first article dealt with new ideas in business and was published in 1991 (Stewart). His second article appearing as a front-page cover story titled "Brainpower" was published spring 1991. As told in the foreword of his book, shortly after his cover story on brainpower appeared in *Fortune*, " ... a Swede who worked for an insurance company named Skandia phoned to say that he was coming to New York and to ask if he could visit me. In my office he handed me his business card ... Director of Intellectual Capital. I was floored. Leif explained that he had been interviewing for a job with Jan Carende, head of Skandia's Assurance and Financial Services division, and had shown "Brainpower" to him saying, 'This is what your company should do: Manage intellectual capital." Carende agreed, and said: 'You do it.'" (Stewart, *Intellectual Capital* ...Foreword, p. xv). After the publication of the "Brainpower" article, Stewart wrote a second cover about knowledge assets published in October 1994 (Stewart "Intellectual Capital" in *Fortune*). And in 1997, he published *Intellectual Capital – The New Wealth of Nations*.

The sequence of Stewart's writing and the interface with Leif Edvinsson reflects an important reality for intellectual entrepreneurs: networking stimulates ideas and information. Stewart cite's Edvinsson's and Skandia's publications. And when Edvinsson addresses groups, he refers to Stewart and others. This is but one example of why corporations invest in sending their employees to conferences, seminars and to trade association meetings to broaden the social exposure of their employees. Much of the literature on creativity reflects the notion that just as computers can be linked through networks to have extraordinary processing power, human creativity and knowledge is a function of the exposure individuals get from travel, reading, and experiences outside of their routines.

Stewart's book offers some helpful definitions of intellectual capital spiced with interesting stories. Starting with Klein and Prusak's definition that intellectual capital is "intellectual material that has been formalized, captured, and leveraged to produce a higher-value asset," Stewart quotes Paul M. Romer of the University of California at Berkeley as stating that "ideas are the instructions that let us combine limited physical resources in arrangements that are ever more valuable." (Stewart, *Intellectual Capital* p. 67). The concepts of human capital, structural capital and consumer capital are built on that foundation. Both Edvinsson and Stewart explore these concepts and they each developed their own system for "navigating" through the concepts. They both selected the term 'navigators' to describe their first attempts at designing a management strategy. However, much of the early writing really focused on the issue of measuring and identifying intellectual capital within large organizations.

Stewart's book gives examples of how the content of tangible products is absorbing more intellectual content. One example he cites is the aluminum can and how it was transformed from a heavy, expensive container to a lightweight, inexpensive and practical solution to the problem of transporting soft drinks and beer (Stewart). His book is full of other stories of how products evolved and improved as more technology and knowledge was invested into refining the design, manufacture and marketing of products. While Stewart does not make this point, one observes that the introduction and leveraging of intellectual capital is an evolutionary process and not a one-time event. This is an important aspect of the conversion process: it is a process and not a single event. This observation is also held by other management scholars (Roos).

The respective backgrounds of these authors of books on intellectual capital help to explain their bias toward large organizations. Edvinsson's early publications include Skandia's annual report containing a detailed explanation of their system of defining the different aspects of intellectual capital and measuring it. The company was explaining to their shareholders why the market should place a higher value on the company – certainly a bit self-serving, but as profits increased, the price to earnings multiple also increased which certainly justified the company's unique policies on intellectual capital. This is not to say that Edvinsson's role was simply that of a publicist for the investor relations department. On the contrary, the quest to develop a way of reporting on intellectual capital resulted in the development of the Skandia

Navigator which became used for individual performance appraisals as well as rewards and appraisals (Edvinsson, "Developing Intellectual Capital at Skandia" p. 371). The goal of Skandia initiative was to "grow and develop intellectual capital as a visible, lasting value, complementary to the traditional balance. The IC function provides a link between other development functions like Business Development, Human Resource Development and Information Technology Development" (Edvinsson, "Developing Intellectual Capital at Skandia" p. 368).

Stewart, like many other journalists and stock market observers, were perplexed by the incredibly high market valuations of listed companies that had little in the way of tangible assets. As a financial journalist, Stewart's fascination with the subject of intellectual capital arose from his observation that the market valuations of companies with few tangible assets were exceeding some very large industrial concerns. For example, at one time, the internet book retailer AMAZON.COM had a market valuation exceeding that of many Dow Jones Industrial Companies. So, Stewart's initial perspective was to account for the valuation differential.

There are many prominent research conferences, articles and research projects on the subject of measuring intellectual capital. For example, the Danish Agency for the Development of Trade and Industry, the Copenhagen Business School, the University Aarhus, Arthur Andersen and 19 firms collaborated in a project to explore how the 19 firms would go about creating intellectual capital statements (Bukh, et al). What is interesting about the study is that each firm developed its own "statement" of intellectual capital with their own stories and metaphors that describe "knowledge-management activities" (Bukh, et al. p. 104). There is an inherent bias in this approach which is that we need to measure what we manage and without being able to measure we cannot manage. "Intellectual capital measurement is an important element of knowledge management"(Liebowitz). Does that sound reminiscent of Taylor and Deming (Taylor, Deming)?

Other approaches include diagramming the relationship between activities of a company and their contribution to human capital, relationship capital, business process capital, and renewal and development capital. The Roos's have proposed "profit and loss" approach to complement the balance sheet approach to help companies monitor the flows among different types of intellectual capital and between intellectual and financial capital (Roos, Measuring...).

Others pursued their interest in intellectual capital by proposing how a company could use measurement tools to better manage their intellectual assets. For example, Brooking writes from a management consultant and artificial intelligence perspective. Her book defines components of intellectual capital as market assets, human-centered assets, intellectual property assets, and infrastructure assets. Each subsequent chapter provides an "audit" system that includes a discussion of methods for evaluating such assets and suggestions on strategies to enhance a firm's intellectual capital assets. The text offers a very pragmatic approach with its checklists, flowcharts, and sets of questions. Chapter 9, "Intellectual Capital Management" presents a flowchart outlining the process of managing intellectual capital which includes identification, development, audit, documentation, protection, growth and dissemination elaborated more fully in later chapters.

Other publications explored the issues of how to train managers in knowledge management. One study used a Knowledge Management Receptivity Survey KMRS, based on Likert-type scales to measure the success of a knowledge management training program undertaken by a public sector agency in Queensland, Australia after they had experienced a tango simulation exercise (Bontis, Giradi). The conclusion was that the KMRS is a valid survey instrument for examining the receptivity of intellectual capital-related phenomena and second, the Tango simulation provided participants with an effective means in heightening their receptivity to intellectual capital initiatives. Some researchers advanced the idea that to gain an understanding of how companies mine their intellectual capital, one should study companies that have successfully converted intellectual capital into profitable activities. For example, Greco describes Dow Chemical's effort to mine their 30,000 patents, Sears's strategy of questioning customers, and Hewlett-Packard's intranet to manage knowledge (Greco).

Knight, a management consultant, offers another attempt to present a new framework for measuring performance. Some of his declarations are not new: "intellectual capital is the sum of a company's intangible assets" and that 'goodwill' is the recognition of a firm's future extraordinary profit potential which arises from the growth of intellectual capital."(Knight). However, his article is useful in suggesting three levels of a framework for building knowledge-based organization. Level 1 being market value; Level 2 Creating a Virtuous Cycle in which investments in human capital result in more competent and capable people to develop better structural capital for an organization, and Level 3 Performance Measurement which he explains are performance indicators that are generic and can be used by almost any organization.

One researcher took a totally different approach by spending a year working in a Japanese firm to observe how they manage for intellectual capital. Fruin's book is drawn on a five-year study plus one year of personal observation of the 60 year-old Tokyo-based Yanagicho Works, one of Toshiba's 27 domestic Japanese factories. Fruin's explores intellectual capital from direct observation of one Japanese manufacturing firm. While the detailed description of intellectual capital and knowledge management strategies within one Japanese company offers useful insight on one company's approach, it is uncertain that all Japanese companies practice "knowledge works." Nor is it possible to conclude that non-Japanese manufacturing companies don't use similar strategies. The value of this work lies not in drawing conclusions about the nature of Japanese management or culture, but in describing the strategies the author observed at Toshiba. Here again, however, is research done at a very large firm (Fruin).

There has always been self-improvement literature on creativity, but it was fairly recent that researchers and business journalists have begun to question how organizations can stimulate ideas. Much of this research can be found under the title of 'intrapreneurship'. Only very recently have the techniques and strategies of corporations to stimulate new ideas been examined from the standpoint of intellectual capital.

In the United States, there are many organizations that help corporations in their struggle to enhance employee productivity. One of these is the American Center for Training in Development. Founded in 1944, ASTD is the world's premier professional association and leading resource on workplace learning and performance issues. ASTD rovides information, research, analysis and practical information derived from its own research, the knowledge and experience of its members, its conferences, expositions, seminars, publications and the coalitions and partnerships it has built through research and policy work. There are than 70,000 people working in the field of workplace performance in 100 countries worldwide. Their members work in more than 15,000 multinational corporations, small and medium sized businesses, government agencies, colleges and universities (ADST web site).

The American Society for Training and Development conducts an annual survey and in 1998, the survey included eight hundred and one organizations, both profit and non-profit. Among interesting results: firms are spending as much as ten times per employee on information technologies as they are on training! Among other findings was that compared with previous surveys, firms are increasing the amount of spending on training, and the proportion of employees receiving training increased. The selection of the sample – those firms that voluntarily join the organization's benchmarking service precludes making conclusions on the extent or nature of training among industries or within the US. However, the study does reveal that many firms have yet to understand that purchasing technology may not produce increases in productivity unless employees learn how to really use it (Bassi & Van Buren).

An American organization concerned with quality control systems within firms is the American Society for Quality. It advertises its mission as advancing "individual and organizational performance excellence worldwide by providing opportunities for learning, quality improvement, and knowledge exchange." (American Society for Quality). This organization offers education and training programs for quality control engineers and ISO 9000 series certification. It sponsors conferences and training programs, publishes several journals, and publishes book for industrial engineers and quality experts.

More recent research and publications have addressed the issue of how ideas are created and how individuals can harness what is known about the structure and function of the brain to increase their own learning and creative productivity. An article by Miller briefly describes a new tool, The BrainStyle Inventory®, Center for Creative Leadership based in Greensboro, N.C. A key principle in the BrainStyles™ approach is that people tend to have one core strength (of four defined) that doesn't change. However, by knowing one's BrainStyle one can leverage one's strength. The article presents a case study of Research Polymers International and how David Cherry implemented a strategy to save the firm from bankruptcy using the BrainStyles™ approach to create a team-based, intellectual capital generating organization. Tony

Buzan, a prolific author and co-author, on the brain, has made a career of teaching people what he calls Mind Mapping (trademarked term). Buzan has been involved as author or as co-author of some 84 materials including books, audiotapes, training manuals, and video tapes interpreting medical and scientific publications on research on the brain (Buzan).

The list of American 'self-improvement' books would fill this publication! But, the connection between individual creativity or learning or memorization, and that of 'intellectual capital' is still a rather unexplored area. It is one thing to memorize the names of all the Monarchs of the British Empire; it is another to be able to create an organization that injects intellectual capital into its products or services to achieve competitive advantage.

Based on the publications cited above and the articles cited in Kozlowski's chapter, it is clear that researchers are fascinated with intellectual capital and its implications for the economy. However, most research and publications focus on larger organizations and not on those who start with 'practically nothing' and develop new organizations rich in intellectual capital. It is this process of converting intellectual capital to financial capital that lies at the heart of intellectual entrepreneurship.

INTELLECTUAL ENTREPRENEUR DEFINED

The intellectual entrepreneur is one who is applying intellectual capital to enhance or define his/her firm's product or service to give it competitive advantage and a unique market niche. The intellectual entrepreneur's goal is to create an organization that will benefit from extraordinarily high growth and profitability. The intellectual entrepreneur seeks to have the firm develop creative ways of responding to changing market conditions thus helping to insure that: (a) the future of the organization will be secure, and (2) the organization becomes a distinctive entity valued at far more than its tangible worth. Under this definition, the entrepreneur's goal is to create a distinctive entity that has a value far more than its identifiable assets. In the United States, most entrepreneurs have a very strong vision and understanding of the process of creating wealth through taking a company public and begin their enterprises with this goal. Another strategy well understood by entrepreneurs even at the earliest stages of starting their company is the potential value of selling out to a competitor. There is a major distinction between a professional service provider ('mom and pop' enterprise) and a true entrepreneurial venture. Some might describe Stewart, for example, as an intellectual entrepreneur. After all, as a journalist turned book author turned management consultant, he has converted knowledge into income in the form of royalties, speaker fees and management consulting fees. He basically used his skills in researching, interviewing, writing, and editing to create articles, books and a knowledge base that has value. In return he earns an income. Consultants, lawyers, doctors, and teachers are examples of knowledge workers whose value is not in typing the will, giving the shot or writing on a blackboard but in solving someone's estate problem, curing their illness or satisfying someone's intellectual curiosity. However, take away the individual due to sickness, vacation or death, and you have an end to the stream of income. True intellectual entrepreneurs are building organizations that create wealth. Remove the entrepreneur and the organization continues. And really great organizations attract or develop their own superlative leaders. Jack Welch, for example, did not start General Electric, but his leadership has created executives at GE that have become successful leaders of other industrial giants. Creating an organization that is valued at more than its fair market value of physical assets requires more than packaging ideas into books or into services that must be performed by their creator. Creating an entrepreneurial venture involves extending one's intellectual capital to others who create systems that allow for replication and expansion to the point of becoming a self-sustaining organization. This conversion process is far more complex than it first appears.

The first step in the conversion process is at the individual level. The individual must do a self-assessment to identify their personal 'intellectual capital.' This is more than merely writing a work history or resume. It is putting on paper one's personal likes and dislikes, life style choices, what they actually learned from their experiences at work, school, family, church or any other organized activities. It involves taking a full inventory of knowledge and technical skills either gained through experience, academic courses, reading, and travel. It also involves documentation of one's personal network of friends, associates, and acquaintances. At the individual level, intellectual capital is more than knowledge – it is a reflection of the individual's personality, ability to solve problems and life style choices. From this self-assessment, an individual learns not only who they are but what they do not know and what they do not like.

The challenge for intellectual entrepreneurs is to look at 'what they know' and find the answer to the question of 'what problem can my knowledge solve?' Too often individuals interested in starting their own business look externally for 'business ideas.' These people are often attracted to purchasing a franchise because they don't want to cope with developing a sales or marketing strategy, they lack knowledge of a particular industry. Purchasing a franchise is nothing more than purchasing a job. Others will find a business idea that may have validity but they remain frustrated because it is doing something they clearly do not enjoy. Looking externally for 'ideas is a deficient approach because a person's expertise is internal not external. A better strategy is derived from research published on the brain and creativity.

The second step is to aggregate or package knowledge in a form that 'solves a problem.' When Stephen Jobs first started tinkering on a computer, he was solving a personal problem of creating a simple machine that he could use to teach his children about computers. The entire premise of Apple Computer: ease of use, simplicity of design, and functionality all stemmed from this perspective. Interestingly, after he left Apple to form NEXT Computers, he designed a machine with no floppy drives and its own proprietary operating system that really wasn't designed to operate application programs from other vendors, but was designed for the sophisticated user who wanted to design their own application programs. Basically, Jobs was creating a machine for his own pleasure without regard for market potential. Many critics called NEXT a 'company in search of a purpose.' Ironically, the machines did not sell, but his so-called operating system had value to programmers because it allowed programmers to select huge blocks of pre-written code to design software.

Many dot.com companies were created during the 1990's based on interesting technology, but they did not offer services that people were willing to pay for! On the other hand, successful firms are those that solve a problem for their customers. A young computer programmer created a company called Porvenir for the purpose of providing mutual fund investment managers; executives of US export companies and other financial managers with the ability to read Latin American corporate web page information in English. This company was sold to Thomson International Publishers at a profit when many dot.com companies were running out of money. The reason was simple. The company was selling subscriptions to their business-financial data base company to major firms like American Express, Bank of America, etc and was profitable. They had a fully functional search engine that worked! And they had acquired a small staff that knew how to accurately translate Portuguese and Spanish.

The third step in the conversion process is to identify the market, and make sure that the proposed 'solution' is one that can be priced and still produce a profit. Selling service or products at a loss will never produce a profit no matter what the volume! In solving a problem, the intellectual entrepreneur needs to understand that the solution must be priced sufficiently high to afford a profit at a reasonable volume. Part of the angst over AMAZON.COM and Office Max is whether they will be able to sell enough products to earn a profit. They have invested so much in their infrastructure that some analysts question whether they can recover their costs.

Fourth. The intellectual entrepreneur must have some knowledge of the industry and some basic understanding of basic business principles. Industry expertise is best acquired through personal contacts – yes, networks. Work experience and reading trade publications are other ways of gaining industry experience. What is interesting about intellectual entrepreneurs is that their technical expertise is surpassed by their broad knowledge and broad contacts and not the other way around. What makes an entrepreneur different from the pure inventor is the ability to network into different communities including but not limited to potential customers, potential investors, potential financial advisers and prospective employees. While there is no research supporting a particular personality requirement, clearly those who are comfortable in communicating to very different audiences will have an easier time than those who can only express themselves in highly technical language. These personal and professional networks are developed over a lifetime. Before investing large sums of money into a business, successful entrepreneurs develop strong personal networks in the industry they are going to enter. Trade associations offer excellent opportunities to make those contacts. Even in transition countries, as the economies have improved, trade associations consisting of competitors within an industry have banded together to exchange ideas and information, and to promote their industry. Some Western European governments even sponsor such organizations to encourage economic development in specific regions focusing on specific industries. The French government has targeted certain regions of France as future 'Silicon Valleys.'

A fifth strategy is to conceive of the business not as an extension of one's personal power, but as an organization with systems and incentives that build a culture capable of sustaining itself without the founder. This is the key distinction between the 'mom and pop' business consultants, attorneys, and other professionals who view employees as an extension of themselves. Like a giant octopus, as the organization grows and more people are hired, the business owner serves as 'controller' or the central brain issuing orders to the task-oriented tentacles. The controller becomes frustrated when things do not turn out as 'ordered' and begin to question whether they can find 'people who will care as much about the business as themselves.' The entrepreneur takes a different approach. The entrepreneur understands that his role is one of master planner, master teacher and spiritual organizer. The entrepreneur understands that the role of an organization is to hire ordinary people and train them to accomplish extraordinary things. They view their organizations as networks of expertise linked together by a common mission. They are comfortable in 'outsourcing' many corporate functions so that they can concentrate their resources and personnel on activities where they can truly 'add value.' Other writers call this strategy "focusing on core competencies." McDonald's is an often-cited example of an organization that has created a management system for taking teenagers who have never cooked at home and putting them into teams that literally cook the same meal, with the same taste, everywhere – worldwide. One might dispute the quality of the taste, but the consistency is nothing short of miraculous! Another example is the Walt Disney theme park organization. They literally saturate new hires with almost one week of intensive corporate history, history of each of the major cartoon characters and customer relations before they begin to train new employees on their specific task. The organization wants every one of their employees from janitors to chefs to people taking tickets that the success of the organization lies in giving their customers a first class entertainment experience. The organization continues to preach the Walt Disney culture so that everyone understands that they are personally responsible and part of making that first class experience happen. These two organizations provide very basic services, but they employ very high technology to accomplish this, in yet, they realize that the Achilles Heel of their operation is in the interface between customer and their lowest level employee. It is the dirty toilet, the face of someone bored while taking a ticket, or the indifferent greeter that can sabotage millions of dollars of investment.

H. Ross Perot, now better known for his political antics, was an early intellectual entrepreneur in establishing a world-class computer software service bureau firm. Perot was employed by IBM when he approached management with the concept of helping customers with the software services they would need to best utilize the equipment they were buying. Concerned that getting into the software service business would place the company in legal jeopardy from anti-trust regulators who were already constantly bombarding the company with legal requests for information pursuant to their investigation over their market dominance in hardware, management declined Perot's suggestion. In organizing EDS, Perot understood that he was creating an organization that had to be capable of literally training its own software engineers, writers, and technical service people. At the time few universities taught computer science to create graduates capable enough to write the complex programs needed. So, Perot ended up hiring accounting majors who understood the use of such data. He literally created teams whereby each individual was responsible for training others. Perot, a former naval officer, understood this very important aspect of leadership training that he had experienced aboard Navy ships and at the United States Naval Academy. He also understood the psychological importance of having a staff that had a professional appearance – a trademark of IBM, which required all men to wear, suits, wing-tipped shoes, and white shirts with modest ties. EDS developed not only the training manuals for each and every job, but imposed a culture that was almost military in its rigidity on its employees.

Another feature of the naval experience was that in the United States Navy, no one is permitted to remain in their same job for more than 18 months. This reality forces an organization to place a very high premium and high incentive system on managers who truly train subordinates to replace them so that they may assume yet higher responsibilities. Perot's company grew so incredibly quickly to have a value on the New York Stock Exchange of almost $1 billion back in the late 1970's. EDS was eventually purchased by General Motors, and Perot personally gained close to one billion dollars for his share in the company. For a short time, Perot was General Motors' largest shareholder.

With the departure of Perot, many financial analysts predicted the demise of his organization. What they did not understand is that Perot put into place an organization that created its own culture and systems to train people and to extract from them feedback necessary for the organization's survival. While some employees found the environment at EDS to be somewhat restrictive and intolerant, most were thrilled to be part of an organization that was growing so rapidly. Perot, like other American entrepreneurs, understood the importance of offering employees stock plans whereby they would participate in the wealth creation process. Sam Walton is another example. His organization created many millionaires because he offered stock early in the company's history. And this practice continues today whereby employees are offered the opportunity to take some of their compensation in the form of stock. Every single store posts the daily price of Wal-mart stock where both the public and the employees may see it (the sign is always posted in the front of the store in plain view of the checkout counters). These are not isolated examples as thousands of firms have rewarded employees with ownership or generous bonus plans. Many successful intellectual entrepreneurs understand the value of creating positive incentive systems.

In contrast, there is the example of Xerox Corporation. Here is a company that sells $19.5 billion in equipment and services that is currently selling assets to cover operating losses. What happened to a company that in 1986 won the Malcolm Baldridge Award? What caused Xerox, the developer of the telecopier (now known as the fax machine) and graphic user interface (the mouse driven format that Windows and Apple's operating system is based on) and countless other pioneering inventions to slide to the brink of bankruptcy? The answers to these questions would fill another chapter, but the lesson is that corporate culture can also serve as cement that dries too quickly and stifles an organization's ability to respond to changing market conditions. Bureaucratic corporate cultures have hierarchical compensation systems that reward employees for maintaining the status quo and discourage them from 'thinking out of the box' and exploiting their intellectual capital for the benefit of the organization. Xerox developed many technologies, but they simply did not have the system in place to reward those capable of translating research into practical application for mass production. Xerox's leaders understood the potential of new technology, but they did not understand how to create reward systems and organizational structures capable of withstanding the risk of applying technological advances to the marketplace. Individuals willing to take the psychological risk of failure are intellectual entrepreneurs.

Xerox's success in the copier industry was comfortably based on having a patent on a unique machine: the first commercially viable copier. When forced by threats of anti-trust suits by the U.S. government, Xerox licensed out their technology to organizations that were quite nimble in 'copying the copier' and improving its performance and cost. Smaller organizations basically invested more intellectual capital into improving Xerox's major product. So, not only did Xerox lose on not having applications engineers to apply their technological breakthroughs, but they failed to recognize that smaller competitors would be able to reduce the size and cost of copiers and threaten their market dominance.

General Electric, on the other hand, took a totally different strategy. They set up their own venture capital fund for the purpose of investing in companies that have promising technologies that they hope will one-day be worthy of acquisition. Their strategy has proven to be financially rewarding for the company even when they did not acquire the fruit from the financial seeds they planted because they simply held stock in companies that went public. They permitted their employees to take sabbaticals to work on their entrepreneurial ventures and would even fund them if successful prototypes were developed.

The challenge for today's intellectual entrepreneurs is that the speed of technological advances may not permit the full return on specific technologies because new technologies emerge so quickly. At the macro economic level, this is the type of challenge that Kodak faces where digital technology threatens a major part of their firm's livelihood. At the level of the intellectual entrepreneur, the threats are even more intense as large and small companies are entering the marketplace with new technologies. Their survival is not based on merely maintaining market share. This is the strategy that almost caused the demise of Motorola. At one point they had a dominant share of the telephone-radio market with their analogue equipment. This company had in place a customer satisfaction system that reflected that their customers were quite pleased with the analogue systems. However, what the system did not have was a way to measure the impact of digital voice transmission systems so the company did not make the type of heavy investment in digital that Nokia made. Now Motorola is playing a catch up game in that they lost valuable market share to competitors who offered smaller, less expensive cellular systems. Today's intellectual entrepreneur must not only keep an eye on developing a strong internal organization, but must also create systems that literally continually scan the horizon for possible threats from new technologies.

The conversion of intellectual capital into financial capital by intellectual entrepreneurs requires at first an individual's understanding of the concept of value and finding economically valuable solutions to problems, coupled with an understanding of the difference between creating an income and creating wealth, and finally an ability to create the type of organization that is self-sustaining and capable of rapid response to changing external and internal conditions. By no means is the above discussion a complete treatise on the conversion process. It merely suggests some of the themes that are worthy of further investigation.

IMPLICATIONS OF THE AGE OF INTELLECTUAL ENTREPRENEURSHIP

Intellectual capital is the ability of an individual or of an organization to use knowledge to leverage human resources and natural resources more efficiently. Intellectual capital is what will continue to distinguish the quality of products and services and the relative degree of 'value added' amongst competitors of even commodity items such as steel, oil, etc. The intellectual entrepreneur is one who understands that increasingly the value of tangible products and services is dependent on the wise application and development of intellectual capital.

The age of intellectual entrepreneurship has only just begun. Barring war or major natural disasters, mankind has the promise of attaining sustainable development and improvement in the standard of living throughout the world. Though the field of intellectual entrepreneurship within the context of management is relatively new, the process of injecting intellectual content to improve productivity is not and the process of creating organizations that create wealth is not new either. Putting the two elements together against a backdrop of rapidly advancing technological developments, however, has positive implications for encouraging sustainable development.

Public policy clearly has important effects on the economic, regulatory, legal and financial environment that intellectual entrepreneurs will face. The intellectual elites who guide such public policy discussions are beginning to recognize the positive role that intellectual entrepreneurs can have in assuring continued improvement on the standard of living and quality of life even while some protest and are actively hostile to new technology as a threat to the natural environment. To some extend, the success of intellectual entrepreneurs is somewhat dependent on the public being able to comprehend what is a threat to the environment and what is not. The public's understanding of basic science is quite important. Witness the current fiasco in California. Under political pressure the state froze prices of electric power while deregulating the purchase of power from external sources. At the same time, the state has had a ten-year moratorium on the construction of any form of electrical power generation. California, the epicenter of intellectual entrepreneurship and home to Silicon Valley is out of electricity! Fears of nuclear power plants, objections to wind mill farms because of the possible but not verified effects on bird migration, dislike of coal power plants, etc all resulted in a political stalemate that is literally causing companies to shut down because of a lack of electricity. Clearly there is a political danger to progress if a public lacks a basic understanding of economics and technology. Intellectual leadership is needed to bridge the ever-growing gap between what the public understands of economics and rapid developments in technology.

A European example of this gap lies in the controversy over genetically altered foods. Corn, wheat and other basic staples of modern society have all been genetically altered since before Christ. What has changed is the technique. Banning research on the implications of cellular genetic alteration of food products is like shutting off the electricity in California. The point is that countries that want intellectual entrepreneurship to continue to make contributions to humanity must have political and educational leadership to advance research and scientific knowledge to the general public.

The concept of intellectual entrepreneurship also has profound implications on the nature of the workplace as organizations seek to develop and nurture their intellectual capital. Some organizations will simply take adversarial view toward individuals who might seek to exploit knowledge they have acquired at the workplace. Others will attempt more enlightened approaches toward human relations to build loyalty. These are some of the very real legal and managerial issues that organizations will face during this age of intellectual entrepreneurship.

The rapidity and fluidity of knowledge thanks to the internet and yet-to-be devised methods of storing, accessing and transmitting knowledge, data, research may result in more competitive between nations. But at the same time, the fluidity and rapid communication of knowledge offers nations and individuals the opportunity to spare themselves the high cost of errors if they can access and learn from other's mistakes. While advances in computer storage capability is reaching the infinite at lower and lower costs, the issues of systems to access and assess such information represent profound challenges to intellectual entrepreneurs.

Barring war or major natural disaster, and assuming that the public will continue to support the notion of free market economics and democracy, the age of intellectual entrepreneurship may be quite significant in human history as we come closer to sustainable development and an improved standard of living throughout the world.

REFERENCES

American Society for Development & Training, web site located at http://www.astd.org/virtual community/about astd/

American Society for Quality, web site located at www.asq.org

Bassi, Laurie J. and Van Buren, Mark E. "The 1999 ASTD State of Industry Report, American Society for Training and Development" *Training and Development*, No. 1, Vol. 53, P. S3, January 1, 1999.

Bontis, N. and Girardi, J. "Teaching Knowledge Management and Intellectual Capital Lessons: An Empirical Examination of the Tango Simulation" www.celemi.com/articles/texts/tangostudy9903.asp

Brooking, Annie, *Intellectual Capital – The Core Asset for the Third Millennium Enterprise*, London: International Thomson Business Press, 1996.

Bukh, P.H., Larsen, H.T., Mouritsen, J. "Constructing Intellectual Capital Statements" *Scandinavian Journal of Management*, Vol. 17, Elsevier Science Ltd, 2001, pp. 87–108.

Buzan, Tony *The Mind Map Book, How to Use Radiant Thinking, Make the Most of Your Mind, Using Both Sides of Your Brain,* are among the books that Buzan has authored with various publishers (list available at www.amazon.com).

Deming, W. Edwards *Some Theory of Sampling*, Wiley Publishers, New York, 1950

Edvinsson, Leif "Developing Intellectual Capital at Skandia" *Long Range Planning*, Vol. 30, No. 3, Elsevier Science Ltd., 1997, p 366–373.

Edvinsson and Malone *Intellectual Capital*, Harvard Business Press, Cambridge, MA. 1997.

Fruin, Mark Knowledge Works: *Managing Intellectual Capital at Toshiba*, Oxford University Press, 1997.

Greco, JoAnn "Knowledge is Power" *Journal of Business Strategy*, March 1999/April 1999.

Knight, Daniel J. "Performance Measures for Increasing Intellectual Capital" *Strategy and Leadership*, No. 2 Vol. 27, March 1, 1999, p. 22.

Liebowitz, J. Wright, K "Does Measuring Knowledge Make "Cents"?" Expert Systems With Applications Vol. 17 Elsevier Science Ltd., pp. 99–103.

Roos, Goran and Roos, Johan "Measuring Your Company's Intellectual Performance" *Long Range Planning*, Vol 30, No. 3, Elsevier Science Ltd., 1997, pp 413–426.

Roos, Johan "Exploring the Concept of Intellectual Capital (IC), *Long Range Planning,* Vol 31, No. 1, Elsevier Science Ltd., 1998, pp 150–153.

Shewhart, Walter A. *Statistical Method from the Viewpoint of Quality Control*, with editorial assistance of W. Edwards Deming. The Graduate School, The Department of Agriculture, Washington, 1939.

Stewart, Thomas A *Fortune* magazine, "Brainpower" April 1991, and "Intellectual Capital", October 1994.

Stewart, Thomas A. *Intellectual Capital, The New Wealth of Nations* Currency Book, Doubleday Publishers, New York, 1997.

Taylor, Frederick Winslow, *The Principles of Scientific Management*, Harper & Brothers, New York, London, 1911.

Amir Fazlagić

THE INTELLECTUAL PRODUCT

======================== *Abstract* ========================

A heuristic framework addressing the link between knowledge applied for the design of the product and the knowledge mediated from the product to the customer is developed, according to the author's proposed Intellectual Product taxonomy. An expanded view of the knowledge contained in the product allows us to begin redefining value to understand knowledge as an competitive advantage factor in the new product development process. The educational product is proposed as the best example to describe the concept of Intellectual Product. However, the research implications of this new concept reach far beyond the education sector. The realization that value can be generated by 'knowledge content' attached to the product can help reconfigure marketing strategies in many other service sectors including medicine, financial services, professional (B2B) services. The concept of mutual knowledge exchange and educating the customer can also be applied for the manufactured products.

This paper describes the application of knowledge management and product design approaches in service and manufacturing sectors. It reveals the economic meaning of the new perspective of the knowledge content.

INTRODUCTION

The purpose of this article is to develop a conceptual framework that explains the phenomenon of intensive use of knowledge in today's market offerings. To do so, I advance the notion of **intellectual product** as a principal bridge linking the theory of knowledge management and market orientation in the Knowledge Economy

Modern management literature abounds in examples of how knowledge capital contributes to the competitive advantage of many businesses. A number of such companies represent service sector businesses (i.e.Skandia ASF, The World Bank, Accenture, KPMG). The traditional capital, which added value in the industrial economy, has become an important but not necessary element of business growth. In 1997 a $1.5 billion company *Barnes and Noble* felt threatened by the small ($18 mln in revenues) internet company *Amazon.com*. And rightfully so. The important feature of knowledge content is determined by the future rather than the past whereas the financial capital built-up is the result of past achievements and investments.

So far the mainstream marketing researchers have not entered the field of knowledge management. E.Gummesson (2000) assumes that knowledge is just an element of the thirty relationships ("From 4P to 30R"). Therefore, further research in this field seems justified.

Is the Knowledge Economy going to bring about a new breed of market offerings? What will the new value drivers be like?

To give a better view of the new construct of intellectual capital it is necessary to articulate and describe the path, which leads from the industrial paradigms to the newly introduced model of the intellectual product.

THE INDUSTRIAL AGE LEGACY
AND THE KNOWLEDGE ECONOMY

Studies on the industrial economy have been conducted since 1930's (Fisher, 1939; Bell, 1959). C.Clark (1957) introduced the term *service industries*. H.Magdorf and D.Weintraub (1940) defined the service sector by enumerating service professions and J.Fourastie (1969) proposed the three-sector model of the economy based on the dynamics of productivity with the service sector having the lowest productivity of all.

Many authors however question the **output**-*based* typology of the sectors. J.Naisbitt as many other authors define the New Economy not as a *Service Economy* but as a *Knowledge-based Economy*, thus focusing on the **input** (resource) end.

As it often happens the pace of the developments in the econo-my is not matched by the pace of advance of economic theories.

Not surprisingly, many present day management dogmas originate from the industrial era thinking. One of the most frequently criticized 'industrial age' concepts is the present accounting system (i.e. Edvinsson and Malone, 1997; Stewart, 1997). It has been widely recognized that knowledge capital requires new methods of accounting. The accounting systems of today has no monopoly for "applying past solutions to solve present problems". It is tempting to seek other parallels. One of them would be marketing theory.

The customers in the Service Economy have valued quality service. The customers of the Knowledge Economy, instead of temporary satisfaction will seek lifelong benefits of their decisions expecting the purchase of the product will positively and permanently transform them. This can be achieved only if the service product is designed in a new way where the main competitive factor of the product is its ability to educate the customer.

Knowledge is perhaps the ultimate source of opportunity : tt is embedded in research and development. Relationships now are so widely viewed as essential to opportunity creation that they are encapsulated in a distinct relationship marketing.

Table 1. Typology of knowledge

Encoded knowledge (know what?)	Written policies and procedures
Habitual knowledge (know how?)	Every day routine activity
Scientific knowledge (know why?)	Technological and scientific knowledge
Collaboration knowledge (know who?)	Interaction and problem solving
Process knowledge (know when and where?)	Cross-functional teams

Source: M.Whitehill, 1997

SERVICES MARKETING: FROM TRANSACTIONS TO RELATIONS

In 1977 Lynn Shostack, wrote an article "Breaking Free from Product marketing":

> "New concepts are necessary if service marketing is to succeed ...merely adopting product marketing's labels does not resolve the question of whether product marketing can be overlaid on service business."

It was around that time that researchers started to realize the fundamental differences between services marketing and manufactured products marketing. The concept of service product was then introduced to mean an intangible equivalent of the manufactured product rendered by a service company.

For the next decade we witnessed an unprecedented growth of interest in service marketing. The majority of authors aimed at developing a separate *'break free'* theories. The most common approach to services theory was, and still is, to point out the main differences between manufactured products and so called service products i.e. intangibility, simultaneity, and heterogeneity.

The traditional view of marketing was that to achieve marketing success every business had to find the right combination of: technical features of the product, its price, and distribution and promotion methods. The traditional view of manufacturing is to seal off production from the outside world by placing organizational buffers (marketing, product design etc.) between the customer and the production system.

The question of a service product and relationship marketing methodology will occupy our attention for some time to come, until we develop a set of tested tools for defining all the dimensions of the new construct.

One of the important contributions of RM is new thinking about the service process. Services are said to be spontaneous, often difficult to define, acts but, on the other hand, services have become subject to deliberate and systematic methods of design similar to those practiced in the engineering sector. Therefore, **designing can be thought of as a bridge between industrial sector and service sector management theory.**

The unquestionable hallmark of industrial products marketing is the marketing-mix. Nowadays, after over 30 years of the dominance of the marketing-mix (four P's) even its most ardent proponents admit the failure of the application of mechanistic models to marketing. P.Kotler (2000) writes:

> "You can never design a marketing strategy using the Four Ps without first knowing what kind of market you are operating in. The Four Ps do not embrace the relationship-building aspect!"

Since knowledge exchange can be classified as a *win-win process* where the transfer of knowledge produces value both on the provider's and customer's side companies should struggle to engage in knowledge creation relationships. The best methodology undoubtedly is that under the name of Relationship Marketing. The past decade has witnessed a major directional change in both marketing theory and practice with the shift toward relationship marketing. Because of the need for interactions in a complex network of producers, marketers, and consumers, relationship marketing is viewed as an interactive process in a social context. Relationship marketing is about healthy relationships characterized by trust, equity, responsibility and commitment.

Service marketing has gone a long way from virtual non-existence before 1970's to its present status. The two important elements of this evolution was first breaking free from the industrial, marketing-mix paradigms and second, adapting a wide range of universal concepts, definitions such as customer satisfaction, service production, service factory and perhaps the most important: service product.

The outcome of the above mentioned evolution is a totally 'non-industrial' branch of marketing theory: **relationship marketing (RM)**.

The main tenets of the RM philosophy are:

♦ new definition of quality where technological features are only a minor component of perceived quality,

♦ the new meaning of the relationships: the value of business depends on the duration and depth and intimacy of the relationships rather then the number of transactions. Organizational performance is increasingly tied to intangible assets such as corporate culture, customer relationships and brand equity,

♦ emphasis on relations instead of transactions. The relationships, which are developed with customers often, generate unique insight into customers' backgrounds, behaviours, and propensities (Srivastava and Sharvani, 1998). Buyers will inevitably treat any offering like a commodity if they feel treated like a mere piece of market. The service provider must spend time interacting with customers to understand their unique needs.

There is growing recognition in literature that customer relationships enhance cash flows by reducing the level of working capital and fixed investments. Consequences of disloyalty are obvious: San Antonio based insurance company USAA has retention rate of 99% compared with industry average of 80%. This means that after three years they must replace less that 3% of customers compared with 50% for industry.

There are a number of specific topics around which service marketing thought is evolving (Lovelock, 1996): service quality; service encounters/experiences; service design; customer retention and relationship management and internal marketing. None of them however has drawn attention of knowledge management theorists. Some attempts have been made to integrate the intangible assets with marketing (Srivastava, Shervani and Fahey, 1998). Achieving the full profit potential of each customer relationships should be the fundamental goal of every business (Grant and Schlesinger, 1995).

Nevertheless, marketing has been considered an element of company's capital (customer capital) – an input necessary for successful strategy and a subset of Intellectual Capital Balance Sheet taxonomy (Edvinsson, 1997).

Relationship marketing prepares ground for looking at marketing relationships as a subject of knowledge management (table 2).

Table 2. Relationship marketing vs. Knowledge management

Relationship Marketing Research area	Common ground shared with Knowledge Management
Service Quality: the single most researched area in services marketing	Knowledge Valuation: the ultimate test for the knowledge quality is the market success of the market offering which has been created with the application of the knowledge of the service provider
Service encounters/ /experiences ("Moments of Truth" by Jan Carlzon of SAS Airlines)	The Knowledge Management literature primary focus is on the internal knowledge of employees. This perspective states that the knowledge created and mediated during service encounter (the dialogue) deserves equally prominent attention. Especially the customer's involvement in service encounters and the customer's role in service production and delivery shed a new light onto knowledge management
Service design	Services are immaterial processes. Originally, the service design was spurred by the growth of total quality movement (TQM) because TQM is process oriented (Lovelock, 1996). Being intangible, services are subject to less rigorous quality design standards. The most mature concepts of service design include service blueprinting and service mapping (Shostack, 1984; 1987; 1992). The paramount difference between service product design and the manufactured product design is the inclusion of the customer. **Service design has not received any attention in the literature nor in practice of knowledge management.** 'Service engineering' should and will be key areas for scholarly and management inquiry (Lovelock, 1996). The incorporation of the customer's needs into design and delivery services will have far reaching implications

Table 2. Relationship marketing vs. Knowledge management (cont.)

Relationship Marketing Research area	Common ground shared with Knowledge Management
Customer retention and relationship management	The idea of retaining 'old' customers instead of acquiring 'new' ones lies at the heart of Relationship Marketing (RM) concept. A prerequisite for a relationship is always mutual trust between agents. Trust building is therefore a common ground for mediation of knowledge and business relationship development
Internal marketing	"Everyone in the organization has a customer" (Gronroos, 1981) and therefore everyone in the organization has someone whom she or he must serve. *Communities of practice* are a good example of how internal marketing works within an organization. In fact, internal marketing encompasses knowledge brokering – an important element of knowledge management
Information asymmetry	Marketing has been viewed as a tool for capitalizing on the inadequate information on customer's side. Information asymmetry may exist between transacting parties in a variety of settings. Knowledge sharing is a creed for streamlining organizational efficiency
Measurement	A frequently quoted criterion for RM effectiveness is the retention rate and loyalty. Aaker and Jacobsen (1994) point out that assets that are harder to measure are also more likely to be underfunded. Market based assets are principally of two related types: relational and intellectual (Shrivastava and Sharvani, 1998). Relational market based assets are outcomes of relationship between a firm and key external stakeholders including customers. Intellectual market-based assets are the types of knowledge a firm possesses about environment, such as the state of market conditions. Lowendahl (1997) writes about relational intangibles, Mallone and Edvinsson (1997) mention the customer capital. All the terms refer to the 'marketing muscle' of the firm.

Table 2. Relationship marketing vs. Knowledge management (cont.)

Relationship Marketing Research area	Common ground shared with Knowledge Management
Strategic Management	Strategic management of the 1970-s and Business Process Reengineering (BPR) (Quintas, 1997; Bertels and Savage 1998; Huseman, Goodman, 1999) paved the way for building more holistic management models covering the complexity of networks and relationships. Resource based view of the firm has been one of most influential concepts so far. Knowledge competitive advantage of a service firm: • the competence of its staff • educational competence of the organization to develop and improve the performance of the front-line staff • the knowledge contained in a process behind the scenes
Growth of business	A firm may develop over time unique facts, beliefs, and assumptions about its customers' tastes, manufacturing process. Intimacy of relationships enables knowledge to be developed (Glazer, 1991). Knowledge Management draws on the Resource Based view of the firm (Itami, Prahalad and Hamel) It assumes that the growth of the knowledge base will have its impact on the knowledge base. Therefore, growth of business can be explained in terms of accumulation of intellectual capital. Knowledge relationships require complex networks including universities, educators, suppliers etc. Learning and knowledge creation are increasingly the purpose of alliances The customer's personality and stock of knowledge becomes enriched (Gummesson, 1999).
Knowledge creation	Knowledge product and Services are those offerings that embody learning and the capacity to create new knowledge in them. In the old days knowledge came out of the R&D function – people inventing new knowledge – Today the whole company become R&D function. Everybody is responsible for contributing to the new knowledge base. The R&D part now is everybody (Botin, 2000). J.Kao (1997) writes: "Creativity is a process that has grammar – a process that's linked to the way knowledge is managed [...] Creativity is not only about new products and services, it's equally about new processes".

Table 2. Relationship marketing vs. Knowledge management (cont.)

Relationship Marketing Research area	Common ground shared with Knowledge Management
Value creation	Marketing activities focus on success in the product marketplace. Increasingly, however, top management requires that marketing view its ultimate purpose as contributing to the enhancement of shareholder returns. Under RM, the firm's offering is seen as a "value carrier" (Ravald and Gronroos, 1996), destined to offer a greater net-value than the offerings of the competitors. The shift from goods to services to knowledge is a shift in the fundamental basis for value added (Morrison, 1998). The knowledge content allows for the formation of huge numbers of one-to-one relationships. Gummesson (1999) writes about the *Value Economy* to describe the present transformation. The value of knowledge can be estimated no sooner than after the service encounter. The application of mathematical methods (Kanevsky, 1998) becomes problematic when it comes to the description and analysis of thousands of incomparable and unique "moments of truth" characteristic to service marketing but only cursory in the consumption of industrial products. Relationship marketing has opened up new ways of formulating even more advanced "down-to-customer" theories. Davidow and Malone (1992) commenting on the changes in the marketplace defined value-based-marketing as: *To exceed customer expectations one must not only design appealing and useful products and deliver them in a timely fashion, but maintain a more than satisfactory level of service for that product through its life cycle ant that of its descendants*
The role of the Internet	The proponents of 4P's assume that the Internet is another tool for reaching the right customers with the right information at the right time. Eventually we will realize the scope of the whole knowledge business and see that the internet part is just a subset. Although the role of ICT cannot be underestimated there is a magnitude of business activities in The Knowledge Economy, which have nothing to do with computers.

Source: derived from Ch. Lovelock, 1996.

However, you cannot ask your customers for information on product improvement. They have no idea of the future (Morrison, 1998). Until recently, such problems were resolved by high satisfaction and high sacrifice situations (see Gilmore and Pine, 2000). Now the responsibility goes back to the "manufacturer". Are we then going back to the into sales oriented business? Is marketing no longer a powerful means of acquiring company-market fit? Certainly not – this time, however, it is the service provider who is supposed to know the future needs of its client. The failure to meet those demands is not the fault of bad marketing (knowledge acquisition) but inefficient knowledge creation and application within the company.

THE CONCEPT OF SERVICE PRODUCT

This paper describes the application of knowledge management and product design approaches in service and manufacturing sectors. It reveals the economic meaning of the new perspective of knowledge content.

One of the contributions of relationship marketing to the understanding of separateness of services is the concept of **service product**. Service products can be subject to designing, market tests and many other engineering tools similar to those known from manufacturing sector. The differences occur when we look at the sequence and interrelatedness of the three main elements of the design and its design process (figure 1). I believe that the background for the formulation of the intellectual product concept is the realization that the service product is designed at the time of production. The service provider is capable of standardizing a number of features so that unqualified personnel can repeatedly provide quality services. On the other hand no two service acts are exactly the same.

Figure 1. New Product Development

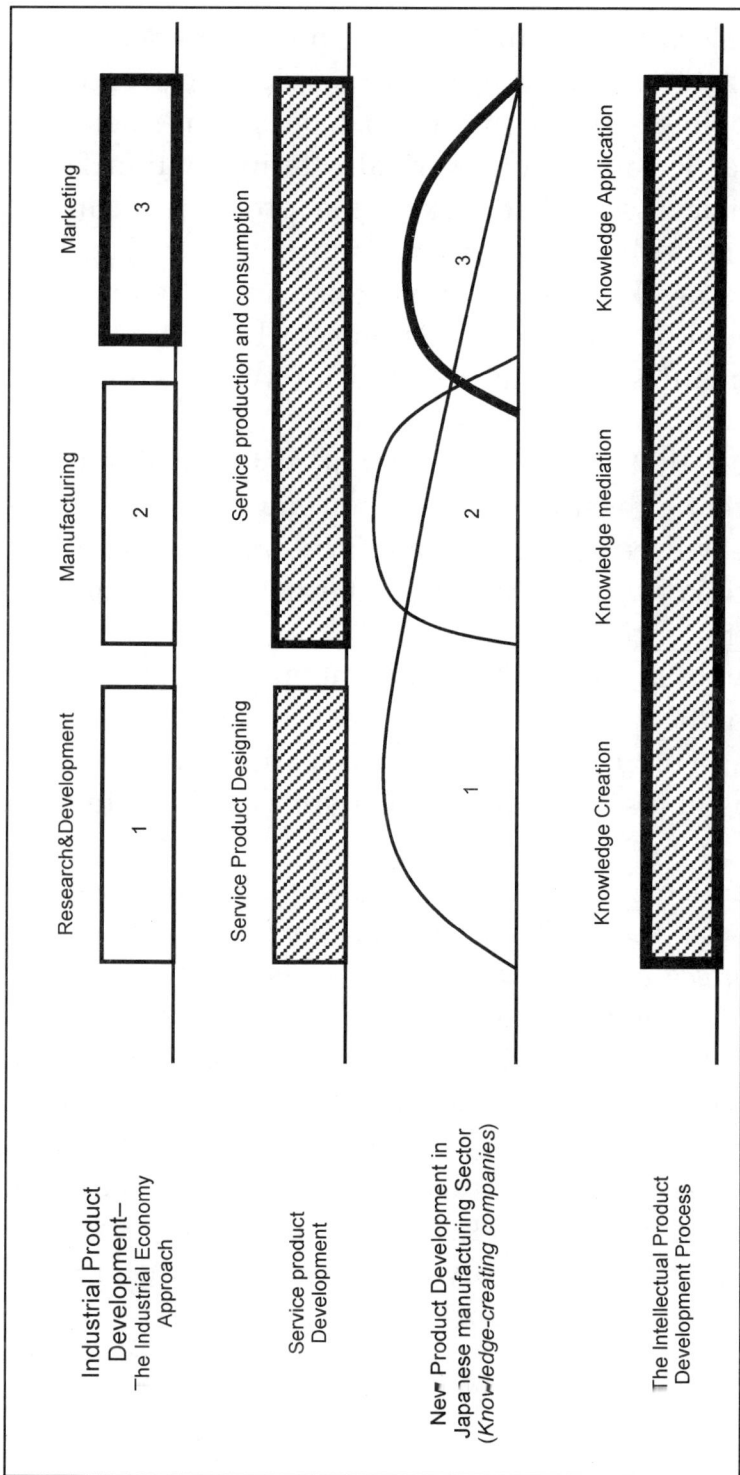

Source: Aothor's based on: I. Nonaka, H. Takeuchi, The Knowledge Creating Company, Harvard Business School Press, Boston, 1995, p. 78. See also: (Laem, 1996); Knowledge Management in The Learning Society, OECD, Paris 2000, p. 59; A. Fazlagić, 2001

The majority of industries are now experiencing rapid commodization of most products, services or even processes for their delivery (Whitehill, 1997). One North American bank boasts that it can copy any rival offering within 24 hours. The tangible assets that make up a product are more and more prone to hostile copying. Traditional barriers to entry are collapsing. The organizations that can move most quickly are those with a store of skills on which to draw. The most agile companies are able to build upon their knowledge assets.

I propose that soon the strategy of customization will be so popular that almost any competitor equipped with the right ICT tools will be able to imitate it by introducing a broader pool of choices. How then will the next battle for the customer be fought?

I believe that the battle will be about the value of knowledge embodied in the product. The customer will stop looking for short-term solutions such as learning a new skill, 'lose 20 pounds in just 3 months' or get your car fixed in less than an hour.

The service provider will be compelled to answer such questions as: *"How will the quality of my life improve in 20 year's time if I purchase your service?"*

In 1968 F.Herzberg put forth his "two-factor theory of motivation". He identified two categories of factors, one he called "hygiene factors", and the other he called "motivators" (Neumann and Jackson, Jr., 1999). If we assume that both categories apply to the present status of the customer, it would be tempting to seek another dimension in time: I propose to add a third category of factors i.e. "transformers" (table 3).

Table 3. Quality drivers in the Knowledge Economy

HYGENE FACTORS (Preventing Customer Dissatisfaction)	SATISFIERS (contributing to customer satisfaction)	TRANSFORMERS (contributing to customer's transformation)
Credibility	Responsivness	Experience
Reliability	Courtesy	Education (Knowledge dissemination)
Accessibility	Empathy	Righteousness
Delivery	Exceptional Quality	Faith
Accuracy	Personnel	Respect

Source: author and Neuman and Jackson, Jr., 1999.

THE MODEL OF INTELLECTUAL PRODUCT

"Product" has come to mean anything offered in exchange for monetary value, rather than only tangible, manufactured goods. The popularity of the term has somewhat blurred the fundamental distinction between intangible offerings for which goods are components. (Pine II and Gilmore, 1997). The economic pyramid introduced by Pine II and Gilmore have proposed a much broader view of the economic landscape. No longer are customers subject to 'a delivery of an offering from the producer'. To stay alive companies will have to offer products, which **transform the customer** (figure 2). Transformation means not only technological correctness of the industrial age or quality service. The new economic offerings on top of the Economic Pyramid are inherently personal (Pine II and Gilmore, 1997), one-of-a-kind. If a child pays a three-day visit at one of the Walt Disney Resorts she not only gets a quality service but also learns about the world (experience) and her personality is ultimately being reshaped (transformed). To achieve such an impact the service provider needs to offer a bundle of benefits which go far beyond a transactional context. The client has to be looked upon as a 'heart and soul matter'. The extent and depth of such transformation relies heavily on the knowledge contained in the product. It is the knowledge itself which has the power to change (transform) people. Therefore, **the competitiveness of business products will depend heavily on their knowledge content.**

Figure 2. From Commodities to Transformations

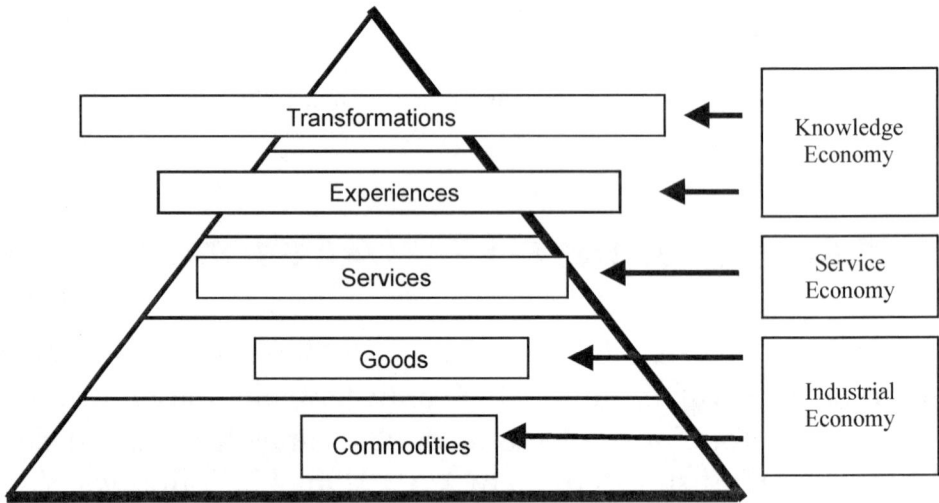

Source: author and Strategic Horizons LLP, 1997

This statement calls for the introduction of a new concept defining the role of knowledge in the product. In my view, the process of new product development (NPD) in the Knowledge Economy will include the decisions about:

➢ what knowledge to include in the product?
➢ what impact will this knowledge have upon the customer?
➢ how will the knowledge be 'packaged'?

What will the interactions be between the core knowledge and the marketing knowledge?

Especially the last question deserves further explanation. Using the Walt Disney example, it is obvious that the transformation which is taking place derives from the wellsprings of knowledge accumulated and applied by Walt Disney theme park specialists. There is also the question of financial backup and infrastructure necessary to 'sell' the core knowledge. No child will be transformed in a theme park packed with restaurants and vending machines if the attractions are no more eye-catching than a billboard.

In the same vain, hiring the best artists, novelists, hosts and comedians will be a shameful marketing disaster if they are not backed up by huge investments in entertainment technology.

Knowledge delivery emerges as the core element of the product, not an add-on element. Now it is not the core and augmented product components that make the distinction between the ordinary and the extraordinary. It is skillful knowledge management, which enables the application of so-called "marketing knowledge" to streamline the flow of professional knowledge from and to the customer (figure 3).

Figure 3. From Service product to intellectual product

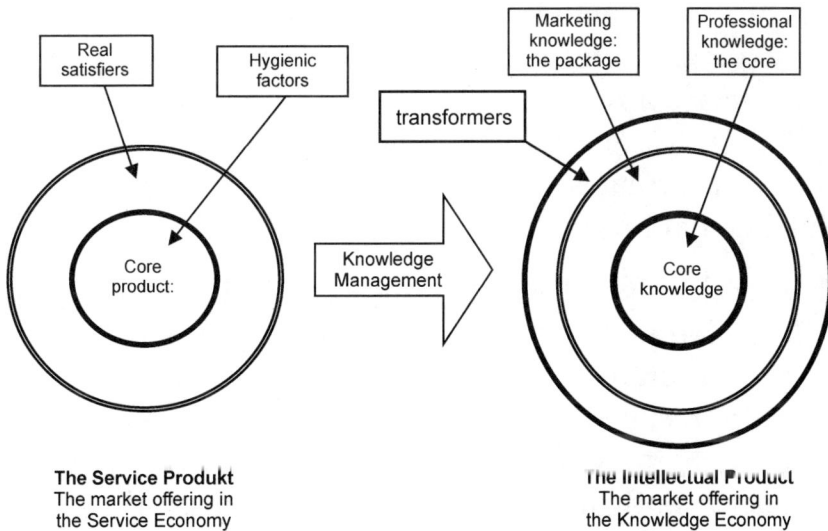

The Service Produkt
The market offering in
the Service Economy

The Intellectual Product
The market offering in
the Knowledge Economy

Source: author.

Time is an inseparable element of value creation as it sets the context for the knowledge. Transformation should be the ultimate goal for every business in the Knowledge Economy. A new construct is necessary to explain for the existence of **active** or 'live' knowledge, which can be contained in services.

The intellectual product is a construct, which us enables to perceive market exchange as a dynamic, multidimensional process where 'the rules of the game change at play'. Intellectual means not only 'knowledge rich' but also emotion-rich (as of "Emotional Intelligence"). An Intellectual product has the power to transform peoples' lives.

Knowledge shared by the organization at the higher levels (values and beliefs) will be far more powerful and difficult to imitate than those of the lower levels (capabilities, behavior). A change at the higher levels of knowledge will cascade down and effectively change the lower level. The reverse process is somewhat more laggard. A change in the environment has to be powerful enough to influence the upper levels.

The elaborate theoretical explanation deserves an empirical explanation. 'Intellectual' is rather a vague term – after all, all results of human activities are 'intellectual'. Why then search for an explanation of such a supposedly common phenomenon. There are a number of examples of products, which can be called *knowledge-rich* but none of them complies with all the below postulates which characterize the new constuct of the Intellectual Product:

- They are designed and produced with **broad application of knowledge** (knowledge-intensity) e.g. pharmaceuticals, modern aircraft, electronics. The value of knowledge has been appreciated in many industries such as aerospace, biotechnology, pharmaceuticals, financial services, semiconductor and many others. The cost of production of a new Boeing 777 is mainly knowledge applied during its design and marketing. This knowledge, however can be described as **passive** or 'dead knowledge'. This knowledge contained in the aircraft has no value to the customers once they have reached their destination safely. <u>Therefore a distinction has to be made between knowledge embodied in manufactured products and services.</u>

- The knowledge embedded in the product is its **competitive advantage** through a unique combination of corporate culture, high HR investment e.g MS Windows or marketing expenditure in brand awareness e.g. Coca-cola.

- **They bring lifetime value.** A proper school, military training or a summer camp can shape a personality of an individual or even a generation individuals (family tradition) for decades.

- Another **characteristics** is that **they are able to interact with the customer** in real or near real time.
    A good example of such product concept is Individual Inc. – a Burlington, Ma. based company, which competes with information-retrieval services, provides published news stories selected to fit the specific interests of each client. The customers effortlessly receive timely, fresh, relevant articles delivered right to their desks. When someone signs up for Individual's service, the company as signs an editiorial manager to determine what sort of information the client wants. Every day the SMART Software System searches hundreds of sources for the information, which will most likely fit the client's needs. On a weekly basis the client rates the articles as "not relevant", "somewhat relevant", or "very relevant". In the first week of service the customers find only 40% to 60% of delivered information relevant. After 5 weeks the ration increases up to 90%. Then the frequency of rating is reduced to once a month.

The new *Nike*™ sneaker that has special material in the sole so that when it feels one is running it starts to stiffen up and when one slows down it gets softer. It is interacting with the foot in real time. This is the basis of the knowledge business when considering products having the ability to learn and capacity to create new knowledge built into them. Another example of interactive product is *Outlast technologies*™ (Boulder, Colorado) a company having patent rights to develop materials (cloth, fabric, car seats). Thus, the PCM they manufacture is genetically engineered to sense cold, which makes it turn hot, when it senses hot, it starts to turn cold.

- **Intellectual products are more art than science**

  Each floor at O'Hare Airport (Chicago, IL) is decorated with murals of different Chicago sports franchises. There is music performed at the background. If we were able to combine all the above-mentioned characteristics in one product it would be a pure exemplification of the intellectual product. Obviously, such an intellectual product in the economic sense would be more a service than a tangible product. As it usually happens in management practice, new concepts devised for one application soon find their way in others. Relationship marketing, was originally developed for services. Now companies like Lexus or Harley-Davidson (Harley Owners Group) introduce a full scale RM methodology. The same is likely to happen with the concept of intellectual product.

THE IMPLICATIONS FOR THE MANUFACTURERS

The concept of the Intellectual Product opens up new opportunities not only for service providers but also, as well as, for manufacturers. The designing of Intellectual products will require new methods of market research, reconfiguration of resources, measurement system and strategic management including mission statements.

Undoubtedly, the human factor, which entails the intellectual content, will enhance the performance and effectiveness of already used methods already used in of management such as:

♦ **brand management**. Brands with the strongest images in the personal computer industry, such as IBM and Compaq typically can expect customers to adopt their next generation products three to six times sooner than brands with weaker images. Intellectual product can be thought of as a vehicle to continue to enhance brand loyalty both in service and manufacturing business.

♦ **Customer relationship management** (CRM),

♦ **Core capability building**

♦ **Knowledge-friendly organization structure** and trust building

The paramount feature of the Intellectual Product will be its long-term future orientation (figure 4). The value creation by the Intellectual Product will be a long term, painful exercise resembling upbringing children. The process encompasses inevitable failures and conflicts but, thanks to strong relationships, trust, care and a strategic vision, the process may contribute to a success.

Figure 4. Value added chain and the Intellectual Product

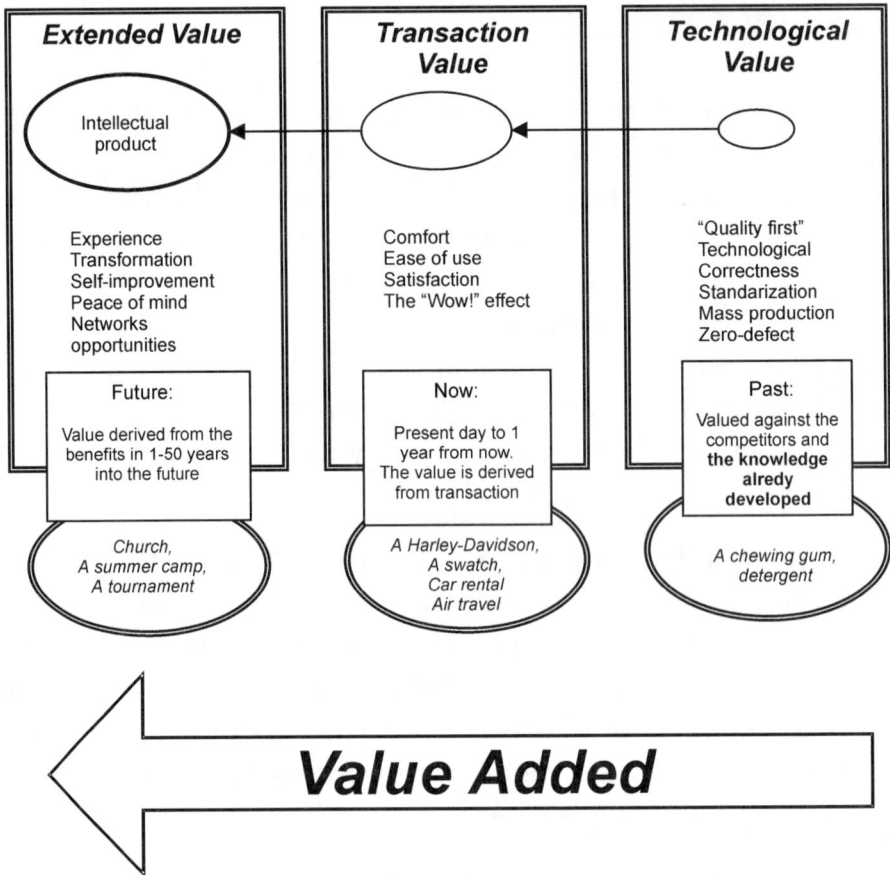

Extended Value	Transaction Value	Technological Value
Intellectual product		
Experience Transformation Self-improvement Peace of mind Networks opportunities	Comfort Ease of use Satisfaction The "Wow!" effect	"Quality first" Technological Correctness Standarization Mass production Zero-defect
Future: Value derived from the benefits in 1-50 years into the future	**Now:** Present day to 1 year from now. The value is derived from transaction	**Past:** Valued against the competitors and **the knowledge alredy developed**
Church, A summer camp, A tournament	A Harley-Davidson, A swatch, Car rental Air travel	A chewing gum, detergent

Value Added

Source: author.

WHAT'S UNIQUE ABOUT THE INTELLECTUAL PRODUCT? WHY IS IT SO SPECIAL ... OR IS IT?

The intellectual product is an outcome of the evolution of management thought (figure 5). The formulation of quality principles (TQM) has paved the way for services marketing. Similarly, knowledge management helped to nourish new thinking about resources and value creation. Finally, the fusion of modern marketing principles with knowledge management has enabled the formulation of a universal concept of the intellectual product. **The concept is also a powerful method explaining the existence of intangible, non-service products** such as computer software or media offerings (television, music, the internet).

The intellectual product is a service product in the sense that it is based on human relationships. The most probable configuration for such products is described in table 4.

Table 4. Intellectual product macroeconomic context

Who:	professional service firms
Why:	to create more value for money, to enhance knowledge resources
Where:	in the Knowledge Economy
How:	by introducing a new thinking about the product design, building social capital (Fukuyama), relationship marketing
When:	ASAP

Source: author.

CONCLUSION

Knowledge management movement has been hijacked by pragmatists prematurely (Botin, 2000). This article was written with an intent to bring fresh ideas into mainstream Relationship Marketing. Neither monetary value of knowledge investment nor the superiority of the knowledge can be the only distinguishing factors of the intellectual product.

The goal of this article is to accentuate the understanding of the marketing-knowledge management interface by developing a framework capturing the linkages between relationship marketing and the knowledge management activities. The framework presupposes that marketing in service organizations is concerned with the task of developing and embedding the organization's knowledge in its intellectual product.

Therefore, the philosophy of the intellectual product is that both its design and its long-term benefits to the customer are knowledge-intensive.

The organizations most predestined for providing intellectual products are professional service firms (e.g. education, health care, consulting etc.) The fully-fledged well-developed, prime, interesting examples are to be found in the non-competitive, out-of-the-market environments such as religious communities (worship), tribal life etc.

Author's hope is that the concept of intellectual capital will ultimately influence the way marketing is perceived and enable marketing professionals to actively collaborate in the knowledge management processes.

What makes an idea a breakthrough is both its broad applicability and its capacity to transform the way we see the world. The ideas behind the quality revolution of the 1980's soon spilt over into the service sector. Applying the knowledge management concepts associated with the *"Knowledge-Creating Company"* concept, it is easy to see the parallel. Using the knowledge creation-application way of thinking, uncovers the various links between quality, innovation and profitability, and focuses service sector managers. As it was two decades ago, now we can experience a similar phenomenon bringing new thinking to service businesses.

FURTHER RESEARCH

Modern organization have immense skill in marketing science – bringing information into the organization through surveys, focus groups and other methods of marketing research. However, all those techniques concern only those products which already exist in one form or another. If a customer is confused as to as to what a given product he/she is about to acquire (is presented to him) is all about, no sensible response is to be expected.

In today's competitive economy there is strong tendency to customize market offerings which takes many forms i.e. one-to-one marketing, customization, "tailor-made solutions" etc. Prime companies, worldwide, struggle put in from of customer a unique set 'pool'- derived bundle of features. The value is created through *the* diversity and *awesome* multitude. This is certainly a step forward compared to the famous Henry Ford's I statement about the variety of body paint available to automobile-hungry Americans.

This paper was written with an intent to stimulate discussion concerning knowledge content in market offerings. Blois (1996) warned against the danger of allowing RM to become concerned "with doing things to customers for the supplier's benefit – as happened with the marketing mix paradigm". The Author has some doubts as this matter may extend, or concern to the issue of so-called "knowledge content". The appreciation for the value of knowledge has a long history. The military prowess of the Roman legions was attributed to the superior training, equipment and leadership. These 'knowledge-based' features enabled them to overcome the enemy lines. Similarly German Panzer divisions were able to encircle Russian armies thanks to the same virtues which we would call "intangible assets" i.e. military expertise and superior engineering. Not surprisingly, the battle of the Atlantic was lost by German U-boat's because of breaking the code of the ENIGMA (n.b. thanks to the contribution of Polish scientists, who as mathematicians had superior intellectual capabilities to German ciphers).

Further research is needed in order to establish and describe the implications of inclusion of customer's knowledge into Knowledge Management models bearing in mind that the production and consumption of services are simultaneous in most non material services (e.g. medical, education, tourism, law, marketing etc). The formulation of new KM models for service firms is a necessity which is well documented in marketing literature.

Figure 5. The evolution: from Scientific management to Intellectual product.

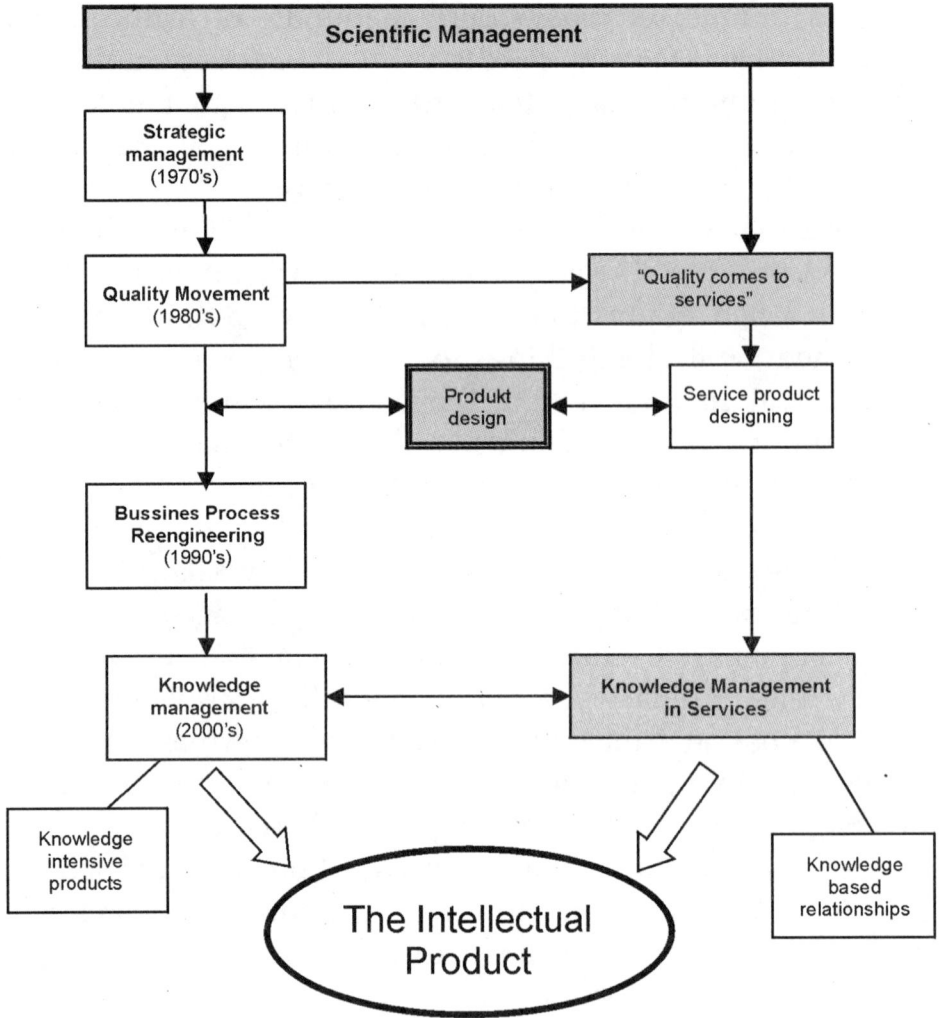

Source: author.

REFERENCES:

Bell D., The Coming of Post-Industrial Society. A Venture in Social Forecasting. Basic Book Inc. Publishers, New York 1973

Bowen D. E., The Customer as Employee Revised, Materiały z konferencji QUIS 7, Karlstad 13–16.06.2000

Building and Sustaining the Sources of Innovation, an interview with D. Leonard, Strategy&Leadership, 6–7/1997

Clark C., The Conditions of Economic Progress, London/New York 1957

Chatzkel J., A conversation with Jim Botin, President of InterClass, *Journal of Intellectual Capital*, Vol.1 3/2000

Davis S., Meyer Ch., An Economy Turned on its Head, *Harvard Business Review*, 11–12/1997

Davis S., Botkin J., The Coming of Knowledge-Based Business, *Harvard Business Review*, 9–10/1994

Edvinsson L., Malone M. S., Intellectual Capital, Judy Piatkus Limited, London 1997.

Fazlagić A., Knowledge Management in Service Firms: (A Call for) a Distinct Research Agenda, Business Information Systems 2000, Poznań, 13–15 April 2000

Fisher A. G. B., Production, Primary, Secondary and Tertiary w: *The Economic Record*, Vol.XV (1939)

Fourastie J., Die Grosse Hoffnung Des Zwanzigsten. Jahrhunderts, Koeln 1969

Gilmore J. H., Pine II, B. J, Beyond Goods and Services, Strategy&Leadership, 5–6/1997

Gilmore J. H., Pine II, B. J, Satisfaction, sacrifice, surprise: three small steps create one giant leap into the experience economy, 1–2/2000

Grant A. W. H, Schlesinger L. A., Realize Your Customers' Full Profit Potential, *Harvard Business Review*, 9–10/1995

Gronroos Ch., Service management and marketing, Lexington Books, Toronto 1999

Gummesson E., Total relationship management, Butterworth Heinemann, Oxford 1999

J. W. Hebeler Jr., D. C. Van Doren, Unfettered Leverage: The Ascedency of Knowledge-Rich Products And Processes, *Business Horizons*, 7–8/1997

Kanovcky V., Housel T, The Learning – Knowledge – Value Cycle, Knowing in Firms, Sage Publications, London 1998

Kao J. J., The Art and Discipline of Business Creativity, Strategy&Leadership, 6–7/1997

Kavali G. S., Tzokas N. X., Saren M. J., Relationship Marketing as an ethical approach: philosophical and managerial considerations, *Management Decision*, 37/7 [1999]

Kirmani A., Rao A. R., No Pain, No Gain: A critical Review of the Litarature on Signaling Unobservable Product Quality, *Journal of Marketing*, April 2000

Kwiatkowski S., Przedsiębiorczość Intelektualna, PWE, Warszawa 1999

Lovelock Ch. H., Services marketing, Prentice Hall, London 1996

Lowendahl B. R., Strategic management of professional Service Firms, Copenhagen Business School Press, Copenhagen 1997

Mills P. D., Moshavi D. S., Professional concern: managing knowledge-based service relationships, *Service Industry Management*, Vol. 10 No 1, 1999

Morrison J. I., The Second Curve: Managing The Velocity of Change, Strategy&Leadership, 1–2/1998

Naisbitt J., Megatrendy, Zysk i S-ka, Poznań 1997

Neuman E., Jackson D. W., Jr., One More Time: How Do You Satisfy Customers?, *Business Horizons*, 5–6/1999

Pine II B. J., Peppers D., Rogers M., Do you want to keep your customers forever?, *Harvard Business Review*, 3–4/1995

Sivada E., Dwyer F. R., An Examination of Organizational Factors Influencing New Product Success in Internal and Alliance-Based Processes, *Journal of Marketing*, January 2000

Srivastava R. K., Shervani T. A., Fahey L., Market-Based Assets and Shareholder Value: A Framework for Analysis, *Journal of Marketing*, Vol. 62, 2/1998

Stewart T. A., Intellectual Capital, The New Wealth of Organizations, Nicolas Brealey Publishing, London 1998

Stowe Ch. R. B., Intellectual Capital – Implications for Venture Capitalists, www.masterpage.com.pl./outlook/intellectual.html, 28.12.1999

Walters D., Lancaster G., Value-based marketing and its usefulness to customers, *Management Decision*, 37/9 [1999]

Weintraub D., Magdorff H., The Service Industries in Relation to Employment Trends w Econometrica, Vol.8 (1940), ss. 289–311

Whitehill M., Knowledge-based Strategy to Deliver Sustained Competetive Advantage, Long Range Planning, Vol. 30, No. 4, 1997

Bohdan Budzan

NEW INTELLECTUAL PRODUCTS – FUTURE OF UKRAINIAN ECONOMY

Abstract

Like many other countries that formed the Soviet Union, Ukraine's economy was heavily invested in the processing of raw materials and heavy industry. Today, Ukraine's economy is beginning to reflect the massive changes and improvements of the 'new economy.' High technology companies harness intellectual capital and information which helps improve the efficiency and market responsiveness of traditional firms they serve. Specific examples of Ukraine's 'new economy' companies are provided to illustrate the changes that portend well for the future of the country.

INTRODUCTION

Economic growth in the twentieth century is characterized by several trends. The main causes for economic development in various times were: the introduction of the industrial assembly line, the development of the combustion engine, the application of nuclear energy, the creation of the world wide web. Paul Zane Pilzer[1] claims that our contemporary economy is primarily based on technologies and not simply on the exploitation of raw material resources.

INDUSTRIAL TO INFORMATION INDUSTRIES

An examination of the industries at the end of the century is most revealing and tends to support Pilzer's observations. According to the data of ratings presented by American consulting company PriceWaterhouseCoopers and Financial Times newspaper (based on data of the magazine Expert #37 from Oct. 02, 2000) the distribution of top-20 companies among branches of industry, is shown below in Table 1:

Table 1. Distribution of top-20 companies among branches of industry

Rating	Mining	Traditional industry	Electronics, telecommunication, Internet	Finance	Other
FT 500 Global	3	2	11	2	2
FT 500 UK	3	0	6	7	4
FT 500 US	1	1	11	2	5
FT 500 Japan	0	2	14	2	2

---

[1] Paul Zane Pilzer Unlimited Wealth. TheTheory and Practice of Economic Alchemy. N.Y., Crown Publishers, 1990

Having analyzed the listed data, at the end of the century those companies that are leading the economy are those which deal with information technologies. Among leaders of the world rating the high technology sector are 11 companies. A similar situation is observed in the United States and Japan, where the number of companies which are in electronics, telecommunication and Internet are among the most significant. Therefore, it can be stated, that the most dynamic companies are those involved with high technology information (knowledge) based firms.

The trend that high technology, information or knowledge-based firms will dominate the economy is not expected to change during the next five years. According to expert opinion, even after five years the same leaders will remain: General Electric, Microsoft, Cisco, Coca-Cola, IBM, and Sony. However, they predict increasing number of telecommunication companies.

Even today information technologies have a profound impact on human living, its education, leisure, and the workplace. Information technology stimulates more efficient and creative solving of economic and social problems. According to Peter Drucker, the theorist of contemporary management: "Within last 50 years in abbreviation IT ... the main was letter T (technologies). New information revolution has removed the burden onto I (information). The main question of this revolution remains: "What is the content of information, what is its assignment?" This kind of question leads to substantial reconsideration of the objectives, being laid upon information, and simultaneous reorganizing of authorities, which implement these objectives".[2]

The status and development of IT not only accelerates, but also changes entrepreneurship in the following ways. With information technology, new products absorb more science. The organization of production and business management are carried out with help of IT. And finally, the role of busi-

---

[2] Peter F.Drucker, Management Challenges for the 21st Century, Moscow, Kiev, St. Petersburg, Williams Publishing, 2000, Translation to Russian

nesspersons more often is played by highly educated scientists who are the authors and owners of IT.

This paper discusses some of the peculiarities of the creation and implementation of intellectual products (services) based on experience of several companies. Without any claim for overgeneralizing, these trends have implications for the Ukrainian economy.

THE NEW ECONOMY – IMPLICATIONS FOR UKRAINE

The economic development in former Soviet Union with the exception of the military sector was guided by quantitative parameters over qualitative ones. In the Soviet Union, the larger proportion of the GDP consisted of so-called "basic branches." During 2000, in the Ukraine the following sectors of the economy were dominant: energy, metallurgy, and chemical industry. According to quarter rating of Information/analytical center "Ä.À.Ð." (the newspaper "Business" , #405, year 2000) the majority of attractive for investments Ukrainian companies involved the production of raw materials. For the third year, "Ukrnafta" held the top rating. The stable place in first fourth of leaders is given to concern "Stirol" (chemistry branch) which exports 3/4 of its production. In year 2000, there was a slight improvement in industrial branches which produce consumer goods such as food, wood-processing, light and also metallurgy and machine-building (the newspaper "Government Courier", #12 from 23.01.2001). Government's attempts to protect investor's rights to permit our economy to catch up with world trends suggests that future economic activity will reflect an increase in strategic investments and a shift of investor's priorities from purely exploitive raw materials industries to those industries fueled by consumer demands.

Table 2. The most successful and well known investment projects of the year 2000 in Ukraine.

FIELD OF INVESTING	Purpose of investing	Amount of pledged investments	Investments made	Investing company
Telecommunications	Development of network of ATS	Over $245 millions	$ 200 millions	"UTEL" Ltd.
Food industry, agriculture sector, trade	Increase volume of production and exports of grain-crops, fertilizers, oil	–	Approx. $85 millions	Company Cargill
Fast-food restaurants network	It is stipulated to expand until year 2004 the network of restaurants up to 85, which would allow to create more than 5,5 thousand jobs	Approx $100 millions	Over $70 millions	Company McDonald's
Telecommunications	Provide with range of telecommunication services, including fixed and cellular connection, and Internet	Approx. $100 millions	$ 60 millions	Company Golden Telecom
Confectionery industry	Increase volume of confectionery production at the factory "Svitoch" (Lviv)	Over $41 millions	Over $20 millions	Nestle Corporation
Brewery ndustry	Re-equipping of three acquired breweries, increase of market share	Over $40 million	Over $40 million	Company Sun Interbrew
Confectionery industry	Increase volume of confectionery production at the factory Kraft Jacobs Suchard Ukraine city of Trostianetz (Sumy region). Renewal of production range	Over $20 million	$19 million	Company Kraft Jacobs Suchard
Oil-chemistry industry	Technical re-equipping of the concern "Oriana", resuming of olefin and polymer production.	Over $37 million	–	Oil company "Lukoil"

Until recently strategic investors in Ukraine dared to invest only in those projects which promised quick gain and could be implemented with less risk. However, Table 2 ("Ukrainian investment newspaper" #7 (279) from 13.02.2001), suggests that the most significant investments were made in the telecommunications industry.

Based on the fact that the world telecommunications market is using $400–500 billion in investment capital per year to support a 10–12% annual growth rate, one can predict that telecommunication technology companies will grow in Ukraine as well.

Therefore it is extremely important for Ukraine to concentrate efforts on reducing factors that constrain the development of information technologies in our country.[3] The most important of them are the following:

Economic:

- Unstable economic situation in the country, state over-regulation of key branches of the economy;
- High investment risk (consequently low level of investments in information technologies);
- Undetermined attitude of foreign stock markets to Ukraine;
- Low paying ability of the population and high (comparative to low average level of earnings) tariffs for Internet services, which causes insignificant use of Internet: less than 1% of population of the country. The State Communication Committee reports that there are 320–370 thousands of constant users and around 300 thousands of irregular users of world wide web in Ukraine;
- Insufficient business turnover, which decreases efficiency of implementation of e-business systems;

---

3 "Kompanion", magazine № 5, 5–9 February 2001

- High level of shadow economy, which brings rejection or even counteraction from the side of business authorities (electronic business stipulates full transparency of operations, which means being open to control authorities).

Organizational/technological:

- Insufficient computer literacy of population The State Communication Committee estimates there are approximately 1 million operating computers in Ukraine;
- Insufficient development of infrastructure and frequently low quality of communication channels, especially in distant regions;
- Insufficient protection of technical solutions, data and information transfer systems;
- Insufficient level of implementation, monitoring and use of high-tech business systems.

Legislative:

- Undetermined state policy concerning Internet;
- Absence of legislative basis in the field of electronic trade.

Social/psychological:

- Social stratification of users in that more that half of Internet users are school children and students;
- Absence of habit of using information technologies, and consequently – mistrust of electronic ways of making business.

Human resources:

- Lack of specialists in e-business field, which have experience of working with implementation of information projects, and which know the way business goes in Ukraine;

- Insufficient business qualification of IT-companies staff, which cannot pay enough attention to business-planning, marketing, budgeting etc.

EXAMPLES OF UKRAINE'S 'NEW ECONOMY'

Despite presence of the above factors which deter the development of information technologies in Ukraine, businesspersons come to understanding that any business requires application of these technologies in order to plan efficiently. Yu. Sivitskiy, the chairman of the board of directors of "Softline" company, believes that the application of high technologies offers many advantages to companies. These advantages include: the opportunity to get fast and true information, the ability to analize information quickly, and the capability to apply competitive advantages due to optimal decision-making. The company "Softline" can be treated as good example of intellectual entrepreneurship. The company offers intellectual products – integrated systems for production management. Being a pioneer of computerizing of business processes, the company itself attempts to optimize data analysis and processes of management decision-making by using IT. Managers of the company are young people with technical education organized into teams. Currently, all managers of the company have been trained through MBA programs.

Softline is among the leading companies-developers of corporate information systems of high complexity. Its customers are – Ukrainian State enterprise "Ukrpost", Ministry of Finance, State center for employment, and the company "KiyAvia", "Chernobyl center for problems of nuclear safety".

The company "Softline" was established in 1995. In 6 years it became the leader in the market of software. The year 2000 was the most successful in its short history. It bought and became full owner of the company NBN Kraft of Khmelnitskiy, which deals with development of billing (for banking transfers) and other program systems. The company has received the certificate of correspondence ISO 9001 for its systems software. Only two companies in Ukraine which operate in the high-tech market have achieved certificates of correspondence. This allows these companies to enter the foreign market and being equal competitor with Western companies. The company established representative office in Houston (Texas, USA) and received investments from the company SigmaBleyzer (USA) in amount of $ 1 million.

The SigmaBleyzer company is another good example of successful intellectual entrepreneurship but on a larger scale. It is one of the leading private foreign investors in Ukraine. It was established and headed by Michael Bleyzer recognized by Forbes magazine as one of the five most successful immigrants in the USA. Bleyzer is from the former Soviet Union (Ukraine, Kharkiv). Having arrived in the United States in mid-70th, he worked for 25 years for Ernst & Young, and for 15 years at Exxon Corporation. In 1990, when Ukrainian economy was opened for foreign investors, he decided to establish an investment fund aimed at Ukraine. In 1994, he created company SigmaBleyzer on the basis of Ukrainian investment group Sigma (Kharkiv). In 1996, SigmaBleyzer established Ukrainian Development fund – the largest foreign investment fund of private capital in Ukraine. Its participants include such financial structures as Merrill Lynch, SBC Warbung, Goldman Sachs, and ING Barings. For 5 years UGF has invested in Ukraine more than $500 million. Its portfolio includes stocks of more than 70 Ukrainian enterprises. In October 2000, the company SigmaBleyzer started the largest investment project in Ukraine "Will" with the motto "I can do anything". The purpose of the project was to establish the infrastructure for high technology information industry in Ukraine. It is offering to fund several groups of companies related to Internet, television, media, leisure, communication.

Another example of high technology, information rich company is the joint-stock company "Ukranalyt-Avto" a leader in the field of gas pollution monitoring systems. The firm manufactures monitoring and analytical equipment and tools for measuring gas emissions from automobiles and industrial settings. With both automatic stations and mobile laboratories, Ukranalyt-Avto monitors the effects of gas pollution in both the atmosphere and at transportation borders.

Because only 2% of the Ukrainian market's needs for these products and services are currently being met, Ukranalyt-Avto is looking at an enormous opportunity to serve the remaining 98%. In addition, 40% of its sales are planned for the international market.

Innna Mikheeva, Head of Laboratory (54 years old, Kyiv Polytechnical Institute graduate, Ph.D. in technical studies) was one of many managers of the project funded by the Science and Technical Committee of Ukraine (STCU) "Station for Ecological Control of Motor transport." In April 1999, "Ukranalyt-Avto" submitted a new project to the STCU. Now the laboratory is working on Danish-Ukrainian project aimed at saving energy and managing environmental control systems for "K. Marks", a confectionery plant in Kyiv. The laboratory is also working on a project for the American "Ekolengs" Program. USAID expert Shrene Vassan visited the laboratory in September-October. He looked through the business-plan with great satisfaction and pointed that it meets the requirements of the world standards.

TAVEKS Ltd. was established in 1993 by scientists of the Insitute of Semi-Conductors of National Academy of Sciences of Ukraine. Oleksandr Stoliarenko (Ph.D. in technical studies) became its director. The main activities of the enterprise are:

- Development and manufacturing of optical holography equipment;

- Importing of optical-electronic components;
- Representing in Ukraine producers of leading world firms in the field of manufacturing video-monitoring production, security signalization, and communication systems (PELCO, ODIETICS, GYYR, IEI, VDS, TESA).

The enterprise has network of representatives throughout Ukraine. In 1999, the management of the enterprise participated in the "Small Business Innovation Research@ Development Workshop" at the "International Collaborative Ventures: Business Opportunities Through S&T Partnership", conducted in Fairfax, Virginia, September 22–23, 1999. Thus, connections are made for cooperation with American firms. The most recent project is to expand into serving the hotel industry. The enterprise is going to manufacture code locks with magnetic cards and software for hotel management.

The largest Internet provider in Ukraine is the company Lucky Net headed by Arthur Gabovich since 1998. Gabovich is twenty-eight years old. He graduated from the Kyiv branch of Moscow physics-technical institute in the field of Biophysics. He then spent three years in the United States doing scientific sresearch and building his management skills. Upon returning home, he joined the company Lucky Net which he had helped start as a student. According to Gabovich: "Basic technical education helps in great degree. The work itself, somehow, looks similar to research activity". In January 1999, Gabovich was elected to be the President of the company.

The company Lucky Net was created in 1994 by the team of young Ukrainian enthusiasts of Internet which at that time was a new development. At the time, these youngsters were not aware of the risks of their investment. In 1995, the company already was among leading Internet providing companies in Ukraine. In 1998, the company Lucky Net was first recognized provider in Ukraine. In January 1999, it received a status of large company which for that time was in use by only 81 non-

American companies. The strategy of the company is explained by the President as follows: "Internet is high-tech fast growing field, and in order to remain a leader we have to develop ourselves together with it. It concerns both expanding services range, and trying to keep high quality level, and comparatively low prices".

THE FUTURE FOR UKRAINE?

These are few examples of companies providing services in the "new economy". Obviously, the Internet is a major feature of the new economy. The Internet represents the convergence of information and high technology. It is likely that the most successful companies will be those which combine their core competence with the leverage that Internet can provide.

In some ways, Ukraine is in a more favorable situation than fully developed Western countries. Ukraine does not have the developed infrastructure with old technology to replace. Ukraine can simply leap forward without worrying about prior investment in dated technology. And, Ukraine is in the enviable position of being able to learn from the mistakes of others in selecting the best technologies and conceptual models. The development of information technologies gives competitive advantages to countries with high creative potential like Ukraine. For Ukraine, the exportation of intellectual products and servi-ces can be more profitable than exporting raw materials.

Mieczysław Dobija, Martyna Śliwa

MONEY AS AN INTELLECTUAL VENTURE

Abstract

Monetary system is undoubtedly a venture, which has developed in the course of the history. Many facts from historical and even pre-historical times testify to a variety of possible ways of understanding the affairs of money, however, the relationship between money and productivity of labour has been known since the early days. Money conceived to be receivables for work is closely related to banking and economic accounting systems within the legal system of a State. Monetary stability depends chiefly upon the productivity of labour of all employed persons: whether clerks or workers. The question of maintaining productivity of labour should be focussed upon, with a view to maintaining monetary stability. Money as an intellectual venture requires also common sense, and may suffer heavily as a result of rendering it either too shallow or overly intellectual.

EARLY HISTORY OF MONEY FROM THE INTELLECTUAL PERSPECTIVE

Money manifests itself in human experience both as a form and as a substance. The two aspects have always been present at each point of the long history of money. The form is close to Plato's idea and has to be intellectually perceived, the substance, however, is strongly emotional as having more tangible roots. We follow the idea of intellectualism as expressed by B. Johannisson, S. Kwiatkowski and Thomas C. Dandridge (1999, p. 31), who perceive intellectual as focused on form rather than on substance. We perceive monetary system as more intellectual when form dominates, as opposed to the situation when the hard, tangible, down-to--earth substance of currencies commands human minds and souls. No matter which factor dominates, at any time of the human experience, there have been some common causes of creating this invention. Any monetary system requires to possess two features: accountability and measurability, since these are fundamental for every exchange, whether equivalent or not.

> ## The Journey Begins

Our journey of discovering money as an intellectual venture starts at the point when human beings first encountered **the problem of how to work collectively, be able to achieve advantages thanks to the specialisation and cooperation, and how to divide the effects of the work proportionally to the contribution of individuals.** Fair pay expectations and well established money systems have been included in any solution to the above stated economic agenda. Although little is known about the ability of conceptual thinking within the civilisations that existed a few millenia ago, archeological discoveries of sophisticated objects manufactured as early as in the sixth millenium B.C., suggest that people at that time had already developed a high level of abstract thinking (Zabłocka 1987, p.33, see also above plate). Thus, it seems feasible to examine the ways of solving the fundamental economic issues in the most ancient civilisations that the researchers nowadays know about, and to attempt to draw some conclusions that might be useful in the context of modern economies.

The evolution of thinking about remuneration and money shows that it has not always been treated as an intellectual venture. However, over the centuries, money has always been a real adventure, both for those who have created theories and for those who have experienced the reality, and there are reasons to believe that *"money makes the world go round."*

> ## Genius of Simplicity

One of the most surprising facts about the history of money is that at the very beginning of the development of people's economic activity money was indeed understood purely intellectually. It was meant to be information as opposed to a material object; it was supposed to help compare the values of different goods or work of different individuals, without constituting any value itself. The most ancient economy that modern researchers know about understood the concept of money as nothing more, and nothing less, than

information. That purely intellectual idea of money was represented by seemingly primitive accounting tools called *tokens*. The appearance of tokens, about 8000 BC, coincided with the beginning of the dome-stication of cereals in the Middle East (Schmandt-Besserat, 1987). Tokens were small artefacts, modelled in clay into various forms either geometric or naturalistic.

Once established, the system of tokens changed little, as the economy remained basically a rural agricultural one. Then, around 3300 BC, cities started to appear, which brought about an increased need for accounting. In consequence, tokens became more complex. Even though the development of the token system is not the subject of this analysis, what is important about those little clay objects in the context of the history of money, is that they carried information concerning different amounts of manufactured goods and that they constituted a real system of accounting. There was not only one type of token carrying a discrete meaning but an entire repertory of interrelated types of counters, each with a corresponding meaning. The system made it feasible to manipulate simultaneously with information concerning different categories of items, bringing a complexity of accounting never achieved before. Tokens made it possible to store with precision unlimited quantities of information about an unlimited number of goods. They played an important role as direct predecessors of another accounting system, represented by pictographic tablets.

Prior to the explanation of the system of pictograms, it seems worth to mention that in the historical period that we refer to, writing was not yet invented, so transactions could not be made credible by a signature. Therefore, according to Ifrah (1990, p.101), stamps made from gemstones were used in the countries of Sumeria and Elam in the case of all economic and legal activities. The symbolic picture on the stamp was characteristic for its owner and the role it played once placed on a clay tablet can be compared to the role of a signature nowadays. This kind of signature was used and recognised in ancient Elam in Mesopotamia until about 3200 BC, when the way of recording quantities of goods was gradually influenced by the invention of writing, which first appeared in the form of pictograms. Since that time, clay tablets would serve enabling a full registration of a transaction: quantities and kinds of goods were placed on the right side of a pictogram, and the total sum together with the reason for the payment on its left.

The system of pictographic tablets, developed and used in ancient Sumeria since 3100 BC, is the first evidence of abstract counting. It inherited from tokens a code based on word signs, a basic syntax and their economic context. Each pictograph was meaningful and communicated a specific kind of information. Pictographic writing and abstract numbers were used to record entries and expenditures of goods in Sumerian temples.

Why are pictographs and the economy of ancient Sumeria worth mentioning? The answer is that the pictographic tablets did not only carry information. It is essential that the information they carried concerned the amount receivable for work of an individual. Money in the form of coins or banknotes was not needed. According to Polanyi (1957, p. 21), the state authorities kept accounts of equities and liabilities of each individual. The work of every citizen was precisely recorded and one was entitled to take as many goods from the temple's storage as his or her amount recorded on an account allowed for. In this way, public authorities could guarantee that everyone in the state would spend no more than what he or she has earned. Tangible money represented by coins was not necessary thanks to the existing system of overwhelming accounting. Sumerian economy enjoyed the situation of zero inflation because the whole supply of intellectually perceived money was equal to the sum of receivables for work of all citizens. Value of goods was based on the value of work needed to produce them. Metals, like gold or silver, served merely to facilitate calculations and exchanges.

Examples of such calculations can be found in old Egyptian documents written about 1300 BC. One of those documents refers to a case where a merchant was walking from one household to another, offering a Syrian slave for sale. The slave was purchased by an officer's wife who paid for her with different fabrics, clothes and dishes. All prices were estimated separately in silver although the metal itself did not appear in the transaction (Saggs, 1973, p.265). Another example of a similar transaction is described by (Ifrah 1990, p.58). The contract is a document of a sales transaction that took place in New State (between 16th and 11th century BC.) The contract states as follows:

"Hay gives to brigadier Nebsmen:
1 ox which is equivalent to	*120 debens of copper*
In return he receives:	
2 pots of lard which is	*60 debens of copper*
5 skirts of fine cotton which is	*25 debens of copper*
1 suit of Southern linen which is	*20 debens of copper*
1 hide which is	*15 debens of copper*

The above contract confirms that the ox was bought for 120 debens of copper but the sum was paid in goods of equivalent value. However, as Ifrah points out, it is not merely an evidence of the existence of barter but of a real monetary system. Thanks to the metal benchmark, the goods were not exchanged according to the preferences of the trading parties nor the tradition, but according to a generally accepted system, in which all goods had their approximate and fair price. What can be added in this context, is that the price was determined by the value of labour input necessary to produce them, which was possible within the system of ancient accounting.

With the development of trade relations between different groups and countries, it became necessary to find a way of measuring value that would be both universal and acceptable by all trading parties. Metals were found useful in meeting these requirements. The method of assessing the value of a product was by weighing it and comparing its weight with the weight of a metal object. Ancient Jews and Phoenicians used to evaluate things with a scale of *shekels*, which stood both for quantity and weigh. The book of *Genesis (Chapter 23)* describes the transactions of Abraham, who paid Ephron the Hittite 400 shekels of silver for a piece of land with a tomb cave in Machpelah before Mamre.

Due to the use of metals as a reference point for measuring the value of goods and services, an actual monetary system was created, where money was understood in an abstract and intellectual way, and not actually represented by any tangible objects. Metals were treated as benchmarks that allowed to evaluate a fair price of all tradable goods and services according to a generally accepted system. At the same time, although it was possible to pay with metals, people would avoid that in the fear of fraud. Ancient Mesopotamian society accepted gold, silver or copper as the carriers of information rather than as means of exchange.

Another question related to monetary issues in ancient countries is the understanding of capital. It is astonishing that the notion of capital was already recognised in Sumeria and the value of capital was also estimated in metals, although it was actually represented by natural products. An example of a contract, in which capital is borrowed for a trade expedition is provided by Saggs (1973, p.245). The contract reads as follows:

"Two mines of silver, (the value of) 5 gurs of olive (and) 30 pieces of clothes were borrowed by Lumeslamtae and Nigisanabs from Ur-ninmark (as) capital of a partnership for an expedition to Dilmun, in order to buy copper (there). After a fortunate completion of the expe-dition he (the creditor) will not be responsible for any trade losses (of the debtors). They (the deb-tors) agreed to satisfy Urninmark with four mi-nes of copper for each shekel of gold as a fair price."

A question corresponding to the problem of capital is the percentage rate as an amount due for the capital. The exi-stence of loans is another feature of ancient Babylonian economy. The payment of a certain percentage rate was considered a fair price for the capital that a person would borrow. For this reason, a percentage rate was guaran-teed both by laws and contracts. Nevertheless, it was not allowed to establish too high a rate for the capital. According to Hammurabi's law, taking a percentage rate of more than twenty percent was forbidden. Such a practice was sanctioned with the loss of capital belonging to the cre-ditor.

Another kind of loan known in ancient Babylonia was cal-led *chubutattu*. Let us quote an example of a 'chubutattu con-tract':

"The governor Shamashnasir received from Ilushunasir and Nannaibni 133 gur, 1 pi, 4 sutu of seeds as a chubutattu loan. No percentage rate will occur within the first two years. If he does not give the seeds back in two years, a percentage will be added' (Saggs, p.260).

What has to be understood about the above contract, is that it actually referred to the loan of 100 *gur*, with a rate of 33,3 % after two years. Having translated this into an equation

$$100 \text{ gur } (1 + r)^2 = 133 \text{ } 1/3 \text{ gur}$$

one can find that the yearly interest rate r was 15% in this case. This means that ancient people clearly understood both **the concept of capital and the capitalisation process**.

The examples mentioned above suggest that in ancient economies monetary systems existed, although money was not represented by tangible objects but it was treated purely conceptually. Metals served as a point of reference in evaluating the prices of goods. The value of goods manufactured was based on the value of work needed to produce them. The lack of coins and banknotes did not disturb the existence of the notions of capital and percentage rate, which were widely used in ancient contracts.

Since the monetary system is undoubtedly an intellectual undertaking, it does not surprise us that the historical development of the forms of money was accompanied by the development of educational institutions. The graduates of ancient schools were different categories of writers, ranging from simple accountants to highly qualified state officers. The function of a writer first appeared in the fourth millennium BC and it flourished on a large scale at the beginning of the third millennium BC. In the middle of that millennium, there already existed organised groups of writers and accountants working for economic organisations concentrated around temples and towns. According to Tyumenew (1969), accounting documents from the archives of the temple of the goddess Bawa show the existence of a well developed system of economic records conducted carefully and precisely. The condition of the documents is very good and they can provide evidence of how the use of labour was registered in monthly reports that were prepared for years. The content of some of the documents is purely demographic and they refer to the registration of people's migrations, as well as their births and deaths.

Struve (1969) provides an explanation of the measurement and labour registration practices in Sumerian economy. He argues that the analysed accounting documents show that workforce was measured in time units (on a daily basis) and productivity ratios. According to Struve (p.152), fractions smaller than one, e.g. 5/6, 2/3, ½, were applied to the measurement of working time. This led to the establishment of a common calculation unit, and in this way created the main function of money.

Coming back to chronology, the category of accountant called *dub-sar*, which meant *'a man with a measuring table'* appeared in Mesopotamia about 2800 BC. In 25th century BC the organisation structure of a temple included numerous posts of accountants divided into sections led by managers called *ugulas*, who were in turn managed by a leader called *dub-sar-mah*. Tyumenew (1969) mentions a person called Igimu, who as a writer received a field to maintain, with an area of about 6 ha (1 bur), which confirmed his high position within the temple administration.

Even though the system of economic administration is not fully understood, its one feature is with no doubt prevalent. The accounting registration concerns mainly the labour, that is, the work carried out according to a plan and norms of activities. Although initially it might be surprising, it seems obvious in the situation where money is an amount receivable for work. This in turn leads to an alternative: either there is a good organisation and control of work or inflation. A good example of the accountancy conducted by the ancient administrators comes form the city of Ur, from a loom workshop located there (Die Wirtschaftspruefung, no. 14/1993).

The importance of the writers is also illustrated by a poem devoted to the king Shulgi, who was the emperor at the end of the great development of the civili-sation of Mesopotamia (2045–2000 BC). The poem praises the king (Bielicki 1969, p. 156):

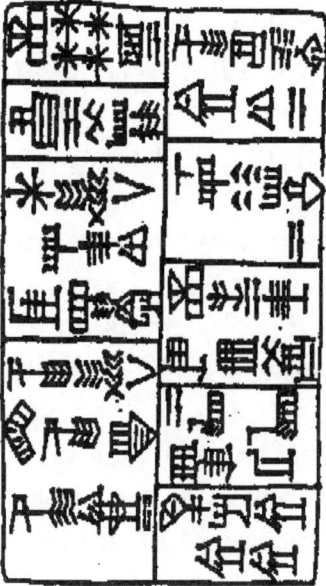

I, king, was a hero before I was born,
I, Shulgi, have been a po-werful man since I was born
An unknown author uses a comparison:
I am like a writer taught by the goddess Nisaba. My knowledge equals bravery and virility.

That king, according to Bielicki (1969, p. 159), built an administration centre in Ur, where the government of the country was located and where the incomes from taxes, workshops and gifts were registered. Also, Shulgi introduced a homogeneous system of measurement, weigh and payment.

A lot of information about the position and role of an administrator can be found in research about ancient Egypt. According to Bator (1993, p. 110), the only way of becoming an administrator (officer) was through a long lasting process of education, which included writing, accounting and the principles of economics, accounting and management. The members of that profession were supposed to meet very high ethical requirements. It should be emphasised that the quality of life of an administrator was much higher than that of a simple worker, and even today it could be wished by many. The above mentioned author describes (p. 116) an old Egyptian workers district, in which the workers' houses consisted of several rooms with the total surface of 70 to 90 m^2. The administrators' flats were much bigger. However, the education process took until about 30 years of age and the percentage of people successful in this field was quite small.

It can be justified to say that highly qualified writers and officers constituted a basis for the functioning of the monetary system and the whole necessary economic and legal environment in ancient economies. Many issues still need to be explained and they are not fully understood nowadays, perhaps because money as an amount receivable for work, and not identified with metal or other material objects, is an abstract category. For its effective functioning, a certain intellectual space is necessary, including the concepts of salary equal to the value of work, capital and percentage rate, receivables and equities, and a fair price, with all these being based on law, organisation and accounting. All this can be found in the ancient economies, in which money was not merely a material carrier of value.

The role of administration as an indispensable component of the accounting system in the ancient empires is highlighted by two outstanding researchers Polanyi (1957) and Oppenheim (1957), who at the same time indicate little importance of the market, which, in that situation, had to be balanced by a certain system of state accounting. That economic system, which is not yet fully known, surprises many researchers occupied with the ancient world. It seems that a wisely elaborated set of labour coefficients, as discussed earlier, was an essential part of that accounting system.

➢ Mykenian and Thebean Puzzle

A well known Polish researcher of ancient Greece Aleksander Krawczuk (1990, p. 67), in his book about ancient Thebes made an astonishing comment on the centrally organised economy in Mykenian times.

> *"Figuring out the tablets from the Mykenian archives gave us a new view of that epoch. Of course, even prior to that it had been assumed that the poetic imagination had given a lot of blaster to its everyday prose. However, when the writing started to talk, it became obvious that the very epoch which was a background of almost all Hellenic myths, was primarily an epoch of extremely precise office activity; the highly centralized economy was controlled by armies of administrators, who were producing tons of accounting documentation. It does not matter whether it is paper or clay that one writes upon. The method of recording does not matter either. Just the opposite, considering the primitivism of the materials it has to be said that with their care to include the whole economic life in their evidence system, the Mykenians could compete with every system of controlled economy".*

The author even argues that one of the reasons for the fall of the Mykenian civilisation to be its extensively developed bureaucracy. On the other hand, he provides an interesting conclusion:

> *"One thing has to be said to justify the writers and the whole system: the Mykenian people did not know coins, salaries were paid mainly in natural goods, therefore precise registration of both the owned fortune and the receivables was necessary".*

It should be added: the receivables for work. The Mykenians, as well as other ancient organisations of states-cities were able to solve, with a great help of accountancy, the ancient economic problems of full employment and payment relevant to the value of work. In order to do this, they needed an accounting system which was not yet understood but which was a guarantee of the economic stability, and of the fact that the receivables for work did not appear merely as a record on a clay tablet. That is why an overwhelming accounting system was necessary.

In spite of their universality and ingenuity, the simple solutions described above and applied to the problems of work, capital and percentage rate were given up by next generations, and never in the history of western civilisation has the concept of money been perceived in so purely intellectual and abstractive way as it was in ancient Mesopotamia. **One is tempted to ask: what causes that the existing monetary theories always lack, and what stands behind their intellectual weaknesses? The simple answer is that these theories focus mainly on the substance rather than the form.** The sound of counted coins and banknotes does not leave any space for more subtle questions. The essential meaning of money as receivables for work is not reflected in quantitative theories, developed after the historical period of the Conquest. In this contest, the remark of Galbraith (1982, p. 397), *who says that after so many centuries of efforts all invented* *monetary systems seem equally far from being perfect, appears to be right.*

In spite of Galbraith's pessimist view on the monetary theorists and practitioners, it seems worthwhile to investigate whether there have been historically any attempts to put the monetary issues in order and to let the oldest idea of money as the intellectual venture come into reality.

➤ **What Kind of Ancient Accounting Organisation Emerges?**

As a result of the above analysis, the following organisation of accounting in prehistoric times emerges. The scheme below is based on a set of assumptions concerning the division of work and redistribution of goods within an ancient economy. The essential components of the system are coefficients of labour productivity, which enable the calculation of standard measures. Standard work hours play the role of an accounting unit, that is, money. Journal entries make it possible to summarise the amounts of receivables for work, and, at the same time, to calculate the product value.

Thus, at the fall of The Heroes' Age, the concept of money was still purely intellectual and it was based on the value created by labour and precise accounting information. This opinion gives some answers to the surprise of many authors who see ancient Sumerians as "obsessive accountants" (Professor Krawczuk shares this opinion in respect to Mykenian economy) or find the developed accounting systems to be a potential reason for the fall of ancient town-states as one of the authors previously mentioned thought. We represent a different view of those times. Although the ancient system of state economy with its predominant role of accounting appears to be very simple, it is on the other hand, very sophisticated. All these meticulously

Scheme 1. Organisation of Ancient Accounting

PAYROLL ACCOUNTING

Journal Entries   **Wage Receivables**

Workers	Records				Workers		
A	10h	x $\frac{7}{7}$	= 10	sh	A	30	sh
B	10h	x $\frac{5}{7}$	= $7\frac{1}{7}$	sh	B	$21\frac{3}{7}$	sh
C	10h	x $\frac{3}{7}$	= $4\frac{2}{7}$	sh	C	$17\frac{4}{7}$	sh
A	20h	x $\frac{7}{7}$	= 20	sh	....	....	....
B	10h	x $\frac{5}{7}$	= $14\frac{2}{7}$	sh	....	....	....
...	....		....		....	....	....
...	....		....				
	Total		**474** $\frac{2}{7}$		Total	**474** $\frac{2}{7}$	

COST ACCOUNTING

Product X	157 $\frac{3}{7}$ sh
Product Y	74 $\frac{3}{7}$ sh
....	....

conducted records were necessary and justified in order for the system to operate well. In other words, money treated as records of payables needed such an elaborate accounting control. Otherwise, those ancient heroes would have to fight against inflation instead of defeating evil in their world. Inflation, however, is a phenomenon of later times.

Scheme 2. General Model of Ancient Economy

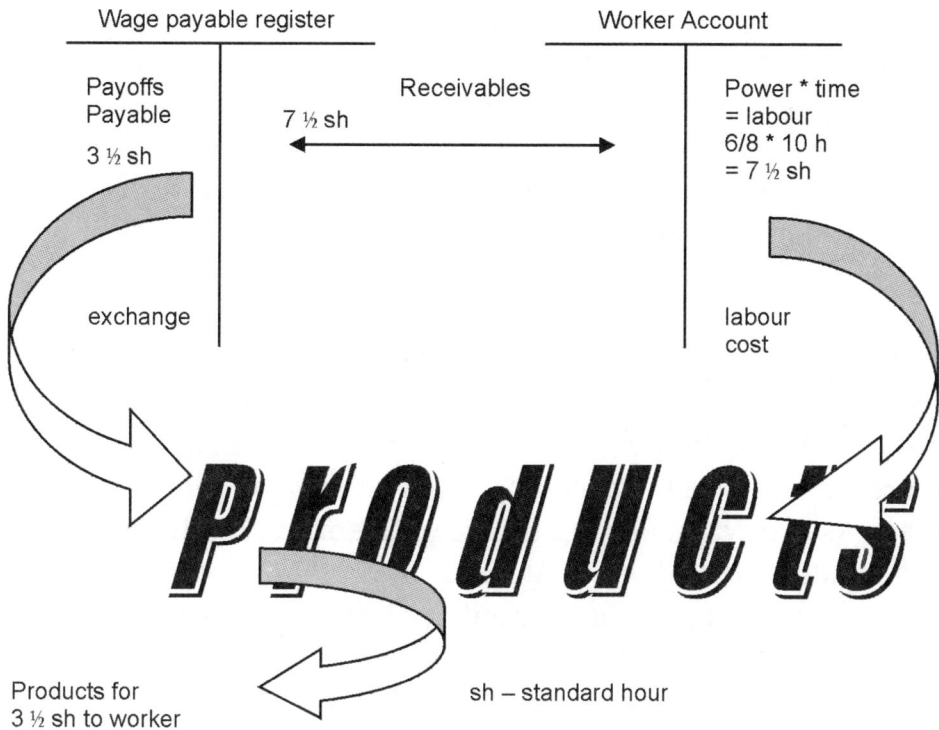

Wage payable register			Worker Account
Payoffs Payable 3 ½ sh	7 ½ sh	Receivables ⟶	Power * time = labour 6/8 * 10 h = 7 ½ sh
exchange			labour cost

Products for 3 ½ sh to worker

Products

sh – standard hour

➢ Thriving on Chaos in Greece and Rome

As an intellectual venture, money was born at the same time as the ancient economies. As a coin, it first appeared in Lidia (Asia Minor) and in China (Ifrah 1990, p. 59) in the 7th century BC. In the opinion of a famous Greek philosopher, Aristotle, the main reason for inventing a coin were problems caused by the necessity of constant checking the weigh and the quality of metals used as a means of payment for goods (Cywinski 1990, p. 22). Given the weakness of the state administration, it was undoubtedly convenient. However, it brought about new threats. **In our view, this triggered the disappearance of the complex understanding of the con-**

cepts of value, price and money, and that initial understanding has not recovered until today.

Once invented, the coin started to become more and more widely used in all Greek cities. It was so practical to pay with coins, and to carry them everywhere, and to influence the economic relations with monetary actions, that the idea of money as an amount receivable for work was easily forgotten. Money started to be something desired in itself, and the habit of keeping gold and silver coins as an evidence of fortune was considered a kind of "financial wisdom".

The three wars with Persia that took place between 500 and 449 BC were another turning point in the economic life of Greeks. A coin became not only a means of exchange but also merchandise itself. Travelling with money at a time of war was risky. It was safer to leave it with someone who was professionally looking after it. This money was subsequently given as a loan, and the percentage rate was pretty high. Due to all these manipulation pro-cesses, money lost its connection with the value of work. Those, whose work contributed the most to the economy, were no longer the rich ones. The rich were those who had the biggest amount of gold and coins. The chaos was overwhelming.

The question that one wants to ask at this point is: did nobody in ancient Greece have a deeper unders-tanding of what mo-ney really is and how it can be used to the benefit of people and the whole economy? Indeed, that figure was Alexander the Great. He was the only one in the old Greek world that gave up the traditional financial policy of gathering unproductive gold and golden coins. The fortune he had gained while conquering the world was circulating and contributed to the economic development. At

the same time, he reserved the gold and the exclusive right to produce coins for the king, and the coins distributed in all regions of the empire were supposed to be homogeneous.

The monetary reforms introduced by Alexander the Great were an achievement on the world scale as they made the trade exchange between distant cities and states much easier. Different cities attempted to heal their monetary systems through associating into monetary unions, assuring the issuing of coins of the uniform quality and according to the same patterns of symbols, as two cities: Syria and Pyksus did around 580 BC. Other cities and states followed these practices when they realised how advantageous for their economies these kinds of agreements were. Thus, Crotona and Sybaris, Crotana and Temesa, as well as Sybaris and Paestum used to place on their coins the same symbols, which they had designed together (Cywinski 1990,p. 37).

The monetary order that Alexander the Great had been trying to achieve was not adopted by the Roman Empire. Because of numerous wars, Roman government needed more and more money, which led to the decision to produce coins from copper, which had to be accepted by the Roman society. That operation allowed the government to earn 500% of profit resulting merely from the discretionary decision concerning a partial substitution of silver and gold with copper. Monetary manipulations of this kind took place many times in ancient Rome, and any time the emperors wanted to increase their income, they would change the proportions between gold, silver and copper in the coins. That policy created a paradox: the wealth of the nation was not determined by its economic development but by a legal act introduced by those who had political

power. Needless to say, that resulted in an economic and social chaos within the Empire.

The monetary chaos that existed in Rome from the middle of the third century, as well as the increase in prices in the country, prompted the emperor Diocletian (284-305) (Cywinski 1990, p. 51) to initiate a monetary reform in year 294. The emperor was going to provide a solid base for the issues of money. His aim was to stabilise the national currency, called *aureus*, through the process of assuring its gold parity and centralising the functions of issuing money. In spite of all his efforts, Diocletian was not successful in putting the monetary questions in order. The coins with a higher content of gold and silver never had a chance to circulate as a means of exchange, since they disappeared as soon as they had been issued. Apart from that, the economy of the Roman Empire in the third century fell into a serious crisis. In the fourth century, the cities stopped to develop and the trade market, that had flourished before, hardly existed. Diocletian realised that in such a difficult financial situation it was impossible to cover the state expenses. In order to suspend the dependence on the monetary fluctuations, he introduced taxes in natural goods. In this way, lack of a stable national currency and an overall economic crisis led to the substitution of money with natural goods. The state started paying the army and the officers with food. Coins were used only in local transactions of minor importance. The prices, however, kept increasing. The Emperor took a final decision. In an attempt to heal the economy, in the year 301 he introduced legislation concerning all prices of merchandises and salaries, including the salaries of lawyers and doctors. His legislation threatened those who would not obey the maximum prices with capital punishment.

The introduction of a consistent system of wages and prices was supposed to bring order to the economy of the Roman Empire, whose most sensitive and most difficult to solve problem was the monetary stability. Nevertheless, the reforms of the emperor Diocletian faced unpredicted difficulties due to the fact that the Egyptian priests, who had possessed esoteric knowledge, especially concerning metallurgy, used to produce gold from different metals on a large scale. As a consequence, according to Holroyd and Powell (1991, p. 159), Diocletian gave an order to burn all ancient books *"concerning the art of producing gold and silver"*. Therefore, only small bits of the ancient knowledge, that by chance avoided the flames, have survived until now. In spite of that, gold and silver have never become either perfect or long lasting as money.

> ## Much Ado About Quantitative Theories

The Conquest and the imports of large amounts of gold and silver from America brought new experiences to the history of monetary issues. The number of metals increased and so did inflation rather than wealth of the countries which possessed metals. This gave reason for developing quantitative monetary theories.

A well known mercantile doctrine assumes that money 'accelerates' the circulation of goods. According to the formula: **MV=PT,** the quantity of money (M) multiplied by the amount determining the frequency of change of the owners in a given period (V) equals to the global amount of trade transactions (T) multiplied by the average level of prices (P). This formula becomes a theory by linking the relevant amount with some determined relations. The quantitative monetary theory is a doctrine connecting M to P and assuming that P must be determined by 'real' forces, whereas V is given at particular payment habits and financial institutions within the economy. In 17th and 18th centuries the central point of the theory was that 'money influences trade'. It was believed that an increased supply of money causes an increased demand for it and, as a consequence, imports of metals influenced directly the amount of trade rather than the prices.

According to Blaug (1994, p.47) the quantitative theory, as it was first expressed by Locke, stated that the price level is always proportional to the amount of money, while the amount of money was understood together with the 'speed of circulation'. Of course, this particular proportion depends on the volume of trade. However, the above statement is a truism rather than a theory, although as a truism it can be useful because it emphasises the function of money as a means of exchange. In this case, two streams are compared: the total amount of money in circulation at a certain time with a total volume of trade at the same time, which shows that the absolute amount of money resources does not matter for the wealth of the nation. The peculiarity of money is that it does not have any value by itself although it serves as a means of exchange. This thesis obviously denies the mercantile assumptions, even though Locke remained a mercantilist because he believed that it was good for each country to possess a larger supply of money than other countries (Blaug, p.41).

In our opinion, the quantitative theory of money it no longer perceived as a symbolic of the value of labour as it was the case in ancient times, but refers to metal coins and bank notes. From this perspective, one can consider **the amount of money instead of considering the sum of receivables**. The money produced or invented in this way is, however, a tangible object rather than pure information about the quantity of work, as it was in the case before. Money as a human enterprise has lost much of its earlier intellectual spirit. At this point, one can quote the saying that "*It was as it had to be*", and admit that the down to earth thinking have replaced the really intellectual ideas.

AN ATTEMPT AT A THEORETICAL DESCRIPTION

Exchanging money for products is a fundamental question of product-money economy. This is the main aim of long lasting considerations concentrated on the equation of exchange and quantity theory of money. Bradford De Long (2000) among others claims that the creation of the exchange equation and shaping of the quantitative theory of money as a prediction tool of price level as well as interest rates, was the achievement of Irving Fisher, despite of the fact that quantitative theory of money goes back to D. Hume if not earlier. The equation of exchange is used to explain the quantitative theory of money but it has no analytical significance since it is true by definition. However, quantitative theorists used the equation of exchange by making assumption about the variables contained in it. The short – run quantity theory results in a direct and proportional relationship between quantity of money and GNP. Suppose that the money supply increases. It must lead directly to an increase in either prices or output or, more likely, some combination of both.

The quantitative theory of money is presently the most widely used tool of controlling inflation, and therefore it is to some extent a point of interest of accounting theory. Financial statements of business organisations have traditionally reflected transaction in terms of the numbers of money units exchanged. This approach is often referred to as historical cost/nominal unit of money statement. The justification for reporting original money amounts is objectivity. Conventional accounting is based on generally accepted accounting principles, the historical-cost principle and stable monetary unit postulate in particular. It is rather universally acknowledged that there are not the best alternative accounting models chosen among well known theoretical approaches based on historical cost, replacement cost, net realizable value, net present value and one of two available unit of measure: units of money and units of general purchasing power. As was suggested earlier, theoretical efforts should be rather more concentrated on the essence of money and the monetary unit in particular. One attempt at a better recognition of money unit stability is a new approach to theory of money and formulation of the wage equation of exchange as a manifestation, and key issue of the general accounting theory.

Scheme 3. Market mechanism equalises stream of products and stream of money

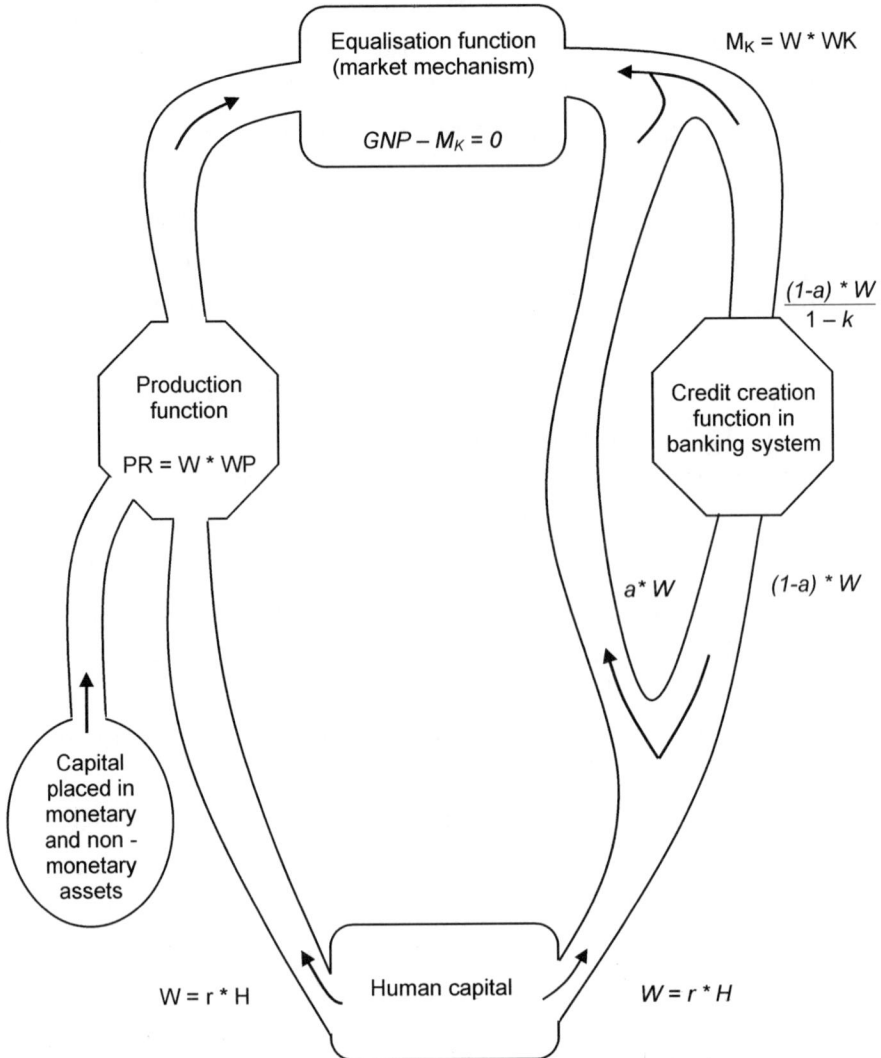

In monetary economy, labour and cost of labour determine two streams as presented on scheme 3. The first stream is a product one created by dynamically linking the labour and the assets. The second stream generated by the labour is the wage receivables stream. The labour is the basic source of money. The two streams can be measured and quantified using of production and credit creation functions. The wage equation of exchange arises as a result of existence of free market where the products are exchanged for money. It can be seen as the essence of monetary economy. The wage equation of exchange is then a theoretical tool for research and actions into stability of a money unit.

Assuming that the market mechanism does equalise value of streams of money and products, following equation can be made and called 'the wage equation of exchange':

$$GNP = GNPR \cdot (1 + i) = W \cdot WP = M_K = W \cdot WK = M \cdot V$$

The last expression refers to the Fisher's equation, thus M is money amount and V is money velocity. Letter (i) denotes rate of inflation; GNP and GNPR denote nominal and real gross national product.

Let us observe that the above-presented process of exchange can be described and explained using the basic accounting concepts. The two streams confront each other (matching principle). The equation refers to basic accounting equation in some way. The left stream represents assets and the right stream discloses liabilities of the state and banking system for value of wage receivable (money). The new accounting issues are involved too. Human resource costing and accounting as a theory that quantifies and assigns value of human and intellectual capital to individuals and determines basis for human capital wage theory, is the starting point of the considerations. Production function reshapes a usage of production factors into value of products, therefore the cost and managerial accounting as a tool of productivity control and growth is distinctively involved. The amount of receivables recorded in bank accounts represents ownership of wealth created by labour of the employees in a given environment.

Labour productivity is an issue quite well recognised in labour economy. McConnel and Brue (1986, p.437), among others have stated that labour productivity is important for at least two reasons:

* Productivity growth is the basic source of improvements in real wages and living standards.

* Productivity growth is an anti – inflationary force in that it tends to offset or absorbs increases in money wages.

Moreover, equal productivity growth helps limit a rate of inflation, while slow productivity growth causes the inflation rate to be higher than otherwise. All these statements can be strongly supported by models including the labour productivity variable as presented in this paper.

> **Compensations as a Return on Human Capital**

Different authors use many forms of description for illustrating the composition of human and intellectual capital. Here intellectual capital referees to that of an individual, and therefore is denoted as:

H(T) – for personal human capital
I (T) – for personal intellectual capital
E – for personal education capital
D(T) – for personal experience capital

The concept of personal human capital cannot be considered without the reference to the general category of capital as discussed in economic texts. Since capital is a basic term in economic thought, it is applied to many forms of economic statements as well as accounting as an area of knowledge, and to financial information systems. Therefore, the definition of capital assumed here is one that had been developed earlier. Let us quote the following view of Ijiri (1995):

> *"Capital" and "resources" are the two financial sides of the same entity... Since current liabilities ...are for the most part generated in the process of managing resources, they are often netted against assets. Following this practice, we state equality of capital and resources as:*

> ### Resources = Capital

> *...Capital is abstract, aggregated, and homogenous, while resources are concrete, desegregated and heterogeneous. The double entry bookkeeping system that has been the backbone of accounting in more than five countries has since its inception recorded recourses and capital in tandem.*

One more feature may be added to Ijiri's description of capital. Capital has an ability to multiply (capitalisation). An entrepreneur cannot multiply his or her trucks directly but is able to multiply the capital embodied in the trucks and then purchase a new truck.

Given the above stated premises for the understanding of capital as described by many authors, especially J. S. Mill, I. Fisher and Y. Ijiri, we apply a balanced definition presented in the work of (Dobija, 1998). This definition embracing the nature of capital is formulated as follows:

> **Capital is the value of economic means capitalised in physical and human resources. The rate of capitalisation is determined through the natural and social conditions of environment.**

Such a definition treats capital as a measure of economic value; thus it must be an abstract and homogeneous category that is a measure of economic value. The nature of capital (i.e., its capitalization ability) is the reason for discounting the expected future stream of inflows. The extended definition may involve natural resources as well.

Capital is the value of economic means capitalized in natural, human and physical resources. The rate of capitalisation is determined through the natural and social conditions of environment.

The value must always be taken at a certain point in time, so that while it may serve as the present value in some cases it ought to be computed as the future capitalized value of the past stream of used means.

Capital defined in the above way may be classified assuming different criteria:

- Equities: equity capital, debt capital;
- Placement: human, physical, and natural;
- Kind of fund: fixed, circulating

The value of capital or the capital embodied in assets will be maintained (preserved), provided the assets generate a stream of inflows that will yield a sufficient rate of return. The rate should not be less than the capitalization rate. Otherwise, the value of capital declines and becomes less than the historical cost value. This is also an essential feature of capital and this measurement process is the main accounting function.

The basic model derived from the above definition involves a set of variables, which can be used as an adequate means of measuring human capital value assigned to a person.

Personal human capital model

$$H(T) = (K + E)\,[1 + Q(T)] \tag{1}$$

$$\text{and} \quad Q(T) = 1 - T^{\frac{\ln(1-w)}{\ln 2}} \tag{2}$$

where: K – capitalized cost of living; E – capitalized cost of professional education; T – years of professional experience; w – learning parameter as assigned to an individual.

From models (1) and (2) stem formulas of measuring intellectual capital and experience capital.

Personal intellectual capital

$$I(T) = H(T) - K = E + HQ(T)$$
$$\text{where: } H = K + E = H(0) \tag{3}$$

Personal experience capital

$$D(T) = H(T) - H = HQ(T) \tag{4}$$

Total personal human capital value

$$H(T) = K + E + D(T) \tag{5}$$

Concept of internal rate of return applied to this particular capital gives:

Equation of personal human capital growth (IRR)

$$H(T)(1 + r) = CF + H(T + 1) \tag{6}$$

where: r – expected rate of return, CF – cash flows gained during one year as wages and fringe benefits. Finding variable CF one can attain to adequate earning model:

Personal earnings model

$$CF = H(T)\,r - H\,[Q(T + 1) - Q(T)] \tag{7}$$

Model (7) confirms Sunder's (1997) opinion that experience is "by-product of doing a job" and thus can modify earnings in the short run. The model reflects an interesting phenomenon. Earnings can be lower in some cases because of the non-monetary benefits in terms of experience the employee gains during the course of a year. An employer may be aware of the resources, opportunities and benefits enjoyed by an employee as well as on the-job-training opportunities. Barron, Berger and Black, (1998) examined the relationship between on-the-job-training and starting wages. Their study suggests that training lowers starting wages but the estimated dimensions are small. According to the above model the gained experience is capitalized, increasing earnings in next period.

A developed earning model can by introduced as scalar product:

Developed personal earnings model

$$CF' = H(T) a + E u_e + D(T) u_t \qquad (8)$$

where: a – average risk rate, $u_e = r_e - a$, $u_t = r_t - a$
r_e, r_t – rates of return on education and experience capital respectively.

Simplified personal earnings model

$$CF'' = H(T) a + I(T) (v - a) \qquad (9)$$

where: a – average risk rate; v – rate of return on intellectual capital.

Minimum wage model (MWM)

$$MWM = H(T) a = (H + D(T)) a \qquad (10)$$

Minimum rate of return on personal human capital (r_m)

$$r_m = a + Q(T) a \qquad (11)$$

The minimum wage model also defines the minimum wage. From the capital maintenance point of view, the minimum wage cannot be less than the product of total human capital as assigned to an employee and the average risk rate. The MWM formula applies in the case the normative statement as well as economic point of view: **"A value of capital should be preserved"**. This is the essence of capitalism in its positive meaning.

The value of capital is preserved, provided the rate of return is sufficiently high. 8 per cent average-risk rate of return as applied in practice is relevant to 12.5 years payback period. It explains better why the rate should not be 4% in respect to human capital accumulated by an employee. In such a case the payback period would be 25 years, and yet which lady would bear wearing the same coat for 25 years?

➤ Production function as seen by an accountant

The general Solow's production function as discussed by Romer (1996) involves four variables. A natural accounting approach to production function leads to greater number of variables tied in a unique composition. Let us denote a market value of an output as (PR), costs of labour are (W), and assets (A) denote capital embodied already in the physical and financial resources. Market value of the output can be generally introduced as the sum of the additive factors:

$$PR = W + zA + rA - sA \qquad (12)$$

where: z – is ratio of the annual usage of the assets; r – is market rate of return on the capital placed in the assets; s – is looseness of the assets in the production processes.

After a simple rearrangement a model composed of the above-specified variables arrives at the production variable:

$$PR = W[1 + A * (z + r - s)/W] = W*WP \qquad (13)$$

where WP – denotes labour productivity variable.
Because W = u * H, where u – is rate of human labour payoff thus the productivity is arrived at as follows:

$$WP = 1 + A/H * (z + r - s)/u \qquad (14)$$

Then, applying a simple math formula ($\exp(x) \cong 1 + x$, for small x) the production (PR) can be expressed as exponential function of considered variables as follows:

$$PR = (W)\exp\left[\frac{A}{H} * \frac{z + r - s}{u}\right] \qquad (15)$$

The above function reshapes input factors into products. The productivity is growing provided an adequate relationship between human and physical resources exists. Variable (z) is asset turnover ratio so the higher the rotation, the higher the labour productivity, and also, the lesser the human capital payoff ratio (u), the higher the labour productivity. Let us note that if A = 0, the production variable (PR) equals W. It is a case of a primitive man working without any tools. The productivity can also be less than zero. This is a case when looseness of assets exceeds the variable (z+r).

The complex of variables written as small letters can be assumed as a one variable Z denoting level and quality of the management. Then the production function is as follows:

$$PR = (W)\exp\left[\frac{A}{H} * Z\right] \tag{16}$$

Now the model resembles Solow's production function, to which so many well-known interpretations can be applied. The general notion is that productivity is growing according to technical means and quality management. Let us take the example of contemporary Japan, and realise again their management efforts in implementing *just-in-time* systems. The force of Japanese yen and the decrease of exchange rate of yen to dollar – close to one hundred yen per dollar – results from the fact that productivity was growing faster in Japan than in the USA. Since 1980s, the effective efforts in the field of productivity, which has been undertaken in the USA, have stopped the process of dollar depreciation.

➤ **Credit money creation function**

On the right side of the scheme there is a stream of money that flows into the market. Both streams (product and money) confront each other on the market (exchange of money for products). During the confrontation, the size of an inflation or deflation variable is disclosed. The money stream can also be quantified as the function of wage (W). Wages paid to employees split into two lesser streams. The first stream has measure aW (0<a<1) and tends directly on the market without entering the banking system. This means that the exchanges are effected immediately. Parameter (a) arrives at this part of wages that are exchanged for products directly, without entering the banking system. The parameter can be interpreted as the welfare level and saving propensity. The second part of the original stream of wages (1-a)W feeds the banking system first. Then, amplified in the banking system (credit money creation), it flows into the market, linking with the first stream. A part of this stream (which is not disclosed in the scheme) is not used by banking system for a basis for credit creation, as it provides mandatory reserves system and requirements of current accounts conditions. Therefore only a part of that stream quantified as (1-a)(1-b)W is the real basis for credit creation (b- is the ratio of reserves). Thus amount of the money M_K which confronts the product stream can be expressed as follows:

$$M_k = aW + \frac{(1-a)+(1-b)W}{1-k} \tag{17}$$

where k denotes a parameter of credit money creation in banking system. The total stream of money is therefore equal to:

$$M_K = W * WK = W \frac{a(1-k)+(1-a)(1-b)}{1-k} \tag{18}$$

The problem of determining the right value of credit money creation parameter k (which minimises the level of inflation) can be solved by using a fragment of the equation of exchange as follows:

$$\text{GNPR} (1 + i) = W*WK \tag{19}$$

Solving for variable (i) we obtain formula:

$$i = \frac{WK}{RWP} - 1 \tag{20}$$

where RWP = GNPR/W is the real wage productivity.

Assuming the condition $i = 0 \Rightarrow WK = RWP$ we can find the value of the parameter k that minimises inflation level. Using the equation:

$$a + \frac{(1-a)(1-b)}{1-k} = RWP \qquad\qquad (21)$$

we come up with the following model:

$$1 - k = \frac{(1-a)(1-b)}{RWP - a} \qquad\qquad (22)$$

Thus the wage multiplier is equal to:

$$\frac{1}{1-k} = \frac{RWP - a}{(1-a)(1-b)} \qquad\qquad (23)$$

The ultimate opinion is that the stream going through the banking system can be increased to a level $W^*(RWP - a)$. The size of credit depends on the wage level, welfare level and productivity level as well.

To keep control over the money supply should only mean a wise wage system and cost control as well as a precise feasibility study in respect to investment projects that involve debt financing in particular. Wages should be derived from the capital value. That to pay less than an average risk rate applied to human capital of an employee is a sin against an individual, but overpaying is a sin against society (inflation and depreciation of wage receivables), is a clear conclusion of the above consideration.

WHAT DETERMINES THE VALUE OF A MONETARY UNIT

The value of a monetary unit manifests itself in two exchanges: domestic and international. The first exchange can disclose inflation or deflation but the second concerns the behaviour of exchange rates.

❖ The value of a monetary unit in domestic exchanges

The inflation variable appears in the dynamic model as an amount created by the market mechanism, which balances the stream of products and the stream of money. Therefore, discussing inflation as a purely monetary phenomenon, as well as taking actions directed solely towards the money stream, is not correct. The essence of the problem lies in the characteristics of the actual stream as well as in the quality and the efficiency of the market mechanism. It is the productivity of labour that is the external variable that modifies the money stream. In order to achieve a better understanding of the nature of inflation, let us consider an actual fragment of an exchange equation to calculate wages:

$$WP * W = GNPR * PD$$

where: $PD = (1+i)$, and 'i' is inflation index.

Thus
$$PD = \frac{WP * W}{GNPR}$$

At this point, it is worth to digress in order to better explain the causes of inflation. As it had already been said, wages are linked to human capital through the relevant rate of return on this capital.

$$W = u * H$$

where: H – value of total personal human capital, u – rate of return.

The number of employees can also be introduced to the denominator of equation (24), on the basis of the following relationship:

$$GNPR = GNPCR * N$$

where: GNPCR - real GNP per employee, N – number of employees.

As a result, the value of PD depends on the following set of variables:

$$PD = \frac{u * H * WP}{N * GNPCR}$$

The only constant of the above equation is the rate of return on human capital. It approximates the value of rate of return on average risk, and therefore it maintains the level of 8%. The H/N variable exhibits a growing trend, which is the result of natural development processes (growing education and experience), while the nominal productivity of wages can vary, depending mostly on the precision of the management system. Therefore, what follows from the latter formula, low inflation is a natural expression of a developing economy, and, simultaneously, a function of management. Such a natural inflation does not usually achieve double figures, unless the process of management fails to achieve its functions correctly, or unless it is stimulated by political activity. If we write the formula as follows:

$$GNPR = u * H * WP / PD$$

we see the significance of actual productivity of wages in GNP creation. It stresses that, given the equal importance of all variables, the key variable of real GNP growth is the value of WP/PD (actual productivity of wages), and again it indicates the role of management wherever remuneration is paid, and not only in enterprises. Labour should be planned, regulated, and controlled, and the wages paid after the evaluation of desired results. We should also note that low inflation is a natural growth-inducing economic factor, while inflation of any level is a challenge to accountancy theory, as financial reporting should present information unburdened with distortions of any kind.

Based on the wages equation of exchange, we can introduce a direct condition:

$$1 + i = WP/RWP$$

According to the above formula, in the situation of zero inflation the nominal labour productivity equals to the real productivity. In other words, all processes are managed in a way that an increase in wages always stems from the growth of labour productivity. Also, the creation of credit money is limited by the real productivity of labour. The concept of inflation understood as a relationship between the nominal and the real labour productivity describes the degree of chaos in a given economy, and this chaos will not be remedied by a monetary policy. Appropriate management systems are necessary in all organisational units of the private and the public sector.

❖ The Value of a Monetary Unit in International Exchange

The behaviour of exchange rates is explained on the basis of several theories such as: the law of one price, purchasing power parity (PPP), International Fisher Effects (IFE). So far, none of these has been universally accepted. Many efforts are put to defend the PPP theory, introducing productivity as an additional variable. The well known approaches as described by (Rogoff, 1996) and others use a concept of productivity limited to the sector of traded goods. This approach, however, is not sufficient to formulate a general model of exchange rate behaviour. The general productivity as defined for the purpose of the wage equation of exchange, is an adequate concept involving wages and GNP as the two most general variables.

Law of one price is the strictest form of the PPP theory. It states that in the presence of a competitive market structure and the absence of transportation costs and other barriers to trade, identical products which are sold in different markets will sell at the same price when expressed in terms of a common currency. Shortness of this theory is confirmed by everyday human experience of people travelling abroad and by additional evidence, coming from BIG Mac index (McDonalds, 1999) or (Pakko and Pollard, 1996). Truly speaking, the Big Mac index was devised as a light-hearted guide to whether currencies are at their correct level, but assuming that the prices of currencies are market-shaped, the only possible conclusion is that the law of one price does not hold.

An auxiliary question may be posed with respect to wages and salaries that determine costs of labour. Is it right to apply the exchange rate only, in determining what salary should be paid to two individuals doing the same job, but working in two different countries? Economists have yet to come up with a clear answer to this question. In order to briefly answer it, we will also take into account the problem of labour productivity. Let us use common sense first and consider two imaginary individuals from Poland and from the USA. Each of them is part worker, part farmer, part clerk, part manager, part teacher, part politician etc. Let Q represent the value (not expressed in monetary terms) of their labour during a given period. What is the result of comparing their effects in terms of labour?

Would the result be $Q_P/Q_A = 1$ where P denotes the Pole and A denotes the American? It is commonly known that the effects are quite different. The relationship should be written as follows:

$$\frac{Q_P}{Q_A} = \frac{1}{U} \tag{24}$$

where U denotes coefficient of labour power comparison.

In each country a wage is paid in a monetary unit. Pay systems arrive at a number of monetary units assigned to a period during which an individual performs a given work. Taking this into account, the next equation can be written as follows:

$$\frac{Q_P * EP_P}{Q_A * EP_A} = \left[\frac{EP_P}{EP_A}\right] * \frac{1}{U} \qquad (25)$$

where EP denotes money equivalent for work.

The product EP*Q is an average pay SP. Let us now consider the situation where, all things being equal, the relationship between the number of monetary units pàid in the two countries in question for equal labour, gives the initial value of the exchange rate, with no other factors coming into play, and where $Q_A = Q_P$. This is simply a case of two identical economies. The only difference lies in unequal amount of monetary units paid to employees (10 DM in Germany compared with $5 in the USA) and the names of the currencies are different too. The required relationship is thus as follows.

$$\frac{SP_P}{SP_A} = \frac{ER\,[^{zl}/_{\$}]}{U} \qquad (26)$$

where ER denotes the exchange rate.

To illustrate the meaning of this coefficient we can estimate the U using rough data. For instance the average pay in Poland in May 2000 was 1,900 zł. The average hourly wage in the USA according to The Financial Times, (May, 7th, 1999) was $11.3 Assuming an average wage in the USA of only $2,200 and taking ER = 4.30 then U = 4.98 times. Labour in the USA is therefore almost 5 times more efficient compared to Poland. What is an economic essence of the U? The labour effect of a country representative as discussed above is nothing more than GNP per capita or per working person. Thus the equation which determines a pay equivalent to a foreign wage may be written as follows:

$$U = GNPC_A[\$]/GNPC_P[\$] \tag{27}$$

The ultimate formula is therefore:

$$SP_P = \frac{SP_A * ER^{zl}/_\$ * GNPC_P[\$]}{GNPC_A[\$]} \tag{28}$$

The GNPCs are expressed in the same money unit [$]. In such a case a model, which describes the exchange rate, can be derived as follows:

$$\frac{SP_P}{GNPC_P[\$]} = ER^{zl}/_\$ \frac{SP_A}{GNPC_A} \tag{29}$$

The above formula may be interpreted in different ways. It should be stressed that per capita income levels broadly reflect differences in labour productivity, the idea which originally comes from early Balassa-Samuelson research. Turning to Big Macs, it is unlikely that there are large differences in the productivity of workers cooking burgers regardless of whether they are working in China or the United States. There are, however, large differences in general productivity measured as relationship between wages and GNP.

The purchasing power parity hypothesis (PPP) is an economic topic that should, according to many economists' belief, be able to explain exchange rate movements. According to the PPP hypothesis, the ratio of domestic to foreign prices determines the basic exchange rate. O'Connell (1998) interprets the PPP theory to mean that national price level should be equalised when expressed in a common currency. Researchers have devised a number of econometric models in order to empirically test PPP as a means of explaining exchange rate behaviour. Such research was designed to confirm the belief that exchange rate would be very stable, not only in the long run, but also over a short period of time, which is easy to predict on the basis of firm economic fundamentals. When exchange rate were floated on a wide scale for the first time in 1973 (Bretton Woods), it was generally assumed that exchange rates would quickly adjust to change in relative price levels. Studies carried out on this topic have yet to confirm these expectations. Fluctuation in nominal exchange rate seemed extreme in comparison with fluctuations in economic fundamentals. As a consequence PPP can no longer be regarded as a reliable theory[1]. Despite the fact that this theory has been put to the test on many occasion, evidence to support it remains elusive, at least with regard to the modern floating rate area. O'Connell (1998) paid attention to a variety of real factors such as productivity and others, which can also determine the exchange rate behaviour.

The formal definition of the PPP relationship as described by Edison at al. (1997) is as follows:

$$ER = \lambda \frac{P*}{P} \qquad\qquad (30)$$

where:

P* – denotes the index of foreign prices (CPI – consumer price index);

P – denotes the index of domestic prices;

λ – is a constant;

ER – denotes the exchange rate.

Most studies have rejected the formula in its strictest form as presented above. Beachill and Pugh (1998) and others indicate that presently done empirical tests have not always rejected productivity-adjusted PPP relationship even though the concept is limited to traded goods sector.

---

[1] See the papers from the workshop "Developments in Exchange Rate Modeling", 1997, written by Koedijk (1998) and Lothian (1998)

As was stated earlier, the exchange rate depends not only on the price level but it is also closely related to general wage productivity. Economic fundamentals such as wages, GNP, and wages productivity have some influence on exchange rates behaviour and movements. In order to derive any relationship between exchange rate and other variables, first we must consider a wage version of exchange equation. In accordance with the exchange equation formula, the GNP deflator is:

$$PD = \frac{WP*W}{GNPR} = \frac{WP}{RWP} \tag{31}$$

The PPP theory focuses mainly on consumer price index. A better way is to consider the GNP deflator in this case. Thus, we determine a relation between the PD of two selected countries for instance Germany and the USA, as follows:

$$\frac{PD_D}{PD_A} = \frac{WP_D * W_D}{GNPR_D} * \frac{GNPR_A}{WP_A * W_A} \tag{32}$$

Establishing USD now as the basic currency, we must express GNPR of Germany in this money unit. To achieve this, the past value of exchange rate is used (ER_0).

$$GNPR_D[\$] = GNPR_D[DM]* ER_0[\$/DM] \tag{33}$$

where: ER_0 denotes the exchange rate at the end of last year.
Subsequently we obtain the formula:

$$\frac{PD_D}{PD_A} = \frac{W_D}{W_A} * \frac{GNPR_A[\$]}{GNPR_D[\$]} * \frac{WP_D}{WP_A} \cdot ER_0[\$/DM] \tag{34}$$

Therefore the end model which explains exchange rate is as follows:

$$PPP_{D/A} = ER\left[DM/\$\right]* WPP_{D/A} * ER_0\left[\$/DM\right] \tag{35}$$

where:
$PPP_{D/A}$ – GNP deflators parity;
$WPP_{D/A}$ – wage productivity parity.

Thus the set of variables which influence the exchange rate (besides current market impacts) are shaped as follows:

$$ER\left[DM\middle/ \$\right] = \frac{PPP_{D/A}}{WPP_{D/A} * ER_0[\$/DM]} \tag{36}$$

Therefore the general model (the adequate form of PPP) which determines exchange rate is as follows:

$$ER = ER_0 * \frac{RWP^*}{RWP} \tag{37}$$

where: RWP^* – real wage productivity abroad, RWP – domestic real wage productivity, ER_0 – a former exchange rate value.

The conclusion is that the greater relative inflation rates in Germany, the higher the USD price. But the higher the wage productivity in Germany, the cheaper is the USD. The PPP theory could explain exchange rates behaviour provided one more parity is included. Besides inflation, the wage productivity variable is needed to determine the purchasing power of a monetary unit. The exchange rate should depend only on the last value, when the above mentioned parities are used.

WHERE ARE WE NOW AND COULD WE DO ANY MORE?

An answer to this seemingly rhetoric question is provided by John K. Galbraith (1982, p. 401) in his work *Money: Whence It Came, Where It Went*. Galbraith argues that the main reason why the monetary systems in the World have been, as he says, unsatisfactory, is that the monetary issues attract very little talented people, who hide behind the mystery that seems to surround the subject of economy in general, and particularly the problems of money. Their indolence is protected by the fact that the failure hardly ever affects those responsible for it. Moreover, very frequently it has been a subject of interesting disputes, or even a source of prestige for those involved. When it comes to monetary questions, one can more easily achieve personal success by repeating widely accepted slogans and conformist behaviour rather than by critical and analytical thinking.

➢ Logic Versus Monetary Policy

An intellectual approach to any issue is always connected with a critique and reflection. It requires a continuous revision of theoretical bases on which the current theory is built, in order to ensure their accordance with reality, as well as an appropriate construction of practice. From this point of view, the monetary policy can be a graceful research field.

The current monetary system and monetary policy, as it has been discussed earlier, lacks a solid theoretical framework. Monetary policy appears to be particularly controversial, since it is conducted as if the implication:

Healthy money $\Rightarrow$ Healthy economy

was absolutely right, in spite of the fact that it cannot be concluded from the experiences of the past and present generations. The human experience is actually the opposite. It is a healthy economy that is a prerequisite of healthy money $(p \Rightarrow q)$. Once the wage questions have been put into order within a given economy, and the wages are equal to the amount of work for each individual (Dobija, 2000), the human and intellectual capital will be paid in the right way, which will result in the state of social peace. A good example of that is the United States of America, where the minimum wage per hour, established at the level of $5.00 refers to the edge 8% rate of return on human capital. The salary systems are based on this right value. Thus, according to the law of counter-position, the logically justified implication ($-q \Rightarrow -p$) is expressed by the following formula:

Weak money (inflation) $\Rightarrow$ improperly managed, weak economy

The logical square constructed from the sentence **p $\Rightarrow$ q** requires, as it is known, two implications located along its sides to be proved. Unfortunately, the monetary policy does not have this logical support and, what is worse, its creators do not feel any intellectual discomfort. The irrelevance that can be observed is the irrelevance in the context of economic reality rather than following the ideal Platonian form.

Apart from that, the intellectual weakness manifests itself in the lack of reflection in following the American monetary policy and Alan Greenspan, its present leading creator. What is distinctive about American economy, is the fact, that in the case of the United States of America the implication **p $\Rightarrow$ q**, which means that a healthy economy is a basis of healthy money, is met. All that Mr. Alan Greenspan has to do is not to disturb the economy, and he is mastering the task. Looking from the Polish perspective at how he is changing the discount rate by 0.5 or 0.25%, always to an extent that does not surpass the risk premium (7-8%), it can be noticed that he is doing a good job without an actual violation of any logical rules. A consideration of wage productivity is not peculiar to him either. Nevertheless, such a policy can not be easily benchmarked, as it has a well managed real economy for its base, as discussed earlier.

Another question is whose merit it is to make the implication **p $\Rightarrow$ q** true. If a practice similar to the above takes place in the situation of failing implication **p $\Rightarrow$ q**, with the idea that 'what is good for America, is good for us', and the discount rate equal to 20%, there can be only one result: a decline of the economy. Benchmarking of this kind means merely following someone else's path, which is not an evidence of a sophisticated intellect. In this way, lack of intellectualism appears to have so far dominated the human experience called money.

COULD WE DO ANY MORE

Neil P. Finnegan, 1995
Critical Perspectives on Accounting, ed. Marilyn Neimark, Academic Press, Harcourt Brace & Co., Publishers, New York, Vol. 7 No. 1-2 February/April 1996.

The world is filled with such sorrow
So much will be gone tomorrow
I'm headed up to the store
Thinking could I do any more?

Any more than earn my keep
Pay the rent so I can sleep
Get a bigger bank account
So those electric bills don't mount

Today a child's life will end
Because her cancer cells won't mend
A man has a heart attack
Another merely breaks his back

Could I do any more
Than merely cry about the poor?
Tears won't get them out of trouble
When cruel life has burst their bubble

I'm a white collar man
The secretaries love my tan
But could I be doing any more
Than swinging a driver yelling 'fore'?

Being of the corporate gentry
I post another journal entry
While homeless people eat
Out of trashcans in the street

Could we do any more?
Time's about to shut the door
Don't just work eight to five
Remember, others are alive!

➢ Money and Contemporary Accounting Systems

Firstly, let us note that accounting systems, especially financial accounting and cost statement, are closely linked to, and use the work-based value theory. The theory manifests itself particularly in the cost statement, which focuses on the inputs of production factors, and similarly, understanding of the value as the sum of work inputs is the essence of the labour theory of value. As Ijiri (1999, p.185) argues:

> "... In contrast to the labour theory of value, which focuses on input, the utility theory of value focuses on output: hence, it does not question how and through what process a product was produced as long as the output possesses the same use value. Thus, the cost principle would not have a common linkage with the utility theory of value as it does with the labour theory of value..."

Therefore, the historical cost principle is fundamental for the accounting system. According to that principle, the value of tangible assets of a given unit is determined by the actual purchase price (or production cost) increased by all costs borne in order to make the asset applicable. In the accounting system, the book value of assets is confronted with the market value at the moment of sales in the same way as labour input is confronted with the social labour input in the value theory. Therefore, the principle of realisation, which regulates the issue of identifying income and profit in accounting, also conforms to the paradigms of work-based value.

This conformity of concepts between accounting and work-based value can be an indication for the research on the influence of an accounting system on the stability of money. The correlation between the condition of accounting and the stability of monetary system can be perceived indirectly. The case of the United States of America is the best example for that, and one can agree to the statement that it is difficult to find a country which has an equally well developed and functional accounting systems and, at the same time, high inflation levels. What is most important here is the controlling function of accounting, actively employed in order to shape the actual use of production factors, in accordance with socially necessary outlays, which is one of the functions of cost statement and managerial accounting. It has to be emphasised that the western countries which achieve the highest level of economic order, first employed standard costing systems in 1920s. In other countries, suffering from a high inflation, accountancy does not normally perform the functions of control and prevention, but it passively reflects the reality. Again, it is worth recalling the practices that existed in ancient Mesopotamia, where the use of standards and ensuring the compliance of real processes with those standards was essential. This question is still poorly understood nowadays. Even in the West, it prevails more in practice than in the economic theory of money.

The awareness of the role of financial accounting shows a growing tendency. A statement by Wallman (1995) can be quoted as an example:

"...For all of the reasons previously stated, financial reporting information flows are a critical component of our system of capitalism and democracy. Without appropriate information, risk increases, as do demanded returns and the cost of capital. Our standard of living will be less than what it could have been. It is clear – obvious – why financial reporting information flows must keep pace with changes in real word..."

The importance of managerial accounting and control is less apparent in lofty statements like this one, than it is consistently proven in practice. Undoubtedly, capitalism needs both financial and management accounting, since it is a system in which capital may be freely multiplied through its location in the right assets, given the lack of legal or social barriers. It is however unquestionable that in order to measure the capital and its movement, economic calculus is indispensable, and it is reflected in precise systems of accounting. In this respect Sombart (Rosenberg, Birdzell, 1994, p. 188) is right arguing that without accounting, the capitalist system would not have developed. Let us emphasise once more that it is not coins that determined the intellectual progress in management, but it is economic thought embodied in accounting systems that systematically builds the path of economic development. However, we must not forget about the remaining factors, since accounting is not the basis of everything in the world.

The role of intellect in the human venture called "money" is depicted in the figure 1, in which the white colour signifies a greater involvement of intellect than the grey colour.

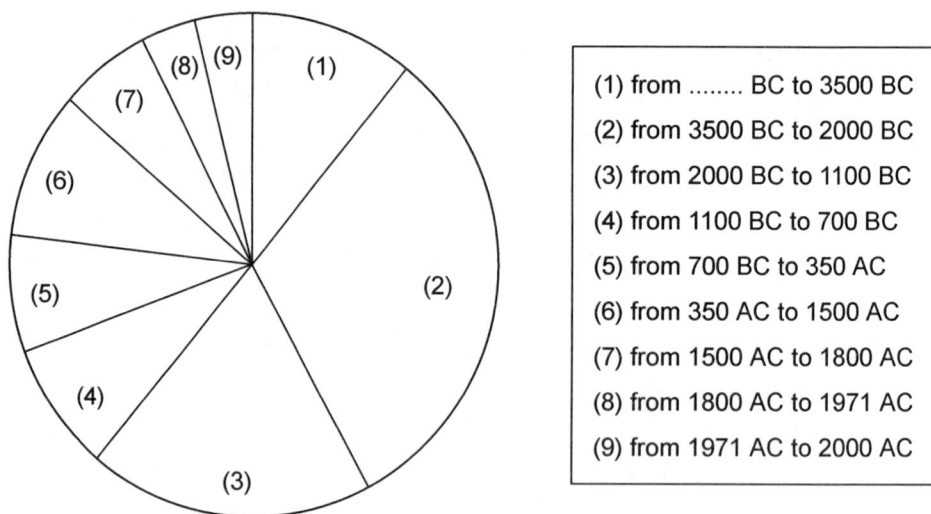

Figure 1. Intellectual perception of money over time

(1) from .... BC to 3500 BC	
(2) from 3500 BC to 2000 BC	
(3) from 2000 BC to 1100 BC	
(4) from 1100 BC to 700 BC	
(5) from 700 BC to 350 AC	
(6) from 350 AC to 1500 AC	
(7) from 1500 AC to 1800 AC	
(8) from 1800 AC to 1971 AC	
(9) from 1971 AC to 2000 AC	

Provisionally, periods and concluding events as showed in figure 1 can be presented as follows:

▶ Beginnings of economic thought and accounting. Tokens

▶ Emergence of town-states. Money as receivables registered in accounting systems. End of Sumerian civilisation

▶ Money based on the system of accounting and calculation against the value of silver and copper. End of heroic age

▶ So-called "Dark Ages" from the end of heroic age until the introduction of coins in 7th century BC

▶ Coins and monetary understanding of money. Diocletian reforms around the year 305

▶ Middle Ages and monetary money

▶ The Conquest and desire for gold. Recovery of accounting

▶ Development of banking, accounting, and quantitative theories of money

▶ Year 1971. Final breakage of the relationship between money and gold. Waiting for new, qualitative theories of money.

➤ In Search of a Universal Accounting Theory

The ideas we have presented here can be summarised in a number of general points:

❑ The first, money is the wage receivable and should be perceived merely as records.

❑ The second, a monetary unit is related to the value of labour and its stability depends on labour productivity.

❑ The third, each employee has her or his own structure of human capital which determines the adequate minimal pay arrived at by average risk rate of return or minimal market cost of capital.

❑ The fourth, the wage equation of exchange describes the two streams that are an essence of monetary economy, which are confronted t with each other within the market.

❑ The fifth, the wage equation of exchange is fundamental for the general theory of money (credit money amount, inflation, stabilisation policy, etc.) and can be a useful tool for keeping control over monetary unit stability.

❑ The sixth, wise pay management is the right tool for controlling the purchasing power of money.

❑ The seventh, to a holder, money is the prime financial asset, while it is also an indispensable obligation of the State.

The above statements open new ways for the economic and accounting thought. The monetary issues are no longer merely of economic character, they become also an important theoretical problem of accounting theory. Indeed, where it not within accounting framework is there the right place for consideration of a monetary unit? Isn't instability of a monetary unit the main reason for different considerations of accounting measures? The unit of measure agenda in money economy framework is a core of general accounting theory.

In this new situation, there emerges a more general framework of accounting fields. Human resource costing and accounting emerge as an indispensable part and parcel of future accounting. Human capital measurement connects wage theories with productivity agenda. Therefore, both should be an integral part of the new accounting framework. A better understanding of the meaning of monetary unit will hopefully enrich the research into fair accounting measures. It is also an essential topic of general accounting theory.

The historical cost measure and conventional accounting as discussed by Ijiiri (1965, 1975), Lim and Sunder (1991) should gain a new light with better understanding of monetary issues. Managerial accounting perceived to be an internally oriented part of accounting should find new external dimensions, as a general tool of productivity control in an organisation, and on the State level as well.

At this moment, a single, generally accepted accounting theory does not exist. However, the theoretical description and stabilisation of a monetary unit can be seen as a solid basis for each more or less coherent system of objectives and assumptions, as well as standards that define the nature and scope of accounting theory and practice.

Monetary unit considerations are closely related to many areas of contemporary accounting: human capital costing and wage accounting in particular. Therefore, the human resources costing and accounting discipline gain a new impulse, as a base for wage managerial accounting, which is a tool for labour productivity stabilisation and, as a consequence, the stability of the value of monetary unit.

Therefore, monetary unit considerations are a common part of both macroeconomics and accounting theory. „**Money is nothing more than wage receivables"** is a new paradigm for the New Millennium. Contemporary money requires a wise and solid accounting theory behind it, coupled with adequate standards that are working in practice – so we believe.

BIBLIOGRAPHY TO PART ONE

1. Bator Wiesław (1993) Myśl starożytnego Egiptu, Zaklad Wydawniczy Nomos, Kraków.
2. Bielicki Marian (1969) Zapomniany świat Sumerów, PIW, Warszawa.
3. Blaug Mark (1994) Teoria ekonomii, Wydawnictwo Naukowe PWN, Warszawa.
4. Krawczuk Aleksander (1990) Siedmiu przeciw Tebom, Wydawnictwo Poznańskie, Poznań.
5. Cywiński Henryk (1986) Z dziejów pieniądza na świecie, KAW, Warszawa.
6. Ifrah Georges (1990) Dzieje liczby czyli historia wielkiego wynalazku, Zakład Narodowy im. Ossolińskich.
7. Holroyd Stuart and Powell Neil (1991) Mysteries of Magic, Polish Ed., PENTA, Warszawa.
8. Galbraith John K. 1992. *Economics in Perspective, A Critical History*, Polish ed., PWN. Warsaw, 80.
9. Galbraith John Keneth (1982) Pieniądz pochodzenie i losy, PWE, Warszawa.
10. Oppenheim A. L. (1957) A Bird's-Eye View of Mesopotamian Economic History, Trade and Market in the Early Empires, The Free Press, New York.
11. Polanyi Karl, Arensberg Konrad and Pearson Harry (1957) Trade and Market in the Early Empires, The Free Press, New York.
12. Rosenberg Nathan and Birdzell L. E. (1994) Historia kapitalizmu, Signum, Kraków.
13. Rachunkowość fabryki włókienniczej Die Wirtschaftspruefung, no. 14/1993 Rachunkowość (1995).
14. Saggs Henry W.F. (1983), Wielkość i upadek Babilonii, PIW, Warszawa
15. Schmandt-Besserat D. (1988) Accounting in Prehistory, Vth World Congress of Accounting Historians, Sydney.
16. Struve V. (1969) Some New Data on the Organisation of Labour and on Social Structure in Sumer During the Reign of the III rd Dynasty of UR, in Ancient Mesopotamia, Nauka, Moskwa.
17. Tyumenew A. (1969), The State Economy of Ancient Sumer, in Ancient Mesopotamia, Nauka, Moskwa.
18. Zabłocka Julia (1987) Historia Bliskiego Wschodu w Starożytności, Zakład im. Ossolińskich, Wrocław.

BIBLIOGRAPHY

1. Beachill. Bob, and Pugh Geoff. (1998). "Monetery cooperation in Europe and the problem of differential productivity growth: An argument for a 'two speed' Europe". *International Review of Applied Economics.* Vol. 12. Issue 3. 445–458.

2. Barron. John M., Berger Mark C., and Black Dan A.1999. "Do workers pay on-the-job training". *The Journal of Human Resources.* Vol.34. no2. 235–251.

3. Bradford De Long J. 2000. "The Triumph of Monetarism?". *Journal of Economic Perspectives.*, vol.14. No 1. 83–94.

4. Dobija. Mieczysław. 1998." How to Place Human Resources into the Balance Sheet". *Journal of Human Resource Costing & Accounting.* Vol. 3. No 1. (Spring); 83–92.

5. Dobija. Mieczysław. 2000. "Human Resource Costing and Accounting as a Determinant of Minimum Wage Theory" *Zeszyty Naukowe* nr 553. Akademia Ekonomiczna w Krakowie. 39–62.

6. Edison. Hali J., Gagnon Joseph E., and Melick William R. 1997. "Understanding the empirical literature on purchasing power parity: the post - Bretton Woods era". *Journal of International Money and Finance.* Vol. 16. No 1.(February); 1–17.

7. Hudson. W. I. 1993. *Intellectual Capital.* John Wiley & Sons Inc, N.Y., p.16.

8. Ijiri. Yuji. 1976. "The Price Level Restatement and Its Dual Interpretation". *The Accounting Review.* No 2. (April).

9. Ijiri. Yuji. 1965. "Axioms and Structures of Conventional Accounting Measurement." *The Accounting Review.* (January).

10. Ijiri. Yuji. 1995. "Segment Statements and Informativeness Measures, Managing Capital vs. Managing Resources." *Accounting Horizons.* (Vol. 9. no. 3): 55–67.

11. Ijiri Yuji . 1999. The Cost Principle and the Labour Theory of Value in Relation to the Role of Accounting Theories and Their Depth, The Japanese Style of Business Accounting, Quorum Books, Westport.

12. Johannisson Bengt, Kwiatkowski Stefan, Dandridge Thomas C. 1999. Intellectual Enterprenuership – Emerging Identity in a Learning Perspective, Published by Leon Koźmiński Academy of Entrepreneurship and Management, Warsaw.

13. Koedijk. Kees G. 1998. "The pendulum of exchange rate economics". *Journal of International Money and Finance*, vol. 17. 1–3.

14. Lim S., and Sunder Shyam. 1991. "Efficiency of Asset Valuation Rules under Price Movement and Measurement Errors", *The Accounting Review.* (no 4).

15. Lothian. James. 1998. "Some new stylized facts of floating exchange rates". *Journal of International Money and Finance,* Vol. 17. 29–39

16. McConnell, Campbell R. and Brue Stanley L.1986. *Contemporary Labour Economics,* McGraw–Hill, 433.

17. McDonalds. 1999. "Big MacCurrencies". *Economist.* Vol. 351. (Issue 8113): 66.

18. O'Connell. Paul G. J. 1998. "The overvaluing of purchasing power parity". *Journal of International Economics.* Vol. 44, 1–19.

19. O'Connell. Paul G. J. 1998. "Market frictions and real exchange rates". *Journal of International Money and Finance.* vol. 17. 71–95.

20. Pakko. Michael and Patricia Pollard. 1996. "For here or to go? Purchasing power parity and the Big Mac". *Review (Federal Reserve Bank of Saint Louis).* Vol. 78. Issue 1. (Jan/Feb 96): 3–19.

21. Rogoff. Kenneth. 1996."The Purchasing Power Parity Puzzle". *Journal of Economic Literature.* Vol. 34, (Issue 2); 647–669.

22. Romer David. 1996. *Advanced Macroeconomics,* McGraw – Hill. 23.

23. Sunder. Shyam. 1997. *Theory of Accounting and Control..* South-Western Publishing. Cincinnati. 36.

24. Wallman Stephen M. H. 1995. The Future of Accounting and Disclosure in an Evolving World: The Need for Dramatic Change, Accounting Horizons, Vol. 9, No. 3, Sept.

ILLUSTRATIONS IN ORDER OF APPEARANCE:

1. A plate made in fifth millennium BC
2. Egyptian Goddess of writing
3. A clay tablet with a poem
4. Greek Goddess - Athena
5. Coins struck by Alexander the Great
6. Coin found at Byblos

Alojzy Z. Nowak

EURO, PURE INTELLECTUAL PRODUCT OR INTERNATIONAL CURRENCY?*

━━━━━━━━━━━━━ *Abstract* ━━━━━━━━━━━━━

Money is sometimes perceived as an intellectual product, and in fact it is. However, sometimes it is only pure intellectual product and another time it plays the role of the real financial asset. This paper is introducing and analysing the conditions that money has to fulfil to be national or international currency, and financial asset. Simultaneously it is answering the question about the role the euro is going to play in the near future, and weather the euro is to be only pure intellectual concept or both intellectual and "real" financial asset.

* This paper was prepared during my stay at the University of North Florida, Jacksonville, as a Bishop Desmond Tutu Visiting Professor of International Economics – in this way I would like to express my gratitude to the College of Business Administration at UNF and in particular to Dean Earle Traynham and Professor Jeffrey Steagall for inviting me, discussions we had, and great work and life conditions.

GENERAL COMMENTS

On January 1st 1999, 11 European Union states introduced the common currency – the euro. Not so long ago, numerous economists, finance specialists, and bankers considered the introduction of the euro a rather unlikely phenomenon. This stemmed from a belief that the bond of governments and citizens of the various European countries to their national currencies is so strong that despite the advanced integration processes in Europe, the introduction and creation of a common currency is practically impossible. As it turns out, things happened otherwise. As of January 1st, 11 European Union countries reached the highest economic and monetary integration level imaginable, precisely by introducing common currency and passing a decision to implement a joint monetary policy by the newly founded European Central Bank. As a result, it has been estimated that during the first year of existence, the new currency "handled" commodity and service turnover of a value exceeding USD 6 trillions. Moreover, this – as referred to by some – monetary revolution has generated the second largest economic power area in the world, with a population exceeding 300 million people. Hence, this fact is not only becoming an economic challenge to the formerly unquestioned economic power – the United States – and to the American dollar in particular, but also to bankers, finance specialists, managers, investors, analysts, lawyers, politicians. In all their calculations and analyses, they should recognise the fact of the existence and use of the new currency (and of the common currency area), as well as the impact of its implementation, both on individual states and on the various business entities party to international trade exchange. Today, the euro is the official currency of Austria, Belgium, Finland, France, Germany, Ireland, Italy, Luxembourg, the Netherlands, Portugal, and Spain.

In professional literature, the introduction of the euro is described as a huge success of uniting Europe, to result in improvement in overall economic management, thanks to an increase in competitiveness in the Community, and thus a growth in prosperity. On the other hand, this fact is frequently described as a „step into a crevasse", "way into the unknown", "unknown future", "dead-end street", etc. Such extreme differences in opinions concerning the introduction of the euro trigger off a need to embark upon a more in-depth analysis of this economic and financial phenomenon of a voluntary resignation of sovereign states from the emission of and price quotation for their own currencies (potentially influencing the condition of the economy), and of resignation from income relating to their senior position, etc. It seems that answers to the following questions may be of help in the understanding of this fascinating phenomenon:

Firstly, what is the euro?

Secondly, can the euro become a European, or indeed global currency?

Responses to these questions shall require a presentation of factors determining the international nature of the currency on the one hand, and – on the other – an analysis of reasons, conditions, and results of euro introduction. Before this is done, however, it would be worthwhile to offer a more detailed presentation of the various euro introduction stages. These encompass three phases.

The European Council decided that phase "A", should encompass states conforming to appropriate economic criteria (inflation rate, interest rates, currency exchange variation rate, budget deficit, public debt volume), and showing an interest in joining the Monetary Union. The European Central Bank was formed, and legal systems of states joining the Monetary Union were adjusted for purposes of introducing a common currency. The first euro banknotes, and first euro coins were emitted. This phase began on May 2nd 1998, and closed on January 1st 1999.

As part of phase, "B", which began on January 1st 1999 and is to last no longer than for a maximum of 3 years, the common euro currency was introduced in 11 European Union states to serve as legal tender. It ought to be emphasised at this stage, that although the currency has not made a physical appearance in business entities yet, many large corporations – albeit unforced by the letter of law – have adopted the euro as a unit of settlement. The following have proceeded accordingly, among others: Daimler-Benz (Germany), Alcatel (France), Nokia (Finland), Chase Manhattan (USA). It is worthwhile emphasising at this stage that although households do not use the euro as a means of settlement yet, this is no proof of a failure of the implementation endeavour for the following reasons: firstly, settlements between individuals form but a minor percentage of settlements total, and secondly, they are to proceed with such action during phase "C" only, that is until 2002. Moreover, phase "B" provides for a definition of exchange rates for the eleven currencies to the euro. A basis for the definition thereof has been provided by the rate of the various currency units to the American dollar on the final business day of 1998. Phase "B" is also the period of Central Banks of the respective states joining the Monetary Union and transferring the task of monetary policy enforcement to the European Central Bank – the successor of the European Monetary Institute.

In conformity to assumptions concerning the implementation of the Economic and Monetary Union, phase "C" shall provide for euro banknotes and coins being introduced onto the actual trade market. Concurrently, this shall be a stage of the national currencies and the common currency being used in parallel (in the physical sense as well), for a predefined period. This means that consumers shall be able to handle cash transactions in their domestic currencies and the euro alike, albeit the European Central Bank will gradually withdraw national currencies from trade, in order for the euro to remain the only currency officially used in Euroland by the end of phase "C". The expected duration of phase "C", however, spanning a term from January 1st, 2002, through to July 1st, 2002, means that domestic currencies are to be exchanged (in the technical sense) for the euro in the various banks for many years to come. The reason for such a brief phase "C" stems from the expected high costs of business transactions, as their register shall be operated in a minimum of two currencies during the said period. Some countries even intend to cut that period down to several weeks (e.g. France wants to transit to the euro over 6 weeks). Some other countries believe to be capable of completing the exercise in a term as short as one week. The future will obviously show the actual results and capabilities.

DOMESTIC VS. INTERNATIONAL CURRENCY

In general, one might say that the term "domestic currency" means a currency commonly accepted and handled by business entities operating within the territory of a state whose monetary authority is the issuer of such currency. The currency serves four fundamental functions: it is a measure of value, means of trade turnover, means of reserve collection, and means of payment. The monetary authority of any given state actually decides what is money and what is not, by introducing a clause for the domestic currency to the effect of the said currency being the sole legal tender for the territory of the respective country. Such clause imposes the mandatory acceptance of liabilities settlement with the use of the respective financial instrument on the one hand, and – on the other – makes the domestic currency the most liquid financial instrument of all. Thus, the monetary authority can at its discretion replace one currency with another. As a rule, however, this right is only rarely exercised (usually during war-time, under occupation of one country by another, in case of a revolution, etc.), as on the occasion of each such change business entities lose confidence in the given legal tender and monetary authorities, and deposit their savings in currencies, the stability of which they are more certain. The aforementioned phenomenon may result in the emergence of the so-called double-currency system – a situation whereby at least part of savings generated in a given state would be deposited in a currency other than the domestic. For any country engaging in independent economic policy, this would carry in-depth consequences.

Firstly, such a phenomenon limits the impact on defining monetary policy, that is the actual volume of money traded, currency exchange rate and interest rates setting, etc. Such a situation may also lead to unfavourable changes in real terms. The main points at issue include a growth in inflation – triggered by excess demand for foreign currency – and resulting in a drop in investment, a decrease in consumption, and a plummet in employment rates, all of which spell a deterioration of the overall economic condition.

Secondly, in extreme cases the double-currency phenomenon can result in a currency crisis, consisting in flight from the domestic currency of the foreign and domestic entities alike. The "birth" mechanism of a monetary crisis as a consequence of a major escape from domestic currency is relatively simple. Business entities losing confidence in the stability of any given currency – and confidence in the option of gaining adequate income from deposit made in such currency – change it for a currency in which they trust more. Experience shows that foreign capital is the most sensitive instrument to confidence in the banking system and in the various currencies; this applies in particular to short-term capital, which – if sensing a drop in income on investment tied to a specific currency – "runs" from it. If the process takes sufficiently long time, the pattern is followed also by business entities (house-holds included) in the given country. Growing demand for foreign currency with a concurrent specific supply thereof makes it significantly more expensive on the one hand, and – on the other – problems may even arise with the "physical" satisfaction of such demand. This results in lower financial liquidity of the respective banking systems, in extreme cases leading to their bankruptcy.

The currency of a given state, however, can under certain conditions serve its basic functions to a scale much broader than domestic currency. Such functions can also be seen as positive. These include such role of money as is accepted by business organisations operating not only within the territory of the state being the issuer of the given currency, but also engaging in transactions abroad. Most frequently, the term "international currency" means tender used on an interna-tional scale as the:

- Means of exchange;
- Unit of financial settlement;
- Means of thesaurisation.

All these functions are closely interrelated, and – as shown in Table No. 1 – can be served by international currency in the private and public sectors alike[1].

Table No. 1 illustrates that as a means of exchange, inter-national currency is primarily a unit of settlement in private transactions and an intervention unit on currency markets, used to ensure a balanced condition within the balance of payments. The settlement function, on the other hand, proves that international money is used to invoice trade turnover in

[1] For more information, see i.a. Kenen, P.B.: *The Role of the Dollar as an Interna-tional Currency*. Occasional Paper No. 13, Group of Thirty, New York 1983; Krugman, P.: *The International Role of the Dollar. Theory and Prospects*. in: *Curren-cies and Crises*, MIT Press, 1991; Cohen, B.: *The Future of Sterling as an International Currency*, London 1971; Friedman, M.: *A Theoretical Framework for Monetary Analysis*. NBER Occasional Paper, No. 112, New York 1971.

foreign operations, and to quote commodity and service prices on international markets in private business. Moreover, it is stability anchor as well as a benchmark for the exchange systems of other currencies in the public sector. The function of international currency thesaurisation, on the other hand, is applied for the denomination of financial instruments and portfolio allocation in the private sector, and the valuation of international reserves in the public.[2]

Table No. 1. Fundamental Functions of an International Currency

Functions	Private Sector	Public Sector
Means of exchange	Settlement in international trade exchange and financial liabilities; Transition currency on currency markets; Parallel currency in third states.	Interventions on currency markets; Official cash flow rates.
Unit of financial settlement	Foreign trade invoicing; International financial transactions; Commodity (e.g., raw stuffs) price quotation on international markets.	Benchmark for exchange rate systems of other currencies; Stability anchor.
Means of thesaurisation	Financial instrument denomination; Portfolio allocation.	Official international reserves denomination.

Source: Bekx, P.: *The Implications of the Introduction of Euro for non-EU Countries. Euro Papers No. 26,* July 1996, p. 2;Krugman, P.: *The International Role of the Dollar. Theory and Prospects,* in: *Currencies and Crises. MIT Press,* 1999, quotes from Szeląg, K.: *Euro w roli waluty międzynarodowej (Euro as an International Currency),* Bank i Kredyt *(Bank and Credit),* Warsaw, December 1998.

---

[2] For more information, see Frankel, J.: *Still the Lingua Franca: The Exaggerated Death of the Dollar, Foreign Affairs,* July–August 1995.

FACTORS DETERMINING THE INTERNATIONAL NATURE OF THE CURRENCY

Of all factors with the strongest impact on the international nature of money, the following are quoted most frequently:
♦ Gross Domestic Product (GDP) value;
♦ Share of the given state in international trade;
♦ Currency (price) stability;
♦ Large and well-developed financial markets.

Tables No. 2 and 3 show fundamental statistics determining the international nature of a currency in Eurozone as against the United States, Japan, and the European Union.

Table No. 2. Population and GDP in Euroland (comparison against selected countries)

DESCRIPTION	EUROPEAN UNION	EUROLAND	USA	JAPAN
Population [mln]	374	290	268	126
Area [square miles]	1,300,000	910,000	3,720,000	150,000
GDP [billion]	8,093	6,309	7,819	4,223
GDP PER CAPITA [$]	21,600	21,700	29,200	33,500

Source: Chabot, Ch. N.: *Understanding the Euro*, McGraw-Hill, New York 1999, p. 16.

Table No. 3. Share of the Euroland in global economy (in selected sectors)

DESCRIPTION	Euroland	USA	Japan
Share in global trade [%]	18,6	18,3	10,3
Share in global GDP [%]	19,0	20,0	8,0
Stock market capitalisation [$ billion]	2,712	10,879	2,063
Bond market capitalisation [$ billion]	4,700	10,200	4,100

Source: *Eurostat*, World Bank, Deutsche Bundesbank, Federation of European Stock Exchanges, New York and Tokyo Stock Exchanges, IIE, *Die Woche*.

Data contained in Tables Nos. 2 and 3 justify the strong global position of the American dollar, chiefly relating to the share of American GDP in the global product, to the share of the USA in international trade, and to the large and well-developed financial markets, in this case measured with their capitalisation expressed in USD billions. Concurrently, the material presented allows an assumption, that for those same reasons the euro does stand a chance of becoming the international currency of considerable importance. The global share of the Euroland in global GDP is indeed comparable with that of the US. Moreover, the share of the United States and the Eleven of the Economic and Monetary Union in international trade is similar as well (Euroland – 18.6%, USA – 18.3%). These organisations, however, show a major (nearly triple) differentiation in financial market capitalisation. The reason for such differentiation relates mainly to the majority of the "Union" countries forming part of the so-called German financial system which is based on banking (credit) sources of economic development financing as opposed to the use of capital acquired on anonymous financial markets, which is the Anglo-Saxon pattern. Hence, the financial markets of the continental system are less well developed *ex definitio*. This has been proven by financial market capitalisation[3] in Germany, for example – ca. 28%, as well as in France – ca. 39%, in Japan – ca. 65%, whereas in the United States capitalisation rates reach approximately 90%.

Moreover, lower capitalisation in Euroland has also been caused by Great Britain's abstention from joining the Economic and Monetary Union, because the United Kingdom is obviously the pillar of the Anglo-Saxon financial system with the best-developed financial markets and a capitalisation rate exceeding 160%. Hence, this has become the reason for lower

---

[3] Capitalisation is understood as the trade volume on equity markets multiplied by their price and divided by the Gross Domestic Product.

capitalisation rates in Euroland in comparison with the USA. It is also noteworthy that the share of American dollar-denominated bonds on international financial markets has been dropping since the early eighties. For example, it reached approximately 62% in 1985, whereas in 1997 it was estimated at a mere 38%[4]. During the same period, the share of Japanese yen-denominated bonds increased to an approximately 16%[5], as did the share of bonds denominated in European currencies. This process does not obviously spell an imminent chance of the Eurozone gaining absolute advantage over the dollar zone in bond trading, especially in case of central government-issued bonds, as a uniform bond market does not exist in Euroland yet. On the other hand, a single federal European Union government shall not be formed in the foreseeable future either. Such government could indeed become the main issuer of the securities in question. Today, it is estimated that bonds issued by European Union member states to finance the public debt in the Fifteen constitute approximately two-thirds of the value of bonds issued during the same period in the USA.[6]

We should also emphasise that European Union states are showing very poor diversification in the area providing only for a very limited purchase of such foreign assets by domestic investors (except for Great Britain and the Netherlands). This proves the existence of a potentially large bond market in Euroland. This assumption has also been proven in a recent survey of European institutional investors and concerning investment preferences. The results prove such investors to be primarily interested in investing in governmental papers issued by Economic and Monetary Union member states, only then followed by bonds denominated in American dollars.

---

[4] Compare Portes, R., Rey, H.: *The Emergence of the Euro as an International Currency, Economic Policy*, April 1998, No. 26.

[5] *International Banking and Financial Market Development*, BIS, August 1997.

[6] *Ibidem.*

Moreover, it is expected that American institutional investors – today focusing on bonds issued by their own government – shall show a greater interest in Eurobonds in the future, if only the European Central Bank enforces proper policy in the area[7], consisting mainly in an offer of interest rates higher than those offered in the USA. Given similar inflation rates, euro-denominated bonds could allow for higher rates of return. The near future is to show the actual state of affairs.

The global position of the US dollar continues to be very strong. Some claim it to be too strong relative to the economic potential of the United States. Table No. 4 shows the role of the American dollar in comparison with other major currencies of the contemporary world.

Table No. 4. Importance of Main International Currencies on the Global Market in 1998 [%]

Name of currency	Public sector		Private sector				
	Foreign currency reserves	Currency anchor	Means of payment on currency markets	Bank deposits	Bank Loans	Treasury bill issue	Unit of settlement
USD	58.9	30.3	42.0	50.8	69.8	45.0	48.0
DEM	13.6	4.5	18.5	14.8	3.3	16.8	17.0
Yen	6.0	0	12.0	5.5	0.2	4.5	5.0
GBP	3.4	0	5.0	8.0	15.6	8.9	15.0
FRF	1.6	22.7	4.0	4.0	5.3	6.4	no data
CHF	0.7	0	3.5	4.1	1.1	2.6	0
ECU	5.9	0	1.0	1.6	0.8	1.3	no data
Other	9.5	42.4	14.0	11.2	3.9	14.5	no data

Sources: Salvatore, D.: *The Euro as an International Currency*, materials of the 4th ECSA Conference, Brussels 1998.

---

[7] See Artus, P.: *L'euro, la diversification de portefeuille et la gestion des reserves, Document de Travail 1997–09/EI, Caisse des Depots et Consignations*, Paris 1997.

As proven by data contained in Table No. 4, a huge share of 58.9% of currency reserves were held in US dollars in 1998[8]; the American dollar was recognised as the so-called stability anchor for more than 30% requiring currency stability. A major share of assets – more than 50% - was denominated in the American currency as well. Concurrently, the American dollar was the basic crediting currency (69.8%), as well as a unit of settlement for 48% of trade transactions. Moreover, approximately 83% of the currency market trade volume is settled in American dollars. For the sake of comparison, German mark serves as a currency of settlement for approximately 37% of currency transactions, with other Eurozone currencies accounting for about 21%, and the Japanese yen – for approximately 24%[9].

Of all the other currencies of international importance, the German mark was the only one of major use both in the private and the public sectors in 1998. Other currencies – the Japanese yen, the British pound, and the French franc in particular – were also relatively significant to global trade, but to a marginal extent against the American dollar, or even the German mark.

Price stability measured with the consumer commodity and service index is another factor commonly recognised as fundamental when determining the international nature of a currency. Empirical statistics prove such stability to be comparable for all the countries analysed. Table No. 5 shows relevant data.

---

[8] It seems worthwhile emphasising that in 1973, more than 76% of currency reserves were denominated in American dollars, hence the obvious drop in the importance of the dollar in the area, with a concurrent growth in the importance of other currencies – of the German mark in particular, whose share in currency reserves grew from 7.1% in 1973 to 13.6% w 1998, as well of the Japanese yen, whose share grew from total insignificance in 1973 to 6% in 1998. Other European currencies also increased their share in currency reserves: approximately 14.3% in 1973 to approximately 21.9% in 1997.

[9] Portes, R., Rey, H.: *The Emergence of the Euro…, op. cit.,* p. 311.

Table No. 5. Consumer Commodity and Service Prices in Selected Countries, 1996–2001 (change – %)

Description	1996	1997	1998	1999	2000p	2001p
OECD	2.0	2.0	1.2	1.4	1.8	1.6
USA	2.9	2.3	1.6	2.2	2.6	2.2
Canada	1.6	1.4	1.0	1.6	1.8	2.0
Japan	0.1	1.7	0.6	–0.4	0.1	0.2
European Union	2.1	1.8	1.4	1.2	1.5	1.6
Germany	1.3	1.5	0.6	0.4	1.2	1.4
France	2.0	1.3	0.7	0.5	1.0	1.4
Italy	3.8	1.7	1.7	1.6	1.4	1.4
Great Britain	2.4	2.8	2.7	2.3	2.5	2.0
Russia	47.7	14.8	27.7	90.0	20.0	11.0
China	8.3	2.8	–0.8	–1.6	1.0	1.0

Source: International Monetary Fund, quote from *Polska Gospodarka. Tendencje, oceny, prognozy (Polish Economy. Trends, Evaluations, Forecasts)*, CASE, Warsaw 1999, No. 3.

Data presented in Tables No. 4 and 5 prove that in the years 1996-1999, the most stable prices in the countries analysed were recorded for Germany, where the inflation rate did not exceed 1.5% over the period researched. It is noteworthy, that although this rate was somewhat worse in the European Union overall than in Germany, it still surpassed that recorded in the USA. Despite the above, it was the American dollar – not the German mark, or the ECU – playing the lead role in global economy. This means that none of the aforementioned factors determining the international nature of a given currency can be considered in isolation; quite the opposite: they have to be analysed jointly. Moreover, as in the case of the Swiss franc, other reasons for elevating a domestic currency to the international position may emerge. The point at issue here is the acceptance of the Swiss currency for international settlement purposes by China, most probably stemming rather from political than from economic considerations. In effect, however, the national currency of this minor state has become the sixth most important currency of the contemporary world (see Table No. 4).

BENEFITS TO A STATE HOLDING INTERNATIONAL CURRENCY

Most frequently, there are two types of benefits gained by a country holding international currency – economic and political effects. Of the economic benefits, special attention ought to be paid to the so-called income gained from the senior position. This is understood as interest-free loans granted to a country holding international currency. The economic sense of such loan is that a country with a currency enjoying international confidence (i.e., used willingly beyond the territory of the issuer state) can acquire commodities and services with no need to produce, then export other commodities and services (within their own territory, usually) for purposes of acquiring funds to purchase commodities and services produced abroad. For example, the United States raises in excess of USD 15 billion annually from the aforementioned source, such money then used for purposes of purchasing commodities and services originating from outside the US. Moreover, the use of the American dollar as an international currency lowers the cost of credit in the USA by approximately 25–50 basic points, bringing in a further USD 10–15 billion[10].

---

[10] Compare Salvatore, D.: *The Euro...*, op. cit., p. 9; Artus, P.: *A Strong or Weak Euro?*, Document de Travail 1996–09/EI, *Caisse des Depots et Consignations*, Paris; Kuntz, D.:, *The Fall of the Dollar Order: the World the United States is Losing*, Foreign Affairs 1995; McKinnon, R.:, *International Money in Historical Perspective, Journal of Economic Literature*, 1993.

The senior position offers the country holding international currency an option of decreasing the value of a loan taken by enforcing appropriate financial policy, enabling the growth of the inflation rate beyond and above the expected level. What I have in mind here is mainly the setting of adequate interest, currency exchange, and tax rates. Notwithstanding the above, it ought to be emphasised, however, that as a rule, countries (the US, in this case), do not exercise this option excessively, for reasons including the fear of a loss in confidence in their own currency, of a flight therefrom, and of the resulting uncontrollable growth of inflation processes domestically. Moreover, in case of the United States, monetary authorities have to proceed with extreme caution in the area, as common estimates show that more than two-thirds of dollars ever issued in the USA are now circulated outside its territory[11]. Their uncontrolled "return" could trigger unimaginable economic turbulence. Other results of holding a currency serving as a "fly-wheel" for the contemporary global economy include commissions received by markets and financial institutions engaging in currency transactions. Such commissions are – among others – a consequence of the commonly applied mechanism of so-called cross-ratings[12].

---

[11] As claimed by the 1999 Nobel Prize winner in economics, R. Mundell. Compare the speech delivered on March 7th 2000 at the Leon Koźmiński High School of Entrepreneurship and Management in Warsaw. C. Sprenkle of the University of Illinois, Urbana-Champaign, among others – claim that more than 90% of dollars ever emitted in the USA are now in circulation abroad.

[12] The cross-rating mechanism consists in currency transactions handling via the USD. Hence, should any given entity hold a currency other than the American dollar – the German mark, for example – and wishes to purchase French francs for any reason, such entity will be forced to buy USD first paying with German marks, and only then sell the dollars for francs. The knowledge that all currency transactions could be handled with the assistance of this so-called two-way price-method means that any entity not being a USD holder and wishing to engage in transactions resembling the above will actually lose twice – firstly, when buying the dollar for the bid (purchase) price, lower than the offer (sales) price. Thus, such organisation receives less dollars for the German marks, only then to pay a higher price when acquiring French francs.

Moreover, an international currency enables the issuer country to limit operational uncertainty for her business entities, largely thanks to the elimination of variations in currency rates and economic conditions[13]. Holding of an international currency provides the issuer country with an ability of covering the current trade deficit and any deficit in the balance of payments alike.

Finally, as Kuntz has it, "… the geopolitical power and role of any given state largely depends on that state's financial power, with one factor supporting the other, while a negligence of the very real economic and political benefits stemming from the holding of an international currency is a tragedy…"[14]

The basic cost of holding an international currency, on the other hand, is the potential danger of losing control over the money supply by the issuer country. The acceptance of the domestic currency by foreign business entities and the capacity of using this phenomenon to finance any commodities and services purchased, and/or to finance the trade deficit actually causes a natural inclination to increase the supply of money on the market. *Ex definitio*, this danger grows along with the share of foreign trade in the issuer country's economy. In case of the United States, the danger is not extreme, as the share of foreign trade in American economy is rather low. With regard to the Economic and Monetary Union, however, making the euro international may cause an incomparably larger problem for reasons of the above, as foreign trade plays a major part in the individual economies of all states in the Community.

---

[13] More on the subject – see i.a. McKinnon, R.: *International…, op. cit.*
[14] See Kuntz, D.: *The Fall…, op. cit.*

EURO AS THE INTERNATIONAL CURRENCY

The euro is likely to be a strong international currency in the future, although at present we are rather dealing with pessimistic scenario of its implementation and in result with declining exchange rate euro against USD. It seems, however, that soon the European Central Bank will want to create a better reputation for itself, and will use all possible tools to reverse present situation. The euro must be strong enough to satisfy Germany, which only reluctantly abandoned its venerable Deutschemark. It is unlikely, however, that the euro will be as strong as Deutschemark has been, because with so many countries at different levels of economic development and stages of the business cycle on its board, the ECB will probably be unable to be as tough on inflation as the Bundesbank has been. Furthermore, the euro cannot be so strong as to discourage growth and exports in the European Union, especially at this time of high unemployment in most EU countries.

Will the euro become an important international currency? Everything indicates that it will. The reasons are following:

♦ EU is as large an economic and trading unit as the United States;
♦ EU has large, well-developed and growing financial market, which is increasingly free of controls;
♦ EU is expected to have a good inflation performance that will stabilize the value of the euro.

As the data in tables 2 & 3 indicate, the 15-members EU has very similar shares of world GDP and exports and its domain or network value of money is more than twice that of Japanese yen. Thus, if the international use of the euro were to match its share of the world exports, the euro would become as important as the dollar as an international or vehicle currency. This would mean that the relative international use of the dollar would fall to 40–45 percent of the total, with an equal share going to the euro, with the remainder going mostly to the yen and a few other smaller currencies, such the Swiss franc, the Canadian dollar, and the Australian dollar[15]. This would involve a substitution of dollars for euros of about $500 billion to $1 trillion and lead to depreciation of the dollar vis-à-vis the euro. But since this is likely to occur gradually over time, it may not undue pressure on the dollar. Furthermore, the increased financial integration in the EU will also expand the supply of euro-denominated assets and thus the tendency of euro to appreciate with respect to the dollar.

It is unlikely, however, that international use of euro will soon be able to match the EU share of world GDP and exports, as some economists believe. First of all, the absence of federal government in the EU puts a ceiling on the integration process in the market for government securities, and so financial integration in the EU will inevitably fall short of that in the United States. Secondly, with a strict portfolio diversification motives, there is less reason for EU investors to increase their holding of euro-denominated assets, while there will be a greater reason for increasing their dollar-and yen- denominated assets as the ECB pursues an independent monetary policy with respect to the Fed and the Bank of Japan. Thirdly, a portfolio shift in favour of euro-denominated assets will occur only if the ECB will conduct a tighter monetary policy than the Fed. However, as suggested above, with the need to reconcile the different monetary-policy requirements of the various EU members, this may not be possible.

There are also other reasons causing it unlikely that the euro can soon displace the dollar as the most important international currency. Among them are:

---

[15] See Salvatore,D., The Euro as an International Currency", Fourth ECSA-World Conference, Bruxelles, Sept.1998.

- Most primary commodities are priced in dollars and this is likely to remain the case for some time to come;
- Non-EU countries are likely to continue to use the dollar for most of their international transactions for the foreseeable future, with the exception of the former communist countries in central and eastern Europe and the former French colonies in Africa, which will, in all likelihood, shift from using the Deutsche mark or French francs, respectively, to using euros.
- Sheer inertia that favors the incumbent (the dollar).

Thus, it is more likely that about 50 per cent of international transactions will be conducted in dollars in the future (down from the present 65 per cent or so), 40 per cent in euro, and the remaining 10 percent in yens and other smaller currencies[16]. That is, the euro will very likely have more weight than the mark has today but somewhat less than the relative weight that the EU has in international trade and finance in the world economy – at least during the first few years of its existence.

CONCLUSION

The introduction of the common currency within the nations is the third attempt since WW II. In 1968 SDR or Special Drawing Right was created by the IMF as "reserve asset" to substitute for gold. The former Soviet Union created so called Transferred Rubbles to substitute for dollars and other "hard currencies". For different reasons, both efforts failed. Hence, we can now state that they were, at least to some extent, only

---

[16] See, Salvatore, D.,....., op.cit....., p.13, and McCauley, R.N., The Euro and the Dollar, Essay in International Finance, No.205, Princeton University Press, Princeton, Nov. 1997.

intellectual products, existing on the paper. Is the same going to happen to the euro? As it was shown, almost everything indicates that it is not. The euro is some kind of intellectual product (as other financial instruments and money in particular) that is going to succeed by becoming accepted international currency. Why? In short, because the euro is both an economic and a political project. Helmut Kohl, former chancellor of Germany and one of the most outspoken proponents of monetary union, views the euro's economic benefits as secondary, instead emphasizing that "The bitter experiences of war and dictatorship in this centaury teach us that the unification project is the best insurance against a relapse of national egoism, chauvinism and violent conflict"[17]. Even today, the legacy of two world wars plays crucial role in the process of European integration.

There are other political motivations. Ireland views the euro as a means of reducing its reputation as an offshoot of England. Italy wants to avoid becoming a political pariah. France desperately wants to diminish its susceptibility to the monetary policy decisions of the Germans. Many enthusiastic German leaders hope monetary union will be the "cart" that drags the "horse' of total political union. Indeed, there are now as many justifications for the euro as there are participating countries, because each EU nation perceives a particular set of advantages and risks.

European leaders are also convinced that single currency is a boon to economic stability and growth. They strongly believe that the introduction of the euro will decrease exchange rate risk and transaction costs and enable better price transparency. Macroeconomic stability of the union will be improved, making the euro a part of the structure of the international monetary system for the 21st century.

---

[17] Kohl, H., „EWWU Ekstein fur Europa", Bank Information und Genossenschafts Forum, Jan. 1997, pp.4–5.

In summary, it is worth recalling that Bismarck once said that the most important event in the 19th century was that England and America spoke the same language. In the same spirit, R. Mundell said that the most important event in the 20th century was the creation of the Federal Reserve System, the vehicle for the spread of the dollar, without that we could not have had the subsequent monetary events[18]. Let us hope that the most important event of the 21st century will be that the dollar and the euro learn to live together.

---

[18] Mundell, R.,A., The International Monetary System in the 21st Century: Could Gold Make a Comeback?, Lecture delivered at St. Vincent College, Letrobe, Pennsylvania, March 12, 1997.

Dorota Dobija

INTELLECTUAL PRODUCT.
A CHALLENGE FOR ACCOUNTANTS
AND A NEW AGE OF ACCOUNTING

Abstract

Traditional financial statements will no longer suffice in an
era where the firm's intellectual resources play a dominant role.
This study investigates the effect of intellectualization of a
product on the accounting and the cost of this product. Traditional statements will have to be modified to include a new component, which is the cost of intellectual assets engaged in production of goods and services. In this paper a model of measurement of intellectual capital is presented in order to introduce
a new element to the costing system such as the usage of intellectual capital. As a result, a human resources statement and
statement of human capital payback is proposed in order to obtain better information which can be used by both external and
internal users of accounting information.

INTRODUCTION

A new era has begun, the knowledge era, which is likely to have a dramatically different terrain and which will require a new business compass to navigate. The compass of the industrial and information eras – the traditional financial balance sheet and income statement – will no longer suffice. Composed of backward looking measurements, the balance sheet is no longer a sufficient tool in the decision making process.

Most organizations have only a vague understanding of how much they invest in their intellectual capital and this do not consider "the return on" those investments. Standard financial accounting systems don't allow for easy estimation of intellectual capital investments, even after such investments have been clearly identified. Without methods for measuring intellectual capital, many firms don't realize its full potential. Instead, they either under-invest or many of their investments are ineffective. And without standards, stakeholders have no way to judge the value and effectiveness of investments in intellectual capitals across firms.

This new environment is also a challenge for accounting, and the accountants who practice it, because its role in the society is rapidly changing. Accounting is at a crossroad as S. Wallman writes in his commentary about the future of accounting and financial reporting (Wallman, 1996, p. 138). In the past century accounting played a dominant role in accountability for capital invested in physical resources, goods and services. In the new millennium, the so-called knowledge era, accounting will be more focused on providing information about the firm's intellectual and social capital. Companies and investors will also be interested in information concerning the human resources of a company as one of the most important elements of the company's overall performance.

Figure 1. The past and the future of accounting

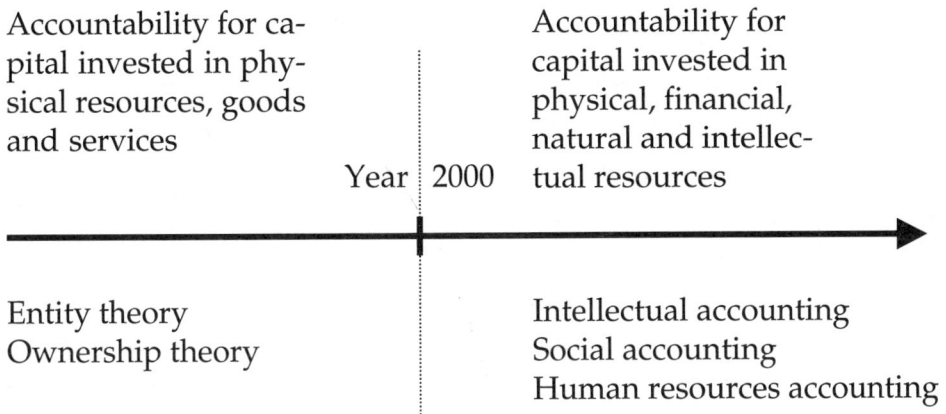

Accountability for capital invested in physical resources, goods and services		Accountability for capital invested in physical, financial, natural and intellectual resources
	Year 2000	

————————————————————►

Entity theory		Intellectual accounting
Ownership theory		Social accounting
		Human resources accounting

Standard accounting models were designed for informing company management and stakeholders on stocks and flows of value. Most of these are quantifiable and subject to generally accepted accounting principles and practices. In contrast, intellectual capital, human resources and social resources are relatively new and enigmatic concepts, relating primarily to the intangible, highly mutable assets of the firm. As such, the current accounting model does not adequately capture their value nor represent them in a concise, meaningful format. Accounting for these "intangible" assets will ultimately require the invention of new financial and management accounting concepts and practices more appropriate for the era of the new economy.

It is worth noting that the product will change as well. It will include a larger intellectual component, because the firm's intellectual resources will be used in the production process. Among many other intellectual resources the one which requires more attention is the work of skilful, well-educated, experienced and knowledgeable employees. To reflect these changes in production, cost accounting systems will have to be modified as we enter the knowledge era.

ACCOUNTING APPROACH TO ECONOMIC ISSUES

The financial statements of a business enterprise are intended to provide both a snapshot of the financial position (assets and liabilities of the business at a specific point in time) and a summary of transactions during the prior period resulting in that picture. The latter is presented in the form of an income statement. Considerable active debate affecting both of these statements concerns the question of what value should be assigned to resources acquired and owed by an enterprise. Accountants may use the historical cost principle or a market value principle to determine the amounts presented in financial statements.

The cost and market value principles of valuation determine the book value of a resource and the price at which the resource is presented in the financial statements. Under either valuation principle, the book value and the presentation price of monetary resources are normally set equal to money equivalent, subject to discounting in the case of long –term receivables and payables, and the translation of foreign currency denominated monetary resources. Therefore, *the differences in valuation principles appear in the book value and the presentation price of nonmonetary resources.*

Under the cost principle, a nonmonetary resource is recorded at its historical cost on the date acquired. Its book value based on this historical cost, and presentation price in the financial statements in not adjusted for subsequent changes in its market value. These adjustments should be made under the market value principle. Professor Y. Ijiri (1999, pp. 178––182) presents four essential points, which emphasize the significance of the cost principle. These are:

❑ Historical cost is derived from the microscopic perspective based on the self-experience of the enterprise, while the market value is derived from the macroscopic perspective based on the experience of other enterprises and from the concept of market that also lies outside the enterprise itself.

❑ The cost principle reflects the market price, albeit with a time lag.

❑ The cost principle helps establish and strengthen "accountability" by its demand for a complete double-entry record. The double entry system does not permit a change in any resource to be recorded, without being matched by another change.

The cost principle requires the use of transactions costs actually incurred by the enterprise in the course of conducting its economic exchanges. It is the "actual acquisition cost" by the accounting entity for which recording and reporting are to be made. Prof. Y. Ijiri (Ijiri, 1999, p. 180) comments also that "...although there may still be many problems in judging and measuring the cost, it is easier, less expensive and more precise for the enterprise to judge the cost of its own specific resources than to judge its market value. This seems to be reasonable especially when we notice that the market for a good can rarely be observed with precision (it is a collection including those who actually or potentially buy or sell the resource and the transactions for the resource among them all)". However, the accounting records created under the cost principle are not totally divorced from market events beyond the direct involvement of the enterprise. As long as the enterprise transacts often enough with the outside world, costs in its records will reflect market values. Therefore, the cost principle does reflect the market price, albeit with a time lag.

The cost principle is also rooted in the double-entry system because this system does not permit a change in any resource to be recorded alone, without being matched by another change. This means that a company needs to trace the historical resource flows in order to present information identifying "which resource was obtained in exchange with which other resource" (Ijiri, 1999 p. 181). The cost principle also strengthens "accountability" of the entity. Financial statements prepared in accordance with the cost principle, provide an assurance that they are supported by double-entry records of the entire network of resource exchanges in the economy.

There is also a connection between the above mentioned principles and the statement that accounting records should reflect the **input-output relationship** faithfully in the production function and other enterprise activities, because they are essential in clarifying charges and discharges of accountability. W. A. Paton and A. C. Littletown (1940, p. 13) state that the cost of a final product is a sum of the different costs of items used in the production process. "When production activity effects a change in the form of raw materials by the consumption of human labor and machine – power, accounting keeps step by classifying and summarizing appropriate portions of materials cost, labor cost and machine cost so that together they become product costs".

Figure 2. Input- output relation in accounting

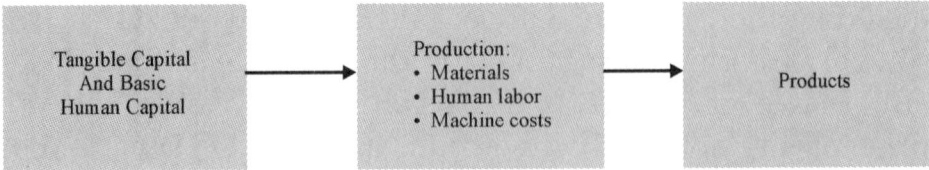

It is easy to notice that the cost principle also has a common linkage with the labor theory of value. According to this theory, the value of a commodity is determined by the amount of labor that is necessary for its production. If factors other than labor are consumed in production, the amount of labor contained in those factors is also transferred to the commodity produced. Therefore, to compute the value of a commodity means to trace the production process and aggregate the labor consumed during production as well as the labor contained in the factors consumed during production.

Value and accounting computations are different in the sense that the former traces the amount of labor, while the latter traces the receipts and disbursements of money. However, neither approach can be applied without tracing the production process in detail. As stated in by W. Kimura "...as one wishes to be objective, one must follow the production process closely, and as one tries to follow the production process closely, one must consistently use cost, namely, the transaction price (see Y. Ijiri, 1999, p.184).

In this paper the usefulness and limitation of these valuation principles will be examined. I will focus on the changes in production processes and the increasing importance of product intellectualization. A new measurement model of human capital will be presented which is based on costs of living, education and experience. This will allow for further discussion of the role of cost accounting in reporting "actual costs" of production. The argument is that cost accounting will need to be reshaped in order to meet the needs of the new economy where the share of intellectual product in the product market is growing.

WHAT DO WE KNOW ABOUT INTELLECTUAL PRODUCT AND INTELLECTUAL PROPERTY IN CONTEMPORARY ECONOMICS?

One of the consequences of intellectualization of production and services is a product, which can be called an intellectual product. *This product can be described as the result of creative processes where the knowledge and ability of a person taking part in the production, together with usage of other intellectual resources in the production process, play a leading role. Intellectual product is strictly connected with intellectual capital of organization.* A discussion of intellectual product and what constitutes such a product begins with the concept of intellectual capital. If we are able to recognize and measure intellectual capital of the organization, we will be able to answer the question of which elements should be included in a cost calculation of intellectual product. This will allow us to discuss the changes in the cost accounting system that will be necessary to provide better information about costs of production of an intellectual product.

As it can be seen in the management literature the term "intellectual capital" has many complex connotations. It is often used synonymously with intellectual property, intellectual assets and knowledge assets. It is widely held that the most important assets possessed by companies are intangibles, primarily represented by intellectual property and other intellectual resources of a company. Some of these intangibles are created by the business and some of them exist under protection of law. In the literature we can find listings of some characteristics of intellectual property which are essential in our further discussion (Smith, Parr, 1989, pp. 93-95):

- It produces an economic advantage;
- It raises some barriers to competition;
- It protects and creates a strong market position.

Intellectual capital can be thought of as the total stock of capital or knowledge-based equity that the company possesses. As such, intellectual capital can be both the end result of a knowledge transformation process or the knowledge itself that is transformed into intellectual property or intellectual assets of the firm (Dzinkowski, 2000, p. 33). From a management point of view, intangible company resources can be defined as „assets" or „skills" as asserted by R. Hall (1992, p. 136). Assets include the intellectual property rights of patents, trademarks, copyright and registered designs, as well as contracts, trade secrets and databases. Skills and competencies include the employees, suppliers, distributors and the culture of the organisation, enabling it to cope with change.

Table 1. Elements of intellectual capital

Human Capital	Customer capital
► Know-how	► Brands
► Education	► Customers
► Vocational qualification	► Customer loyalty
► Work-related knowledge	► Company names
► Occupational assessments	► Distribution channels
► Psychometric assessments	► Business collaborations
► Work-related competencies	► Licensing agreements
► Entrepreneurial skills, inno-vativeness, changeability	► Favourable contracts
	► Franchising agreements
Organisational capital	
Intellectual property	**Management philosophy**
► Patents	► corporate culture
► Copyrights	► management processes
► Design rights	► information systems
► Trade secrets	► networking systems
► Trademarks	► financial relations
► Service marks	

As previously stated, there is no consensus concerning what constitutes an „intangible". From management point of view it seems that it will be difficult to reach a commonly accepted definition for intangible assets from management point of view. But at least there is a common agreement among managers and consultants that the items of intangibles should be identified and separated in order to control, measure and manage them.

Efforts to address the measurement challenges surrounding intellectual capital fall into two basic but overlapping types: measuring stocks of intellectual capital and measuring its effectiveness. The simplest form of this type of measurement is a straightforward enumeration of the intellectual capital of an organisation – the number of patents, Ph.D. professionals or Fortune 500 contracts. The result is an inventory of intangible assets that account mainly for the type and amount of assets an organisation has, but little else. Organisations are interested in measuring not just the quantity, but also the monetary value of their intellectual capital stocks. Because the intangible nature of these assets makes such valuation extremely difficult, most attempts at valuation provide only an approximation of the total aggregate of an organisation's entire intellectual capital stocks, without enumerating each and every element.

The accountants' approach towards intangibles is different from the manager's view discussed above. It comes from a conservative attitude towards reporting. Accountants seek to present information about a business enterprise that reflects a value of the assets dedicated to that enterprise. For many reasons (which have been previously stated) an historical cost principle prevails as a solution for fair reporting. So far, the traditional balance sheet includes tangible assets (current assets, plant, property and equipment) but provides no information about intangibles in such a statement (except goodwill). One of the reasons for this is the lack of a commonly accepted definition of "intangibles" and, the lack of an approach for valuation of such items. As a consequence no information is generated about intellectual assets used in a production, so the product costs are not fully valued and reported.

However, in response to the growing concern for intangibles, in 1989 the International Accounting Standards Committee initiated the project for an accounting standard. After three revisions, the IAS 38 was finally issued in the autumn of 1998. The big issue in the development process of this standard were the three questions of (IASC, 1998a):

* Whether internally generated intangible assets should be recognised at all in the balance sheet, and if they were to be recognised, whether the recognition criteria for these internally generated items should differ from the recognition criteria for externally acquired assets;

* Whether an intangible asset's "fair value" could be reliably determined; and

* Whether the intangible assets should be amortised and, if so over what period.

The definition of intangible assets given by IAS 38 (1998b, p.37) is formulated as follows:

> „An intangible asset is an identifiable non-monetary asset without physical substance held for use in the production or supply of goods or services, for rental to others, or for administrative purposes. An asset is a resource: (a) controlled by an enterprise as a result of past events, and (b) from which future economic benefits are expected to flow to the enterprise. „

This definition requires that the intangible asset is identifiable, such that it can be clearly distinguished from goodwill. The control aspect is important in this standard. When an enterprise has insufficient control over the expected future economic benefits arising from a team of skilled employees and from training, there might be serious problems in determining whether these meet the definition of an intangible asset. This also applies to management and technical talents in a company, unless such assets are protected by legal rights to their use and unless the company can demonstrate that it will obtain the future economic benefits expected from them. According to the definition of intangibles, the standard fails to recognise such items as portfolio customers, market shares, and customer relationships and customer loyalty.

OECD has tried to produce a standard practise concerning intangible investments. In 1992 OECD (OECD, 1992, p.114) offered the following definition.

> „Intangible investments cover all long-term outlays
> by firms aimed at increasing future performance other
> that by the purchase of fixed assets „

Such a definition, however, does not actually specify what constitutes an intangible investment and, although it does mention the goal of these investments, it still remains unclear what is meant by further performance as stated by M. Croes (1997, p. 202). Therefore Croes proposes the following definition:

> „Intangible investments are all new goal-oriented
> activities of a firm or disembodied tools use by a firm,
> on a strategic and tactical level, during the reference
> period. On a tactical level, they are aimed at quantita-
> tive change or extension of existing knowledge, while
> on the strategic level they are aimed at the acquisition
> of completely new knowledge".

Such items include marketing, technological, informational and organisational activities or tools. They must be separately identifiable and measurable in financial terms.

The definitions cited above do not allow focusing on intangible processes, activities and phenomena. They are restricted only to intangible assets or investments.

Some companies are making inroads in measuring and leveraging their intellectual capital assets. Skandia and Dow Chemical are examples (Edvinsson, Malone, (1997). Some of those organizations have made their measurement system available publicly in one form or another. However none of the systems is widely accepted. These company-tailored measurement systems developed in isolation, do little to create measurement methods that are robust enough to be adopted across the board in diverse organizations. Greater strides on intellectual capital measurement can only come from collective action. Measurement standards require formalized information sharing, common definitions and metrics, and shared methodologies.

INTELLECTUAL CAPITAL AND COSTING SYSTEMS

S. Sunder (1997, p. 178) wrote that human capital is an inalienable entity. It is physically impossible to detach the stock of human or intellectual capital from its owner. There can be no market for such resources in their capitalised form; nevertheless they can be measured because capital is a measurable category.

Turner (1996, p. 304) contends that since accounting for the enterprise's human resources was first discussed more that 30 years ago, it has encountered two main barriers that impede it from entering into mainstream accounting. The first obstacle is that employees do not qualify as assets and the second is an inability to establish a meaningful system of measurement.

During the last decade authors dealing with this topic have suggested that Human Resources Accounting could benefit users of financial statements. External and internal decision - makers must know changes in human assets in order to evaluate assets, wages, salaries and income properly. Grojer J. E. and Johanson U. (1996, p.17) assume that human capital is defined as *"...knowledge and ability a person possesses lead to the future production of useful items in the form of goods and services.*

The total value of these goods and the services may then be seen as the value of the person in the economic sense, that is, his human capital..."

T. W. Schultz (1981, p. 21) wrote: "*consider all human abilities to be either innate or acquired.... Attributes of acquired population quality, which are valuable and can be augmented by appropriate investment, will be treated as human capital...*". W. J. Hudson in his "Intellectual Capital" (Hudson, 1993, p. 16) defines intellectual capital as a combination of four factors: (1) genetic inheritance, (2) education (3) experience and (4) attitudes towards life and business. M. Dobija (1998, p. 87) adds that to reveal the genetic inheritance, a human being needs a body that represents at least the capitalised costs of living and the cost of basic education.

The quoted authors consider the problem of human capital valuation and reporting within the framework of conventional financial accounting principles and concepts. The entity concept is still maintained in their work. However, for human capital and human assets measurement, a system must be found to show a value from the person's perspective and not from the firm's point of view. A person who can be employed has his/her own value independent of the firm's value and its income. In human resources framework there is no longer only one accounting component. Both the entity and the employees create two equal components. The new function of accounting is to preserve the capital embodied in physical and financial assets as well as to preserve human capital.

A debate about human and intellectual capital can not be continued without discussing some ontological prerequisites. In accordance with a commonly accepted paradigm, a human consists of a body and an intellect, which is a function of the body. Considering human capital, researchers respect also a third element – experience. So a person is a triad of "body – intellect – spirit" (M. Dobija, 2000, p.44). From the economic point of view a human is valued as a present value of past living expenses and the intellect is a result of investment in education, the ability of that person to learn and the attitude toward life itself. It is measured as a present value of investments in education. The third element of the triad, although connected with – for example – creativity, is not a subject to a measurement system in the economy. If the creativity will lead to a new invention or patent, a person (author of the innovation) will be paid extra accordingly to the profits achieved from that invention (patent).

In order to synthesise the measurable model of human and/or intellectual capital as discussed by M. Dobija (2000, p. 49), we apply the following variables:

K – physical human capital measured as capitalised cost of living (involves a particular set of genes as discussed by T. Schultz and W. Hudson);

E – education that creates an important part of intellectual capital (measured as capitalised costs of education);

Q (T,w) – experience which definitely depends on time of professional job (T) and individual skills (learning parameter w). These variables increase the sum of K and E.

The sum of human capital H(T,w) is then:

$$H (T , w) = (K + E) [1 + Q (T, w)].$$

The existence of the sum and product in function H shows an existence of interrelation and synergy between the set of variables. The new set of measurable categories can be obtained on the basis of the above written model. We denote H= H (0)= K+ E – human capital at the threshold of a professional career. Subsequently:

$$D (T, w) = H * Q (T , w) - \text{experience capital};$$

$$I (T, w) = E + D (T , w) - \text{intellectual capital}.$$

Therefore:

H (T, w) = K + I (T , w) = K + E + D (T, w) – total human capital.

Illustration: Valuation of human capital in 5 employees at different stages of carriers

Let us consider 5 separate cases. There are 5 persons, with the same starting point – 18 years of basic education, with similar capabilities of learning. One of them has just finished his basic education – is at the beginning of his professional carrier. The second case depicts a person with 2 years of experience who started his job right after he finished his basic education. The third person has the same basic education and 5 years of experience and also has completed an additional 2 years of vocational training. The next person is an MBA graduate with 14 years of experience, a CEO of a big company. After his basic education, he went to a college and then after some years of work experience went to a university and completed an MBA. The last case depicts a professor (with a Ph.D.) with 16 years of experience. The calculation done in order to value human capital of these 5 persons is given below.

Table 2. Basic data for human capital calculation for each discussed case

	case 1	case 2	case 3	case 4	case 5
Costs of living					
Monthly costs of living	400,00	400,00	400,00	400,00	400,00
Interest rate	8%	8%	8%	8%	8%
Annuity factor	37,45	37,45	37,45	66,76	66,76
age (number of years)	18	18	18	24	24
Costs of education					
Cost of education	0,00	0,00	2 000,00	10 000,00	10 000,00
Interest rate	8%	8%	8%	8%	8%
Annuity factor	0,00	0,00	1,00	8,92	14,49
age (number of years)	0	0	1	7	10
Experience					
Learning rate	10%	10%	10%	10%	10%
Learning parameter	0,00	0,10	0,26	0,33	0,34
Years of employment	1	2	7	14	16

Calculations of the total costs of human capital in 5 described cases and subsequently a value of human capital is given below.

Table 3a. Calculation of human capital for 5 cases

	case 1	case 2	case 3	case 4	case 5
Capitalized costs of living	179 761,17	179 761,17	179 761,17	320 470,84	320 470,84
Capitalized costs of education	0,00	0,00	2 000,00	89 228,03	144 865,62
Experience	0,00	17 976,12	46 540,34	135 383,74	160 029,21
Total human capital	179 761,17	197 737,29	228 301,51	545 082,62	625 365,68

The total value of intellectual capital embodied in a human body is a sum of capitalized costs of education and experience.

Table 3b. Calculation of intellectual capital for 5 cases

	case 1	case 2	case 3	case 4	case 5
Intellectual capital	0,00	17 976,12	48 540,34	224 611,78	304 894,84

The calculation results can be presented in a form of a picture.

As we can see, the value of costs of living increase in the case of the MBA and the professor, because the time span before their first job widens from 18 to 24 years. Assuming the same abilities of learning, the intellectual capital increases as the investments in education increase. This applies to work experience as well.

Figure 3. Value of human capital in case of 5 different carriers

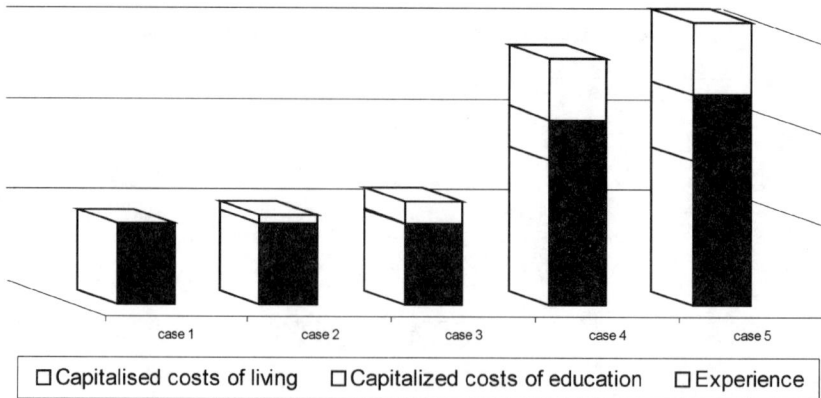

| case 1 | case 2 | case 3 | case 4 | case 5 |

☐ Capitalised costs of living   ☐ Capitalized costs of education   ☐ Experience

---

Human Capital is a sum of physical capital, education and experience

$$H\ (T, w) = K + E + D\ (T, w)$$

We can now pose a question. Having assigned values to the intellectual capital of employees, how is it possible to use these figures in cost accounting and reporting? It seems that the financial information about human capital could be included in a balance sheet-like statement presented as follows:

Applying an appropriate rate of return to the factor of human capital one can obtain a pay formula.

$$CF = H\ (T) * a + (v - a) * I\ (T)$$

Where: CF – employee compensation
        a – average risk rate of return
        b – rate of return on intellectual capital.

G. Becker (2000, p. 45) and others have researched the rate of return on intellectual capital. This research estimated the size of this rate. Therefore one can be tempted to introduce intellectual capital into periodic reporting. The shape of such a report can result from the above formula.

Figure 4. Human Resources Statement

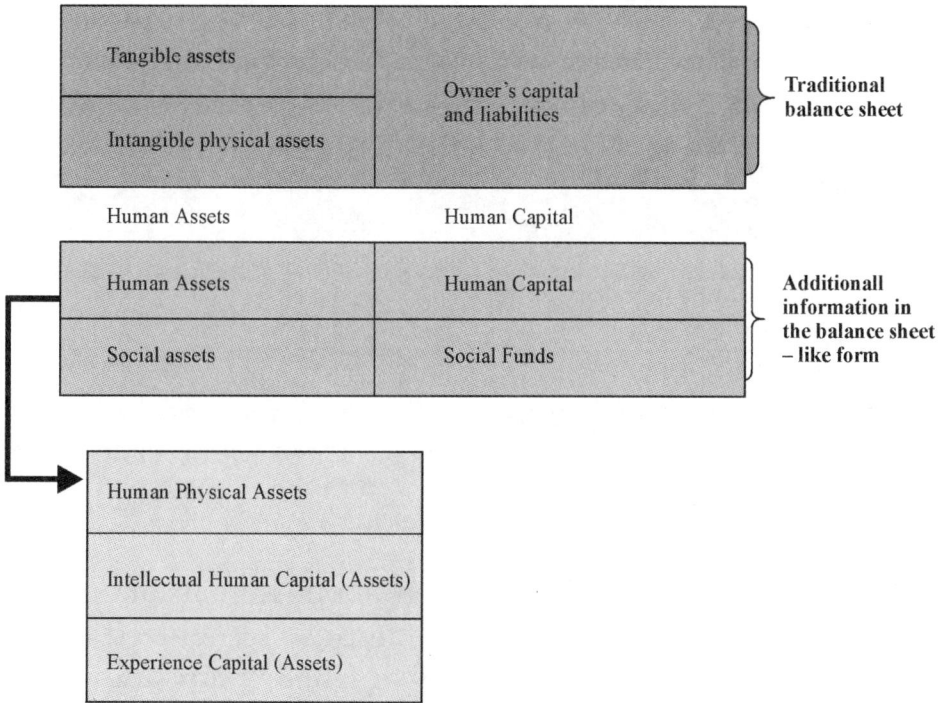

Tangible assets	Owner's capital and liabilities	Traditional balance sheet
Intangible physical assets		

Human Assets	Human Capital	
Human Assets	Human Capital	Additionall information in the balance sheet – like form
Social assets	Social Funds	

Human Physical Assets
Intellectual Human Capital (Assets)
Experience Capital (Assets)

Taking into regard variable CF as the actual amount paid to employees of a company, the mentioned report on human capital payback could be arranged as follows:

Table 4: Statement of human capital payback

Actual compensation (cost of labour)	Minimum wage	Pay for intellectual capital	Payback on intellectual capital
W	$H(T) * a$	$W - H(T) * a$	v

Using the data related to the earlier example of the calculation of the human capital and the intellectual capital (see table 3a and 3b), the statement on human capital payback for those five cases is presented in table 5 (assuming 8% of average risk of return):

Table 5. Statement on human capital payback for the 5 employees

case	mon-thly salary	yearly com-pen-sation	human capital	minimum wage	pay for intellectual capital	intel-lectual capital	pay-back on intel-lectual capital
		CF	H(T)	H(T) * a	W – H(T) * A	I(T)	v
1	1100	13200	179 761,17	14 380,89	–1180,89	0,00	0
2	1500	18000	197 737,29	15 818,98	2181,02	17 976,12	4%
3	1900	22800	228 301,51	18 264,12	4535,88	48 540,34	1%
4	10000	120000	545 082,62	43 606,61	76393,39	224 611,78	26%
5	8000	96000	625 365,68	50 029,25	45970,75	304 894,84	7%

Introduction of new information about human and intellectual capital as resources of an enterprise recognized in the balance sheet, leads to the question of whether any additional elements should be included in the income statement.

The cost concept and the matching concept, in general, govern the measurement of costs applicable to an accounting period and to the product manufactured in those periods. The common cost object in business is a product. The principles discussed earlier give much guidance on how total product costs are to be assigned to individual products or groups of products. Product costing involves determining the cost assignable to goods and/or services as they flow through the production process. In the traditional product costing system, direct materials, direct labor and factory overhead costs are assigned to specific product. In such cases product cost information can identify weak production areas, control costs, support pricing decisions, and set inventory values on the operational level.

Although most product costing applications involve physical products, in recent years many applications of job order costing and process costing have been developed for organizations that produce services rather then inventoriable products. The major issues in designing the cost system in a service environment still relate to identifying direct costs (primarily labor) and determining how to assign overhead costs to the units of service. The key to developing a good cost system is to understand the particular production environment and tailoring the system to reflect the characteristics of that environment in order to meet the needs of its managers.

A CPA firm, for example, accumulates the actual hardware and software costs of an accounting system installed for a client, along with the actual wages earned by employees while working on the job and any related travel expenses.

W. Morse, J. Davis, A. Hartgraves (1996, p. 522) point out that there is a new trend in cost accounting. Contemporary cost measurement systems, emphasize the measurement of all costs and not just manufacturing (inventory) costs as in the older traditional systems. Consistent with the process focus, contemporary cost systems use activities and operations as critical cost objects in building a cost measurement system. They also provide better information to help managers understand what drives the costs of each step in the process of developing, producing and delivering products to customers. By analyzing costs at the detailed level of activities and operations involved in the cross-functional flow of work, these newer systems make visible how activities in one processing step may affect costs at the other processing steps, thus enhancing the visibility of cost-driver relationships. The four important differences between traditional and contemporary approaches to cost measurement are as follows:

A contemporary system:

- Provides comprehensive product cost information by including in product cost not only manufacturing costs but the costs of all activities and operations that create, produce, deliver and support the product or service. This includes both preproduction (upstream) costs and postproduction (downstream) costs;
- Emphasizes management of the activities and operations that make up the process rather than the department that performs the work;
- Allocates indirect costs to activities/operations and from there to products rather than the department that performs the work;
- Supports strategic costs management by making cost driver relationships visible as opposed to emphasizing external financial reporting.

Although the contemporary cost measurement systems expand the definition of costs, it is still not a complete picture of all costs incurred to serve a customer. All entities along the value chain are dependent on the final customer's perception of the value and cost of a product or service. It is the final customer who ultimately pays all costs and provides all profits to organisations along the entire value chain. The goal of every organisation should be to maximise the value while minimising the cost of a product or service to final customers. In more advanced environment where intellectual capital plays a dominant role in value creation it is also important to include information about intellectual items in the cost calculation. This will also increase the accountability of the production process along the entire value chain.

S Sunder (1997, p. 212) wrote that managerial capital is used in the job, but it does not get used up. The same can be said about the intellectual capital. S. Sunder continues "...on the contrary, much of it (managerial capital) is acquired as a by-product of doing the job. No more than a small part of this capital can be acquired off the job, for example by getting a university degree". If some part of intellectual capital is used in the production of goods or services accounting, should be able to identify this part to include it in the cost calculations. Seeking a solution will lead us to the earlier described model of intellectual capital that is defined as a sum of the costs of education and experience of an employee. Calculation of the value of intellectual capital engaged in a person employed in production will lead us to better information about the costs of production (where part of intellectual capital was used).

According to the division of total human capital into two categories, two different items of the cost of labor should appear in the income statement: wages as cost of labor depending on size of variable K (costs of living) and salaries derived from value of intellectual capital (I). In such an approach, product costs no longer cover the traditional cost items but also include the costs connected with engagement of intellectual capital. The idea is to some extent in accordance with R Abdel-khalik's (2000) concept of intellectual capital measurement on a basis of incentive pay. In his work R. Abdel-khalik has measured a value of intellectual assets (intellectual capital) of a firm on the basis of the excess of the pay over the normal, regular salaries.

Figure 5. Product costing in HRCA framework

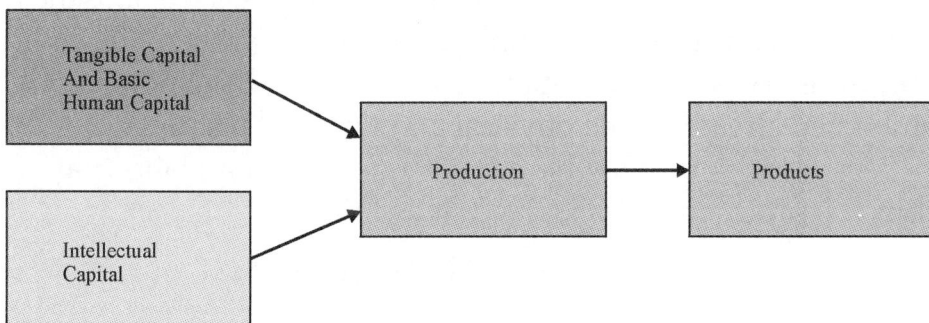

For a better calculation of the entire costs of intellectual product, the modification in presenting the cost of all labor should be extended to the value chain of that product. The cost sheet should include not only information about intellectual capital engaged in the production but also information about intellectual capital engaged in preproduction and post-production, which can be reflected in downstream and upstream costs of intellectual capital engaged in creation of intellectual product.

Having determined the above modification, a new way is open to value added statement reformulation. Human and intellectual capital measurement models enable us to analyze the actual earnings paid to employees from a capital preservation point of view as discussed by M. Dobija (2000, p. 55). A new function of the value added statement is an accounting for a rightful compensation system and its consistency with minimum wage standards resulting from human capital measurement.

Cost accounting should be organized to adequately represent the production function. (Schweitzer, 2000, p. 199). M. Dobija (2000, p. 59) has proposed a production function, which includes human capital. The proposed function is a sum of production costs categories including labor costs (W). The formula is as follows:

$$PR = W + zA + rA - sA$$

where: z – is ratio of an annual usage of the assets; r – is market rate of return on capital placed in the assets; s – is looseness of the assets in production processes; PR – market value of an output as; W – costs of labor; A – assets which denote capital embodied already in the physical and financial resources.

Because $W = u * H$, where u – is rate of human labor payoff thus the productivity is arrived at as follows:

$$WP = 1 + A/H * (z + r - s)/u$$

Reshaping the formula leads us to a production function, which can be expressed as exponential function of considered variables as follows:

$$PR = (W)\exp[\frac{A}{H} * \frac{z + r - s}{u}]$$

The above formula can be rewritten with using one variable Z, which denotes a level and quality of the management.

$$PR = (W)\exp[\frac{A}{H} * Z]$$

The variables included in this production function show relationships between company assets (A) and human capital of employees (H). It is worth noticing that variable A involves not only physical assets, but also intellectual capital of the organization as discussed earlier. Distribution of the variables underline well known requirements of productive (efficient) economic process. Employees' human capital should be supported firmly by organization's intellectual capital such as information systems, management control processes and so on. The independent variable Z, which can be interpreted as management, is indispensable factor of successful results.

CONCLUSIONS

As the growing demand for knowledge-based products and services is changing the structure of the global economy, the role of knowledge in achieving competitive advantage is becoming an important management issue in all sectors. While there is little consensus as to what knowledge actually is, many do accept that knowledge is a primary competitive factor in business today. Its accumulation, transformation and valuation lie at the heart of intellectual capital management. Employee know-how and innovative capabilities play a pre-

dominant role in defining the productive power of the corporation and account for an increasing proportion of the capital
in traditional industries.

Intellectualisation of the product will be followed by
changes in accounting costing systems. Stakeholders are interested in receiving information about the costs of production, which include the cost of intellect in the product. In order to obtain this, there is a need for a measurement model of
intellectual capital and ways of including measurement in the
financial statements.

In this paper a measurable model of human/intellectual
capital was presented. Human capital in this case is regarded
as a sum of capitalised costs of living, capitalised cost of education and experience. After measuring human capital, a proposal for inclusion of such information into financial statements was presented.

In conclusion, the traditional balance sheet and backward
looking indicators are no longer tools in the decision making
process. A new knowledge era will force accountants to focus
on providing information about the firm's intellectual
potential and capital – the most important element of company's success. Information about intellectual product and
its cost elements is one of the challenges accounting faces today.

REFERENCES

Abdel-khalik A. R., 2000. *Incentive Compensation and Human Capital Assets*, paper
presented at the 23rd Annual Congress of the European Accounting Associations, Munich.

Becker, G.S., 1975, *Human Capital*, Sec. ed., National Bureau of Economic Research, N.Y., p. 45.

Croes M., *Classification of intangible investments*. Working paper, EUROSTAT and
. Statistics Netherlands;

Dobija M., 1998. How to Place Human Resources into the Balance Sheet, *Journal
of HRCA*, vol. 3, nr 1, p. 87.

Dobija M., 2000. Human Resource Costing and Accounting as a Determinant of Minimum Wage Theory, *Zeszyty Naukowe Akademii Ekonomicznej*, Kraków, pp 39–62.

Dzinkowski R., 2000. The Measurement and Management of Intellectual Capital, *Management Accounting*, vol. 78, no. 2, February, p 32–34.

Edvinsson L, Malone M. S., 1993. Intellectual Capital, Harper Business, p.31.

Hall R, 1992. The strategic analysis of intangible resources, *Strategic Management Journal*, vol. 13, no 2, pp 135–144.

Flamholtz E., 1976. The Impact of Human Resource Valuation on Management Decisions: a Laboratory Experiment, *Accounting, Organisations and Society*, vol. 1, no 2–3, pp 153–165.

Flamholtz E., 1985. *Human Resource Accounting*, Jossey Mass Publishers, Los Angeles.

Grojer J. E., Johanson U., 1996. *Human Resource Costing and Accounting*, Joint Industrial Safety Council, Stockholm.

Hudson W. I., 1993. *Intellectual Capital*, John Wiley and Sons Inc., New York, p.16.

IASC, 1998. International Accounting Standard IAS 38; Intangible Assets, London.

IASC, 1998. Basis for Conclusions: IAS 38, Intangible Assets, IAS 22 (Revised 1998) business combinations, and summary of changes to E60 and IAS 22, London.

Ijiri Y., 1999. The Cost Principle and the Labor Theory of Value in relation to the Role of Accounting Theories and Their Depth in: Sunder S., Yamaji H., *The Japanese Style of Business Accounting*, Quorum Books, Westport, Connecticut, London, pp. 177–190.

Morse W. J., Davis J. R., Hartgrave A L., 1996; *Management Accounting*. A Stategic Approach, South-Western College Publishing.

Mouritsen J., 1998. Driving Growth: Economic Value Added versus Intellectual Capital, *Management Accounting Research*, pp 461–482.

OECD, 1992. *Technology and the Economy. The Key Relationship*. The Technology/Economy Programme, Paris.

Paton W.A., Littleton A. C., 1940. *Introduction to Corporate Accounting Standards*, Sarasota, Fl; American Accounting Association, p. 13.

Schultz T. W., 1981. Investing in People, *The Economics of Population Quality*, University of California, p.21.

Schweitzer M., Znaczenie teorii produckji i kosztów dla systemów rachunku kosztów w XiX i XX wieku, Zeszyty teoretyczne Rady Naukowej SKwP, Zeszyt Specjalny, no 56, Warszawa, 2000.

Smith G. V., Parr R., 1989. *Valuation of Intellectual Property and Intangible Asstets*, John Wiley & Sons, pp 93–94.

Sunder S., 1997. *Theory of Accounting and Control*. Cincinnati, South-Western Publishing.

Turner G., 1996. Human resource accounting – whim or wisdom? *Journal of Human Resource Costing and Accounting*, Vol. 36, no 3, pp. 303–320.

Van Buren Mark E., 1999. A yardstick for knowledge management, *Training and Development*, vol. 53, issue 5, p.71–78.

Wallman S., 1998. The future of accounting and financial reporting. Part II. The colorized approach. *Accounting Horizons*, vol. 9, no 3, pp 81–91.

Andre Helin

QUALITY AND MEASUREMENT OF INTELLECTUAL CAPITAL AT AN ACCOUNTANCY FIRM SUPPLYING AN INTELLECTUAL PRODUCT

Abstract

The traditional financial statement model, based on historical pricing, concentrating mainly on the measurement of material values (measurable), and the financial effects of executed transactions, omits certain key factors for determining the value of an enterprise, such as the significance of intellectual capital, and the capacity for creating future value (earnings drivers).

This general problem has inspired BDO, especially at our organisations in the United Kingdom and Denmark, to develop a model (in a form similar to the traditional financial statement) that reflects the growth of intellectual capital.

This paper presents this model developed to determine the quality and measurement of the intellectual capital of the accountancy firm as the intellectual product supplier.

ACCOUNTANCY FIRMS AS INTELLECTUAL PRODUCT SUPPLIERS

Our main purpose is to present a model developed to determine the quality and measurement of the intellectual capital of the accountancy firm as the intellectual product supplier.

The model, *Accounting For Growth (AFG)* is developed by BDO Accountants and Consultants.

BDO is a worldwide organization of professional accountancy and consulting firms serving global and national clients. The firm leads the market in advising growth-oriented, owner managed businesses and, is positioned as the world's sixth largest multinational accounting and consulting organization.

Accountants have been part of one of the most successful professions of the 20th century. The qualification has not just been only relevant to traditional finance and accountancy work, but has been relevant for many successful businessmen and women.

However, past success offers us no guarantee for the future. As a profession we face a much more competitive market for professional services. Unless we recognise these changes and rapidly develop business and individuals strategies to exploit them, the profession faces inevitable decline.

Accounting firms sell know – how. Our product is intellectual capital – the knowledge we possess and for which clients are willing to pay. Whether we bill by the hour, by fee or by transaction, the work we do is the application of our intellectual capital. Consequently, accounting firms are highly dependent on the know-how existing amongst their professionals.

Accounting firms should cherish the know – how in their ranks and make sure that it meets and will meet client needs. For his reason, attention to the development and maintenance of the intellectual capital is the must. It should be (and almost is) an integral part of any professional firm's management, especially in light of the fact that existing know-how rapidly becomes outdated with internationalisation and changes in legislation.

The intellectual capital of any enterprise is closely connected with the kind of business, the business environment and with its history and culture. Before the presentation of BDO's way to monitoring growth in intellectual capital it is important to understand the intellectual products we provide, the accounting business environment and the history and culture of our profession.

Selling intellectual products

The aspect and character of accounting firms have dramatically changed in the last few decades. From inaccessible, somewhat statically operating firms focusing on personal practice, accounting organizations have developed into dynamic, multidisciplinary client-facing enterprises. From conservative followers in the financial services sector, larger and medium-sized firms are increasingly developing into suppliers of new services. Next to quality and price, the availability of products and services has become a determining factor in market strategy. The market is subject to great fluctuations and, as result the organizations operating in this market are subject to such fluctuations as well. Innovations and adaptations are no longer being introduced on an ad hoc basis. Rather, they are an on going reality, involving the entire organization and all the people working in it, on a continual basis.

Basically, the services provided can be classified in assurance services and nonassurance services.

Assurance services are independent professional services that improve the quality of information for decision makers.

Individuals who are responsible for making business decisions seek assurance services to help improve the reliability and relevance of the information used as the basis for their decisions. Assurance services are valued because the assurance provider is independent and perceived as being unbiased with respect to the information examined.

The need for assurance is not new. Accountancy firms have provided many assurance services for years, particularly assurance about historical financial statements information. More recently accountancy firm have been expanding the types of assurance services they perform to include engagements that provide assurance about other types of information, such as assurance about company financial forecasts and assurance about web site controls.

Assurance services includes:

- Audit of historical financial statements

- Review of historical financial statements

- Other attestation services (financial forecast, quality of the companies assets, assurance about the effectiveness of a client's internal controls over financial reporting etc.)

Nonassurance services includes:

- Accounting and Bookkeeping

- Tax services

- Management consulting

- Financial services (consulting in respect of merge & acquisitions, selling and purchase of business, selling of securities etc.)

Relationships among Assurance Services, and Nonassurance Services are shown in Exibit 1.

Exhibit 1. Assurance and Nonassurance Services

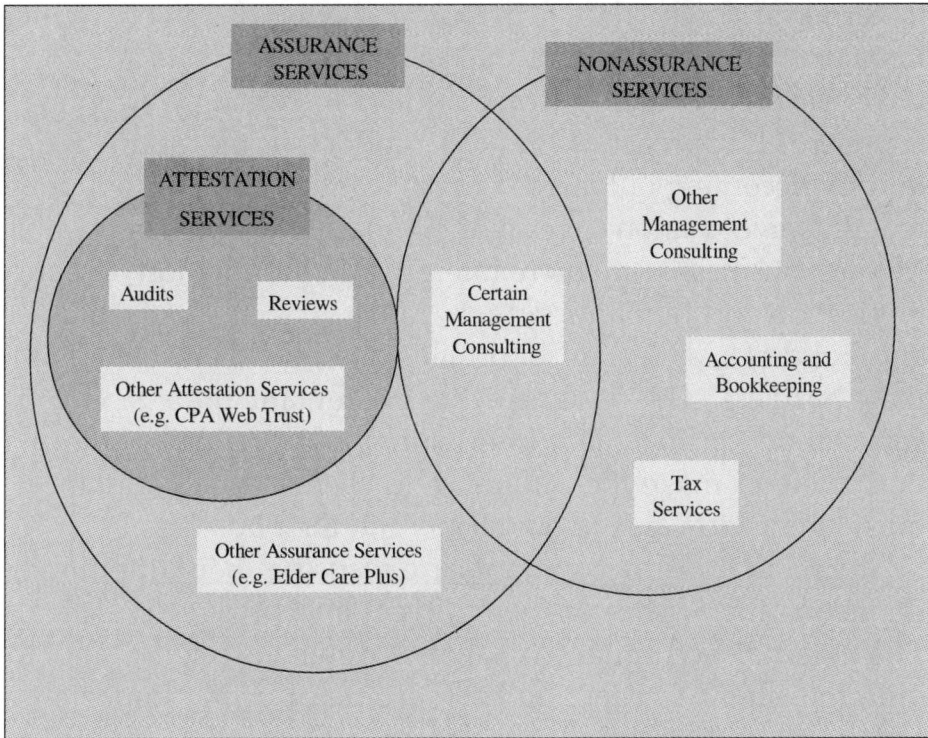

```
                    ASSURANCE
                     SERVICES                 NONASSURANCE
                                                 SERVICES

         ATTESTATION
                                                      Other
          SERVICES                                 Management
                                                   Consulting

       Audits         Reviews        Certain
                                   Management
                                   Consulting           Accounting and
                                                          Bookkeeping
     Other Attestation Services
       (e.g. CPA Web Trust)

                                                     Tax
                                                   Services

              Other Assurance Services
                (e.g. Elder Care Plus)
```

Source: James K. Loebebecke, Auditing, An Integrated Approach, Prentice Hall International

Accounting business environment

A key feature of the environment in which accounting firms operate is that it is first and foremost regulated by rather strict statutory rules. The accountant has a social function regulated by law that requires many entrepreneurs to co-operate with an external accountant or auditor. In addition, the accountant has to comply with the rules and requirements of his own professional association regarding methodology and qualifications.

Unlike other industries where competitors may be able to cut corners to compete, accounting firms, regardless of their size, cannot afford to cut corners. Cutting a corner to save on an expense can end up costing a great deal more at later date in terms of costly claims from the clients, damaged reputations or even revocation of the license to perform as auditor.

However, accounting firms are also increasingly adopting a commercial approach. Our key product is the audit and is quickly becoming outdated. Clients want custom, drilled-down real time information to reach their goals as quickly as possible. Modern businesses are more interested in information, research, innovation and human resources rather than stock, fixed assets and buildings, and want information to give them the edge in their business. This is where the accountant profession must concentrate – using client information and producing information that will make the difference to clients. As accountant we must today add value to our clients and their business.

More and more, accountants are focusing their attention on the needs and wishes of their current and prospective clients. The external accountant has come down to reality, and for him, too, client satisfaction has become of prime importance. Certainly, end especially in the case of smaller accounting firms, there will usually be a strong and often personal tie between the accountant and his client.

This greater attention to the client sometimes produces tension with regard to the abovementioned statutory rules and those of the professional association. Staff members of accounting organizations must be able to operate in this field of tension.

All of these environmental factors make numerous demands on the professional working within accounting firms. As regards their specialization, they will have to cultivate the required skills. As far as their general practice function is concerned, they should not give in to the temptation to undertake activities that are actually outside the scope of their training.

Operating in a professional way also requires a clear understanding and acceptance of one's own limitations with regard to professional knowledge and abilities, particularly now that the risk of claims in on the increase.

Moreover, staff members should also possess social and commercial skills, as well as counselling skills. Finding such staff members is no easy matter. High-quality people are relatively scarce and more firms than ever want to hire them.

History and culture

The owner of an accounting firm is either one person or a partnership of more persons. If they are not the actual founders, they are at least strongly committed to the fortunes of their firm.

The emphasis is usually on maintaining good contacts with clients and on financial issues within their firm. They tend to work extremely hard to serve both interests properly. This has a number of consequences for development and maintenance of the firm's intellectual capital, especially Human Capital and Client Capital. Staff members are, for example, expected to adopt a flexible attitude towards working hours and lengths of working time, and to be able to operate and make decisions independently.

There is a strong emphasis in accounting firms on meeting (often short-term) productivity goals in the form of chargeable hours. The level of remuneration of staff members is linked to whether they meet these goals. The style of communication tends to be pragmatic, open and direct, and aimed at the matters in hand. For these reasons, the style of management is task-oriented.

In this prevailing culture, and in the process of adding value to our clients, all parts of the intellectual capital have been made subordinate to the clients' interest and the financial interest of them.

Attention to the personal interest of individual staff members and other aspects of the social dimension of management are usually only present to a lesser degree. Staff members are expected to be sufficiently independent and assertive to stand up for themselves. Those who can get along with this operational style can derive a lot of satisfaction from their work. On the other hand, in accounting firms job consists of a broad set of duties that offer varied challenges and wealth of internal and external contacts. This stimulating environment constitutes an important advantage for recruiting young professional.

The larger accounting firms offer many internal promotional opportunities and require continuous advancement. 'Up or out' is a principle often heard and employed. Career stagnation when rising from an entry-level professional to a supervisor often means the end of career in a larger firm.

But it can also mean a good re-start elsewhere on the job market due to the broad experience acquired within the accounting profession as well as the extensive training received.

Quality of services provided by accountancy firms

Quality is not a strictly defined idea with outlined content. The designation "good quality" or "high quality" looses its meaning without a closer consideration of relative and comparable values.

Instead of a deeper and more theoretical discussion of an ultimate and moderately objective definition of the quality of services offered, accountancy firms, especially those in the United Kingdom and Scandinavia, quickly consolidated their focus on constructing a system of Quality Management (QM), adapted to the specific demands of the profession, based on the assumption that good quality of the service creation process (a high level of essential knowledge), and the good quality of the service provision (associated services) automatically assures a high quality of the final product.

Typical QM at accountancy firms is divided into a general quality system relating to the accountancy firm in its entirety, and more specific quality programmes relating to the concrete execution of services. The following are subsystems of such a program (established policies):

Policies established at the firm level

- Strategic development of the firm (mission, scope of operations, market segment, pricing policies)
- Impartiality (prohibition of employment at other organisations, prohibition of holding stock in a company being audited)
- Trade secrets and client confidentiality
- Rules defining the acceptance of new contracts, and the acquisition of new clients
- Personnel policies divided into: recruitment, employment regulations, salary policy, and employee classification
- Special units
- IT system
- Financial management within the firm

Policies established at the contract execution level

- Audit manual (based on generally accepted auditing standards)
- Accounting standards (based on generally accepted accounting standards)
- Review standards
- Business evaluation methods
- Documentation guidelines
- Quality control of assignment

The effectiveness of QM, which ultimately affects the quality of intellectual capital, is measured indirectly as feed back from the degree of satisfaction expressed by clients, employees, and shareholders in the firm. From BDO's point of view, the following are the most significant attributes for measuring intellectual capital:

- Degree of customer satisfaction

This degree is measured directly on the basis of analysis conducted by a third party independent of BDO, from sales volume growth, and a low ratio of customer attrition.

♦ Degree of achieved profitability
This degree is measured directly from typical financial indicators for the sector (operating profit, the share of remuneration funds in sales revenue, work to time use ratio, etc.),

♦ Stability and low turnover of the senior technical staff,
A high degree of rotation among younger employees is normal for this sector, and is even welcome.

♦ Recognition in professional circles (chartered auditors, banks, lawyers, etc.)
Shown through the influx of new, well qualified staff, in professional publications, the preparedness of other companies to merge or begin cooperation with BDO, etc.

The practical AGF model applied at BDO for measuring quality and the growth of the value of intellectual capital is presented below.

QUALITY AND MEASUREMENT OF INTELLECTUAL CAPITAL AT AN ACCOUNTANCY FIRM.

The traditional financial statement model, based on historical pricing, concentrating mainly on the measurement of material values (measurable), and the financial effects of executed transactions, omits certain key factors for determining the value of an enterprise, such as the significance of intellectual capital, and the capacity for creating future value (earnings driver).

The result of this is a gap in the disclosed information between the value of the company estimated by the capital market, and its adequate balance-sheet value. This, as a consequence, makes it difficult to estimate the significance of intellectual capital, and also, over the long term, the inevitable practical limits of the usefulness of financial statements.

The size of this gap is presented in table 1, which compares the market value of chosen companies in specific sectors, with their book value obtained from their official financial statements:

Tab. 1. Share of intangible assets in the market value
for chosen companies

Company	Market Value (%)	Net Book Value (%)	Value of Intangible Fixed Assets (%)
Shell	100	75	25
US Steel	100	65	35
Hewlett Packard	100	40	60
Hugo Boss	100	21	79
Unilever	100	20	80
WM-Data	100	15	85
Microsoft	100	13	87
Reuters	100	12	88
SAP	100	10	90
Oracle	100	8	92
Rentokil	100	5	95

Source: Market value and business line, Sveiby 1997

The main cause of the revealed discrepancies can be traced to the traditional general accounting definitions of assets and liabilities, which concentrate on historical events and measure their material value (tangible assets).

The traditional financial statement of a company offering intellectual products, based on the common accounting principles, is simply not sufficient. Financial statements prepared in such a way do not provide satisfactory information on whether or not a given company has a sufficient foundation for development, and as a consequence, makes it difficult for the managers of the company to make proper decisions.

Therefore, in the context of the significance of intellectual capital for the development and management of a company selling know-how, it is necessary to apply alternative measurement mechanisms and present the on-going changes in the quality and growth of intellectual capital.

Innovation regarding financial statements should not be limited to the financial data from the balance-sheet and income statement. The ultimate solution in the field of financial statements must come from outside the fundamental framework of financial statements as we know them today.

The practical application of a modified concept of accounting, revealing the capacity to create future value, requires not only the identification of the appropriate operative solutions, which could fulfil the previously identified conditions, but also one that can stand the test of time, and can ensure that the criteria commonly accepted today for proper accounting are adhered to. The solutions are:

- Clarity
- Transparency
- Credibility
- Impartiality
- Comparability
- Continuity

The above mentioned developments inspired BDO International, especially at our organisations in the United Kingdom and Denmark, to develop a model (in a form similar to the traditional financial statement) which reflects the growth of intellectual capital.

The justification and principal goal for developing the model is to achieve a continuous controlled growth of the value of BDO as a firm generating added value.

BDO in United Kingdom has developed a model of business growth. The model provides a universal template against which the progress of any commercial enterprise can be measured. It illustrates the characteristic of growing business in general, regardless of their size or the industrial sector in which they operate.

Based on the work and experiences gained in the United Kingdom, the Danish office of BDO developed a financial statement model which includes an estimate of the quality and attributes for measuring the growth of intellectual capital in a consulting firm.

This model has been used to measure the firms own intellectual capital for the past two years, and despite certain controversial conclusions, was publicly presented for the first time for the fiscal year 1999/2000.

The main assumptions of the model as well as the practical experiences gained by the management staff during its preparation are presented below. The data relates exclusively to BDO's office in Denmark.

BDO is one of the largest accountancy firms in Denmark. The firm has a history of almost 100 years of operation. As a result of the mergers and acquisitions over the past 15 years, the firm has achieved impressive financial results. Sales revenue during the fiscal year 1999/2000 amounted to almost EURO 50m. As at the end of August 2000, the firm employed almost 700 people, of which 100 are chartered auditors. The Danish office has 48 partners.

CONCEPTUAL ASSUMPTIONS OF THE AFG MODEL

Entrepreneurship and Earnings Drivers

The essential goal of BDO as an economic entity is to achieve continuous, stable, and controlled growth of the value of the firm. In our opinion, only this type of a development scenario ensures long term interest of and commitment from all groups of society (owners, managers, employees, clients, etc.) in the every day operations of the firm.

The term "value of the firm", as used in this discussion, is broadly understood and means the total sum of the satisfaction the firm's operation brings to all the groups of society involved in its operations.

As a firm offering intellectual products, the management of the firm is aware that intellectual capital, broadly understood, is one of the firm's most important resources.

Financial statements should therefore strongly present the intellectual capital and fundamental growth factors (earnings drivers), through which the firm will achieve its established goals.

Entrepreneurship, a clearly formulated development strategy, a logical organisational structure, well qualified committed and loyal employees, and the ability to obtain and keep valuable clients, all guarantee the firm's success.

As a consequence, BDO has outlined the following success factors, which should create the conceptual assumptions of the AFG statements:

- ► Entrepreneurship
- ► Clearly defined mission of the firm
- ► Precisely defined development strategy
- ► Target operational programme
- ► Motivation and commitment

- Communication (capacity to distribute information)
- Energy and reasonable impatience
- Innovation, a barrier breaking way of reasoning

Entrepreneurship

According to BDO, entrepreneurship is the fundamental and driving force of any economic entity. Without an appropriate dose of entrepreneurship among the management and employees, continuous growth in the value of the firm is not possible. Individuals possessing characteristics of an entrepreneur are creative, innovative, believe in their own abilities, are inclined to take risks, and know how to achieve their stated goals.

A challenge for the management of a professional firm is to ensure that the organization has exactly the right number of the entrepreneurial leaders.

The AFG statement should therefore inform the management of BDO, whether or not the firm employs the appropriate number of people with these enterprising characteristics.

Goal (mission) of the enterprise

BDO is an organisation based on held knowledge and the transfer of know-how. The operations of the firm are grounded in public trust, the State's authority, essential knowledge, and a clear definition of its operational scope. Companies desiring long term growth, should have a clearly defined mission and development strategy.

Our mission is to serve entrepreneurial businesses and the people behind them.

Precisely defined strategic goals

The strategic goal of BDO in Denmark is to achieve significant growth in the value of the firm over the next three years. This goal will be achieved by increasing the degree of:

- Satisfaction of clients cooperating with BDO
- Satisfaction of our employees
- Achieved profitability of the firm, measured by the proportion of operating profit to sales revenue

Target operational programme

The achievement of established goals requires a target operational programme. In the planning stage, a firm should concentrate on:

- Building a flexible and decentralised organisation which will be in the position to absorb growth
- Increasing the flow of information and the division of knowledge, through the implementation of a modern IT system
- Building electronic libraries (Knowledge Database)
- Expanding and improving the quality of internal training programmes, and establishing contacts within the academic community
- Improving the quality of the applied internal reporting systems

Applied definitions, information sources, and measurement attributes

In the AFG model, the following definitions, information sources, measurement attributes, and databases were used:

Degree of employee satisfaction

In the Spring of 2000, an analysis was conducted by an anonymous electronic survey consisting of 30 questions relating to:

- Strategy and mission of the firm
- Personnel policies

- Salary policies
- Management systems

The analysis was conducted by independent consultants, following earlier conversations with the Executive Board, partners, and employees of the firm. Throughout the entire procedure, participants were guaranteed anonymity. The survey was completed by 86% of employees.

Degree of client satisfaction

An analysis of the degree of client satisfaction was performed by an independent market research institution, Aalund Business Research. The research was conducted in May 2000.

Aalund Business Research has been conducting this type of research for several years, independent of the informational needs of BDO. Their research consists of 2,100 interviews, conducted at companies employing from 10 to 499 people.

The research concentrated particularly on the degree of customer satisfaction, their loyalty to the accountancy firm, and their competitiveness in comparison to other accountancy firms. The comparative analysis was conducted with regard to other large accountancy firms in Denmark.

BDO Intranet

BDO has its own corporate network, BDO Intranet, both on domestic and international levels. The goal of this corporate network is to increase the flow and exchange of information, which will ultimately make more information available. The firm monitors and treats network use as an indicator measuring employees' interest in the network, and as an indication of the quality of the information gathered in the systems.

Administration and financial management systems

Financial information was received with the assistance of the financial systems employed by the firm, including, among others, client and employee files, and the records of executed contracts.

Measurement attributes

Measurement attributes were established *before* receiving information and processing data. The measurement attributes and quality characteristics were established in accordance with the firm's own ambitions, established earlier during meetings with employees, internal discussions with partners, and conversations with clients, etc.

Measurement attributes were established at three levels:
- G –green colour, meaning a satisfactory situation,
- Y – yellow colour, meaning a situation requiring attention,
- R – red colour, meaning the need for immediate action.

Schedule

After developing the specific elements of the AGF model, but before the actual initiation of work, a schedule was developed for the execution of particular phases. This schedule was presented to employees. The areas of particular analysis take into account the natural cycle of an accountancy firm operations. The fiscal year of the firm is October 1 to September 30.

	Month	1	2	3	4	5	6	7	8	9	10	11	12
Mission and strategy			O	O									
Client Capital						O							
Human Capital							O						
Process Capital (QM)									O	O	O	O	O
Budget							M	M	O	O			
Annual Financial Statement											O	O	
Accounting for Growth										O	O	O	

M – Performed by Management,
O – Performed by others

BDO ACCOUNTING FOR GROWTH

The conclusions of the conducted analysis are presented below.

GROWTH PARAMETERS		INTELLECTUAL CAPITAL	
2000			**2000**
ENTREPRENEURIAL SPIRIT		**CLIENT FOCUS**	
No entrepreneurial leaders	Y	Clients' satisfaction	G
		Clients' knowledge of BDO	R
		Clients' image of BDO	G
		Potential clients' image of BDO	Y
EARNINGS DRIVERS		**EMPLOYEE FOCUS**	
Clarity of BDO's mission	G	Employee satisfaction	G
Clarity of BDO`s strategy	G	Employee experience & education	Y
Motivation and engagement	Y	Employee turn over	Y
Quality of Communication	R		
Healthy impatience	R		
Innovation			
		PROCESS FOCUS	
		Use of IT	Y
		Knowledge sharing	Y
		Quality Management Systems	G
		Organization Efficiency	
		Research and product development	
		FINANCIAL PERFORMANCE	
		Organic growth	G
		Profitability	G
		Costs control	Y
FINANCIAL FOCUS			
			2000
Financial performance comparing with forecast			G

R – Needs action
Y – Requires Attention
G – Satisfactory

ENTREPRENEURIAL SPIRIT

Note 1 – Degree of management holding entrepreneurial characteristics

For the purposes of the analysis, entrepreneurial characteristics were defined as: creative personality, ability to take initiative, quick decision making capability, moderate impatience, ability to manage people and the ability to clearly present information.

The survey requested that respondents reply to the following question:

"Does the management staff of BDO hold the entrepreneurial characteristics specified in the attached definition?"

Preliminary quality indicators (measured as the sum of the number of positive responses in comparison to the total number of respondents) were established at the following levels:

R <10% and > 50%, Y 10%-20% and 30%-50%, and G >20% and < 30%,

Obtained result - Y (19%) is a little below the preferable results.

Too little entrepreneurship in such a dynamic sector as the auditing sector creates the risk that the firm will not achieve the necessary degree of innovation and will not keep up with the developing market.

Too many entrepreneurial managers creates the risk of chaos, uncontrolled development and a superficial execution of contracts.

The optimal level of entrepreneurship oscillates between 20%–30%. Such a combination, according to BDO, ensures the necessary innovation accompanied by stable functioning of the firm.

EARNINGS DRIVERS

Note 2 – Goal, development strategy, and operational plan

The task of management is to define the mission and development strategy of the firm, and specify the detailed plans for its execution.

BDO's basic mission is to be the leading adviser to entrepreneurial businesses and the people behind them.

Without a clear mission and strategy, as well as a target operational plan, substantial growth in the value of a firm is seldom possible.

In 1999, BDO approved its mission and an updated development strategy based on the concrete operating plans. This mission and the firm's strategic plans were subsequently published in the form of a brochure. The Executive Board of the firm believes that publishing the firm's strategic goals obligates the management and employees of the firm to achieve these goals.

In 2000 an analysis was performed of the awareness of the mission and development strategy of the firm among its employees. Employees were asked to express their opinion on the firm's mission and operational strategy by taking part in a survey.

The survey requested that respondents reply to following question:

"Do you know the primary mission and development strategy of BDO?"

Answers provided were classified into three categories:

a) Yes

b) In principle yes

c) No

Preliminary quality indicators (measured as the sum of responses to a) and b), in comparison to the total number of respondents) were established at the following levels:

Red < 60%, Yellow 60% - 80% and Green > 80 %

More than 85% of employees were able to precisely define the firm's strategy.

Note 3 – Degree of motivation and commitment

In the opinion of BDO the degree of motivation and commitment plays equally essential role as entrepreneurship. Research was conducted in the form of a survey including three Yes or No questions:
1. "Are you satisfied with your job at BDO?"
2. "Does your direct supervisor motivate you to a greater degree of commitment?"
3. "Does your section (the smallest operating unit) work with an appropriate level of commitment?"

Respondents were given the choice of three answers:
a) Yes, b) In principle yes, and c) No.
Answers a) and b) were counted together.

Re: 1)
Initially established measurement criteria: R < 60 %, Y 60-80%, G > 80 %.
The actual degree of employee satisfaction was 86%.

Re: 2)
Initially established measurement attributes: R < 60 %, Y 60%-80%, G > 80 %.
Actual percentage 44 %

Ad 3)
Initially established measurement attributes: R < 60 %, Y 60%-80%, G > 80 %.
Actual percentage 77 %

In addition, the research included a factor for employees absent because of sickness.

The applied indicator here was calculated as the number of sick hours in comparison to the total number of work hours during the research period.

Initially established measurement criteria: R >3 %, Y >2-3%, G < 2 %.

Obtained indicator: Y – 2.4 %

The low appraisal of supervisors by their subordinates should be noted. The firm's management claimed these results to be unsatisfactory. As a consequence, incentive and training programmes will be developed and implemented over the next two years. These programmes will include lower and middle management.

Note 4 – Communication and the flow of information

The Danish management abides by the principle, that what was not communicated does not exist.

The proper distribution of information is a condition that results from management policies. An appropriate communication system is especially essential taking into account the way work of chartered auditors is organised, as a rule, spending most of his or her time outside the office.

Employees and partners of the firm were asked to answer two questions:

1) "Do you feel that you are well informed concerning all essential matters in our firm?"

2) "Before beginning work on a contract, did you receive satisfactory instruction from your supervisor?"

Initially established measurement criteria: R <60%, Y 60%-80%, G >80 %.

Obtained results for the first question: R 39% and the second question: R 53%

The results regarding the first issue were not satisfactory, but they did not come as surprise for the management of the firm. In a dynamically developing company, the flow of information does not always reach every corner of the organisation in due time. These problems were also identified earlier, and on this basis, the management, in 1999, decided to speed up the implementation of the corporate intranet.

Very unsettling is the low indication of employee satisfaction with the instruction received from their supervisors. A lack of appropriate instructions increases the risk of making errors, and lowering the work capacity. After obtaining these results, the analysis was turned over to a working group established for the purpose of additionally analysing the problems, and presenting management with appropriate solutions.

Note 5 – Healthy impatience and operating effectiveness

The next challenge for management is the creation of a healthy atmosphere and moderate impatience in the organisation, according to the principle, why wait until tomorrow to do something if you can do it today.
The effectiveness of operations is, similarly to entrepreneurship, a very important parameter in the development of a firm.
Employees of the firm were given three questions:

1) "Do you think that the Executive Board acts dynamically and effectively?"
   Initially established measurement criteria: R < 60 %, Y 60%-80%, G > 80%
   Obtained results: R 35 %

2) "Do you think that your direct supervisor acts dynamically and effectively?"
   Initially established measurement criteria: R < 60 %, Y 60%-80%, G > 80%
   Obtained results: R 57 %

3) "Were you given the necessary responsibility and competency to solve the problems you encounter everyday at work?"

Initially established measurement criteria: R < 60 %, Y 60%-80%, G > 80%

Obtained results: G 88 %

Simultaneously, this research was supplemented with financial data regarding work in progress. Long periods needed for completing contracts (and, as a consequence, the reduction of the firm's liquidity) are often caused by lack of decision making - "closing the issues".

The management of the firm established the preferred indicators: R > 150 days, Y 120-150 days, G < 120 days.

Obtained results: Y –120 days

Similarly, as in the case of the appraisal of direct supervisors, the Executive Board of the firm was also found a little ineffective.

On the other hand, the results from the responses regarding responsibility and competency to fulfil their obligations were very satisfying. In organisations offering intellectual products, the effective completion of contracts is directly connected with a large degree of employee independence.

Note 6 – Degree of innovation

Dissolving the barriers to creativity, the existence of the desire to improve, and a belief in the possibility of its execution, are the successive parameters in the fight with competitors.

Knowledge is not a fixed product. The development of new products and the solutions of real problems require a deeper knowledge.

In 2000, BDO began cooperating with the Aarhus Business School, the first private institution in Denmark to establish and fund a faculty in the field of researching growth enterprises and their financial accountancy.

CLIENT FOCUS

Note 7 – Degree of client satisfaction, knowledge and image of BDO in the eyes of its clients and other businesses

The fundamental condition for achieving growth is maintaining, and over time expanding the client base. Without clients, no economic operations are possible. In addition, practical experience from marketing research shows that at firms providing professional services, satisfying existing clients is the most effective way of attracting new ones. The degree of client satisfaction is ultimately the most reliable assessment of the quality of services offered, and is also a good indication of the future prospects for the development of the firm.

An analysis of the degree of client satisfaction was performed by an independent market research institution, Aalund Business Research. The research was conducted in May 2000.

Aalund Business Research has been conducting this type of research for several years, independent of the informational needs of BDO. The results of their analysis are commonly accepted by accountancy firms. This research consisted of 2,100 interviews, conducted at companies employing from 10 to 499 people.

On the basis of 13 parameters (including held knowledge, type of services offered, overall service, price of services and employee commitment), annual analysis is performed in five areas:

1) Degree of client satisfaction with their own auditor,

2) Preparedness of the client to recommend its accountancy firm to other entities,

3) Degree of popularity of the accountancy firm in the eyes of other clients,

4) Image of the accountancy firm in the eyes of the clients, including:

a) innovation capabilities,

b) degree of internationalisation,

c) attractiveness of the firm as a place of employment in the eyes of qualified specialists,

d) societal commitment of the accountancy firm,

e) how accountancy firms solve client problems through their own initiatives.

5) Reputation of the accountancy firm in the eyes of other economic entities, including the same criteria as in Point 4 above.

BDO has included the market research of Aalund Business Research into its own model. The initial measurement attributes were established on the basis of analysis conducted years earlier, and their own level of ambition.

Re: 1) Degree of client satisfaction with their own auditor.

Established measurement attributes: R <80%, Y 80%-85 %, G > 85 %

Actual obtained results: <u>G 86%, the highest in the sector</u>

Re: 2) Preparedness of the client to recommend its auditor to a friendly entity.

Established measurement attributes: R < 40%, Y 40%-45 %, G > 45 %

Actual obtained results: G 46 %

Re: 3) Degree of popularity of a given auditor in the eyes of other clients.

Established measurement attributes: R <20%, Y 20%-25 %, G > 25 %

Actual obtained results: R 17%

Re: 4) Reputation of the auditor in the eyes of its <u>own</u> clients.

4a) Degree of innovation capabilities of BDO
Established measurement attributes: R <5 0%, Y 50%-60%, G > 60 %
Actual obtained results: G 66%

4b) Degree of internationalisation at BDO
Established measurement attributes: R <5 0%, Y 50%-60%, G > 60 %
Actual obtained results: G 81%

4c) Attractiveness of BDO as a place of employment in the eyes of qualified specialists
Established measurement attributes: R <5 0%, Y 50%-60%, G > 60 %
Actual obtained results: G 64%

4d) Societal commitment of BDO
Established measurement attributes: R <5 0%, Y 50%-60%, G > 60 %
Actual obtained results: G 74%

4e) Degree of how BDO solves clients' problems through their own initiatives
Established measurement attributes: R <5 0%, Y 50%-60%, G > 60 %
Actual obtained results: Y 52%

Re: 5) Reputation of the accountancy firm in the eyes of other economic entities

5a) Degree of innovation capabilities of BDO
Established measurement attributes: R <5 0%, Y 50%-60%, G > 60 %
Actual obtained results: Y 51%

5b) Degree of internationalisation at BDO
Established measurement attributes: R <5 0%, Y 50%-60%, G > 60 %
Actual obtained results: Y 50%

5c) Attractiveness of BDO as a place of employment in the eyes of qualified specialists
Established measurement attributes: R <5 0%, Y 50%-60%, G > 60 %
Actual obtained results: R 30%

5d) Societal commitment of BDO
Established measurement attributes: R <5 0%, Y 50%-60%, G > 60 %
Actual obtained results: Y 58%

5e) Degree of how BDO solves clients' problems through their own initiatives
Established measurement attributes: R <5 0%, Y 50%-60%, G > 60 %
Actual obtained results: R 48%

Established measurement attributes: R < 20%, Y 20%-25 %, G > 25 %
Actual obtained results: 17%
The results achieved caused mixed feelings.
On one hand, BDO has the highest client satisfaction of all accountancy firms in the country, but on the other hand, is very anonymous in the eyes of other enterprises.
Considering the high level of respect and recognition in the eyes of its own customers, the following table presents the obtained indicators against the background of the competition:

Year	2000	1999
BDO	**86.5**	**85.0**
Deloitte & Touche	85.3	84.0
KPMG	84.0	83.5
PriceWaterhouseCoopers	83.0	82.8
Ernst and Young	81.0	80.0

The high degree of anonymity of the firm, and the high level of respect and recognition from its own clients, forced the management of the firm to seek assistance from professional marketing organisations. In this context, the Management of the firm is aware of the great significance of its clients' opinions concerning the motivation and commitment of the firms' employees.

EMPLOYEE FOCUS

Note 8 – Degree of employee job satisfaction, the development of their competencies and experience, and employee turnover indicators.

Degree of employee job satisfaction

Research was conducted in the form of a survey, in which employees were asked a series of questions relating to their daily responsibilities, and if they are satisfied with fulfilling their function.
Established measurement attributes: R <60%, Y 60%-80%, G > 80 %
Actual obtained results: G 82%
The obtained results are satisfactory.

Responsibilities and scope of competencies

The essential development and scope of an employees competencies was estimated on the basis of four questions:
1) "In general are you satisfied with your job at BDO?"
2) "Does the firm have an effective training programme?"
3) "Do you solve problems every day related to your knowledge and competencies?"
4) "Have you had a conversation with your supervisor within the last 12 months concerning the development of your professional career?"

Preliminary established measurement attributes (measured on the basis of a YES or NO answer in comparison to the total number of questions) were initially established at the following levels:

Re: 1)
R < 60%, Y 60%-80%, G > 80 %
Actual obtained results: G 82%

Re: 2)
R < 60%, Y 60%-80%, G > 80 %
Actual obtained results: Y 72%

Re: 3)
R < 60%, Y 60%-80%, G > 80 %
Actual obtained results: Y 79%

Re: 4)
R < 85%, Y 85%-95%, G > 95 %
Actual obtained results: R 57%

The overall employee assessment of their jobs is quite satisfactory. The harsh assessment resulting from a lack of discussions between supervisors and employees, results from, among others, the fact that the BDO's regulations require that such discussions take place, at least once a year.

PROCESS FOCUS

Technological progress can open new possibilities/opportunities for consulting firms. This is conditioned by the following features of the progress:

♦ It provides access to effectively obtained, processed, and classified information.

♦ It allows for using and distributing knowledge, independent of geographical distances (very important aspect given the mobility of most auditors).

- Declining costs of IT services, and growing labour costs favourably impact the profitability of consulting firms.

In assessing the capital structure, emphasis was placed on the following essential areas within an accountancy firm:

1) Electronic systems for receiving and processing data, including the corporate intranet and the knowledge database. The firm also uses these additional systems: Customer Relationship Management and a Benchmarking financial ratios system.

2) Work load and knowledge sharing.

3) Quality management in the area of procedures for auditing financial statements, and accounting standards, as well as professional standards and guidance from the Danish Chamber of Chartered Auditors.

Re: 1) Degree of new technology use in everyday work
The analysis was based on the questions:
"Do you believe that the firm provides you with sufficient access to the computer equipment and software necessary to maintain the quality and efficiency of your work?"
Established Measurement attributes: R < 60%, Y 60%-80%, G > 80 %
Actual obtained results: Y 70%

Re: 2) Knowledge Sharing
Research was conducted on the basis of a personnel survey and a measurement of the frequency of use of the corporate intranet (discussion lists) and the electronic library, known as the Knowledge Database
The research yielded the following results:
A) Assessment of the exchange of information among the employees of the firm
Established measurement attributes: R < 60%, Y 60%-80%, G > 80 %

Actual obtained results: R 30%

B) Average number of *employees asking questions* per employee in the discussion lists on BDO's corporate intranet (number of network contacts in comparison to the average number of employees during the research period)
Established measurement attributes: R < 0.75, Y 0.75-1, G > 1
Actual obtained results: Y 0.93

C) Average number of readers in the discussion lists (number of network contacts in comparison to the average number of employees during the research period)
Established measurement attributes: R < 15% Y 15%-20%, G > 20%
Actual obtained results: Y 16.4%

Re: 3) Quality Management
Pursuant to professional standards in Denmark, and on the basis of BDO's internal regulations, the firm is subject to periodic quality control by:
• The Danish Camber of Chartered Auditors,
• BDO International,
• The Executive Board in Denmark.
   In 2000, the firm was subject to inspection by the Danish Chamber of Chartered Auditors. The results of this control showed no violations of the professional standards. According to our own appraisal of the firm, and against the background of the competitors, the implemented quality control systems are of very high standard.
Over the next few years, BDO intends to expand the elements of the quality control system by efficiency factors, and a quality indicator for research and development work. A working group has been established to prepare the appropriate guidance.

FINANCIAL PERFORMANCE

The financial condition of the firm was evaluated at a level established by the firm, which generally places the firm near the top of the sector. The following financial indicators were established as quality parameters:

1. Annual growth of sales volume in fixed prices
2. Improvement of the operating margin
3. Allowable deviation of the growth in general management and administration costs

Re: 1)
Established measurement attributes, sales volume (organic) growth in fixed prices:
R < 0%, Y 0-2.5% G > 2.5%
Actual obtained results: G 2.9%

Re: 2)
Established measurement attributes, growth of the operating margin, measured as the ratio of the operating profit to total sales: R < 0%, Y 0-1.5% G >1.5%
Actual obtained results: G 1.5%

Re: 3)
Established measurement attributes, the degree of cost control, allowable growth of costs in comparison to the planned growth: R > 5%, Y 0-5 % G <0 %
Actual obtained results: Y 4.9%

SUMMARY

Assessing BDO exclusively on the basis of the Accounting For Growth model, the report confirms the reputation of a healthy and forward thinking organisation, but also indicates a series of weaknesses, especially regarding the established goals and mission that the firm wants to achieve. In relation to its fundamental mission as a leading consultant to dynamic enterprises, the low degree of managerial entrepreneurship at BDO as perceived by its own employees must be unsettling, and may even expose the firm to ridicule.

Despite the controversial conclusions, the Executive Board of BDO decided to publish the report in Denmark. As expected, the controversial content of the report caused many significant organisations in Denmark to express different reactions to the press. Discussions were centred on both the applied parameters and measurements of the appraisal, as well as the usefulness of the conclusions by the management of BDO. The self-evaluation of the organisation by its employees was highly criticised (according to many too flattering) as well as being too socially committed.

Despite the evident weaknesses of the model, the management at BDO has a different opinion.

According to the Executive Board of the firm, the preparation and publication of the report exposed existing tensions, initiated essential discussions, and what is most important, obliged and encouraged the management of the firm to eliminate the weaknesses shown.

Mariusz Strojny

KNOWLEDGE MANAGEMENT IN CREATING AND DELIVERING INTELLECTUAL PRODUCT: KPMG AND OTHER LEADING CONSULTANCIES APPROACH

Abstract

Knowledge has become the most powerful economic resource and the only source of competitive advantage in business nowadays. This paper presents how leading consultancies master knowledge management to harness their market positions, how they build knowledge management systems, and how they use IT to facilitate knowledge creation, mediation and use.

Presented examples are widely recognized as "global best practices" in the field of knowledge management. They can serve as benchmarks or even inspiration for both professional service firms and a broad array of companies that are still rooted in Industrial Economy.

INTRODUCTION

The global business community has realized the value of knowledge as an essential element in the process of transformation from traditional industrial economy, which is based on capital to knowledge-based economy, where increasingly it is what organization knows is much more important than what it owns. However, there is still no strong consensus as to the best, or even acceptable, mechanisms for deploying knowledge to improve competitive position. **Knowledge management (KM)** should, therefore, become not only a new business concept but a brand new way of thinking about doing business nowadays.

The major goal of this paper is to present how leading consultancies shape KM strategy and build KM systems to facilitate the process of creating and delivering **"intellectual product"**. By "intellectual product" I understand any kind of knowledge-based services that create lasting value for the company's clients, people or communities. We should be aware that knowledge management is not only about creating and applying knowledge but, what is far more important, about turning this knowledge into value.

Intellectual product in order to exceed client's expectations needs to be created and delivered in the most effective and efficient way. Therefore, the leading consultancies developed **"intellectual environment"** – KM tools, which link, on one hand, KM strategy, KM processes, KM functions and, on the other, organizational culture, structure, technology and people. Today, KM system is an essential element not only for consultancies but for every knowledge -intensive firm aiming at harnessing its competitive edge in New Economy.

KNOWLEDGE MANAGEMENT IN CONSUL-TING INDUSTRY – HISTORICAL BACKGROUND

Professional service firms have been among the earliest and the most enthusiastic implementators of the principles of knowledge management, as they have long recognized that their key resource is the knowledge held in people and structure. As noticed by Rian Goray from Arthur Andersen KM Practice: *"knowledge is 99% of what consultancies sell to its clients"*. Therefore, it is not a surprise that concultancies' impact on development and popularization of knowledge management was crucial. This was due to the following three factors:

♦ Leveraging knowledge has been always the core compe-tence in consulting industry.

♦ Consultancies were among the first organizations that po-ssessed the ability to apply knowledge to effectively solve clients problems, create new business opportunities and deliver the highest quality, knowledge rich services (intel-lectual product).

♦ Consultancies mastered knowledge management for inter-nal purposes but in recent years they have also developed advanced KM solutions for clients in different industries. According to Ernst & Young recent study between 1994 and 1999 the total value of knowledge management pro-jects jumped from 0, 5 to 4,5 billion dollars.[1] IDC research suggests that company expenditures on KM will increase up to 12 billion dollars in 2003.[2]

Knowledge has been always an essential part of consulting industry, which roots go back to Egypt 2 000 years BC. Also,

---

[1] Rudy Ruggles, Why Knowledge? Why Now?, Ernst & Young Center for Bu-siness Innovation (http://www.ey.com)

[2] The future of KM, *Knowledge Management*, Volume 4, Issue 3, November 2000.

in ancient Rome, consulting in form of *information* ("presenting or describing something"), *commendatio* ("giving instructions") and *consilium* ("giving advice") was very popular.[3] However, the first consulting firms, as we understand them today (Sanderson Partner Inc., The Emerson Consultant Inc), were established very recently – both in 1899[4].

I believe that four consultancies were the early pioneers in knowledge management movement: Arthur Andersen and McKinsey & Company in 1960s and 1970s and then Ernst & Young and KPMG in the 1990s. Let's start with a closer look at their initial knowledge management activities:

At Arthur Andersen a formal knowledge management program started in the early 1960s, when the Audit practice began collecting Subject Files, an indexed repository of white papers written by AA people who were experts on certain subject.[5] It became the first knowledge base gathering collective wisdom of the company. Later, gradually over the years other knowledge management systems dedicated to capture and disseminate knowledge were developed. In late 80s the firm moved to CD-ROMs in order to better store, browse and transmit huge amount of data, information and particularly codified knowledge. In 1992 Arthur Andersen began its Global Best Practices (GBP) initiative, which gathered and made available information on best practices in the management and operating processes. During six consecutive years AA spent around 30 million dollars to maintain and develop this repository. As the result of heavy investment and leadership dedication and support, in 1996 GBP reached 12 000 pages describing in details 40 business processes, such as surveying

3 Leopold Stecki, Consulting, Towarzystwo Naukowe Organizacji i Kierowania "Dom Organizatora", Toruń 1997.

4 Zbigniew Chrościński, Konsulting w Zarządzaniu, Polska Fundacja Promocji Kadr, Warszawa 1997.

5 Susan Elliott, Arthur Andersen Maximizes Its Core Commodity Through Comprehensive Knowledge Management, *Knowledge Management in Practice*, August-September 1997.

customer satisfaction, developing and training employees, understanding markets and customers. Two years later, GBP grew three-folds to over 30 000 pages encompassing 100 processes[6]. Once available only on CD-ROMs, GBP went online in November 1996 with the roll out of KnowledgeSpace Arthur Andersen's online knowledge management repository. Currently, approximately 7 000 external users have access to KnowledgeSpace along with more than 60 000 Andersen employees worldwide.

McKinsey & Company is another consulting firm that has been relying strongly on its knowledge management strategy. The strategy was formulated in 1987 to capture knowledge gained from client work, which is stored on computer databases of client projects, documents and specialists. The company's move towards an emphasis on knowledge accumulation really started in the early 1970s, when it first created 15 centres of competence in particular areas and set up work groups to develop knowledge in two areas at the heart of its practice: strategy and organization (one of the first recruits of the organization area was a young graduate holding Ph.D from Stanford Business School named Tom Peters). In spite of deep initial suspicion about codifying knowledge that since then was mostly rooted in personal networks, knowledge infrastructure and formal knowledge management program was a huge and very successful initiative. McKinsey was one of the first companies that established a new position of Chief Knowledge Officer in 1991. Brook Manville who held this position until 1994 helped to enhance knowledge-sharing culture throughout the company and built knowledge management infrastructure with Firm Practice Information System, PGNet, McKinsey Yellow Pages (the company's knowledge map) and Rapid Response Network in its heart[7]. Today Mc-

---

[6] David Pearson, Where Are They Now? Arthur Andersen: Knowledge Base, *CIO*, May 15, 1998.

[7] Tom Peters, Liberation Management, Pan Books, London 1993.

Kinsey spends around 10% of its annual revenues on knowledge management activities.

10 Most-Mentioned Knowledge Consulting Firms by *Knowledge Management Magazine*:

1. Ernst & Young
2. KPMG
3. Deloitte & Touche, Andersen Consulting
5. Arthur Andersen
6. IBM Global Services
7. PricewaterhouseCoopers
8. Barnett International
9. ICM Group
10. Stanford Research International (SRI)

Source: KM Magazine, December 1999.

According to the ranking of "The Most Admired Knowledge Enterprises" by *Journal of Knowledge Management* and *Teleos* in 1998 and 2000 the world most advanced consulting firm in field of knowledge management was Ernst & Young. Its KM program started in 1993 when Roger Nelson, Managing Partner of E&Y's United States consulting practice, announced a new strategic plan called "Future State '97".[8] The plan envisioned $1 billion in revenues up to 1997 (roughly doubling

---

[8] Thomas H. Davenport, Knowledge Management at Ernst & Young, Working Paper, University of Texas, 1997.

the 1993 figure) and described five key processes to achieve this goal: sales, service, delivery, people and knowledge. Some of the most important knowledge management goals in Future State '97 included capturing and leveraging knowledge from client's engagements, having every consultant contribute to the firm's stock of knowledge, and becoming known by clients as a valued source of knowledge and thought leadership (not surprisingly E&Y advertising slogan says: "From Thought to Finish"). Several different knowledge-oriented organizations within E&Y were created: Center for Business Innovation (creates new knowledge), Center for Business Technology (structures this knowledge into methods and automated tools), Center for Business Knowledge (gathers and distributes both the firm's acquired knowledge and external knowledge and information throughout Kweb, Infolink etc.).

KPMG has become one of the most widely recognized knowledge management leader quite recently. In 1999 *Knowledge Management Magazine* announced this company the second "Most-Mentioned Knowledge Consulting Firm" just behind Ernst & Young[9]. KPMG decided to implement knowledge management system because of two reasons. First, at the beginning of the 1990s the company's knowledge was highly fragmented, compartmentalized, and largely unfocused. As the result, KPMG could not effectively solve clients' problems. Second, KPMG's Big Five competitors like Arthur Andersen and Ernst & Young have already implemented knowledge management systems and the company did not want to lag behind. Therefore, to meet client demands and to take the lead in the knowledge race KPMG decided to create state-of-the-art knowledge management system built around the company values and supported by sophisticated information technology. What KPMG needed most was a highly scalable knowledge management solution that would help

---

[9] The KM Year in Review, *Knowledge Management Magazine*, December 1999.

the organization compete and allow 100 000 employees in 160 countries to collaborate – even if their offices are oceans apart. Mike Turillo was nominated as the company's first Chief Knowledge Officer and KPMG declared to spend 1% of its annual revenues on KM (this amounts to over $ 100 mln a year). In early 1998, senior leadership within KPMG decided to develop KWorld – a world-class knowledge management system that would unite all firm employees, enable them to share their knowledge and the firm's intellect on a global basis and in the real time. Also, to support knowledge management and KWorld deployment process, KPMG created International Knowledge Management Organization composed of Knowledge Innovation Center, Global Knowledge Exchange and Intellectual Capital Organization among the most important. Knowledge management implementation went faster and easier than in other "Big Five" consultancies because of the company's knowledge-sharing culture expressed by its mission statement saying about: *"turning knowledge into value for the benefit of its clients, its people and its community"*.

KNOWLEDGE MANAGEMENT DEFINED

There is no widely accepted definition of knowledge management. Different consultancies developed different approaches and definitions. However most of them believe that knowledge management is a fundamental change in the way the company is being managed. KPMG's CEO Paul Reilly says: *"We are betting our feature that knowledge management is going to leap us ahead of our competition"*. KPMG Knowledge Management Report 2000 revealed that KM plays extremely significant role in improving competitive advantage of the company[10].

---

[10] Knowledge Management Research Report, KPMG Management Consulting, London 2000.

Knowledge management is usually understood as the effective use of intangible assets such as knowledge, information, company image and its reputation, good relationships with customers and suppliers but also intellectual property rights, licenses, technology etc. – in other words, knowledge management is perceived as managing the stock of Intellectual Capital possessed by the company. Knowledge management is based on the assumption that if companies learn how to use these "hidden assets", they will be able to significantly improve its economic performance and, therefore, increase its market value.

Within KPMG, knowledge management is defined twofold as: *"the systematic and organized attempt to use knowledge within an organization to improve performance"*[11] or more often as *"the set of policies, procedures and systems associated with the creation, collection, safeguarding and dissemination of the firm's intellectual capital".*[12] Among intellectual capital three general categories are distinguished: human capital (possessed by individuals) organizational capital, and relationship capital (the last two are exclusive property of the company). KPMG's intellectual capital comprises not only patents and other legally protected intellectual rights but also skills, knowledge and experience of the whole company as well as its individual members. Intellectual capital encompasses also concepts, ideas, methods, tools, methodologies, procedures etc. as presented on Figure 1.

---

[11] Knowledge Management Research Report, KPMG Management Consulting, London 1998.

[12] KWorld Deployment materials.

Figure 1. Intellectual Capital Tree

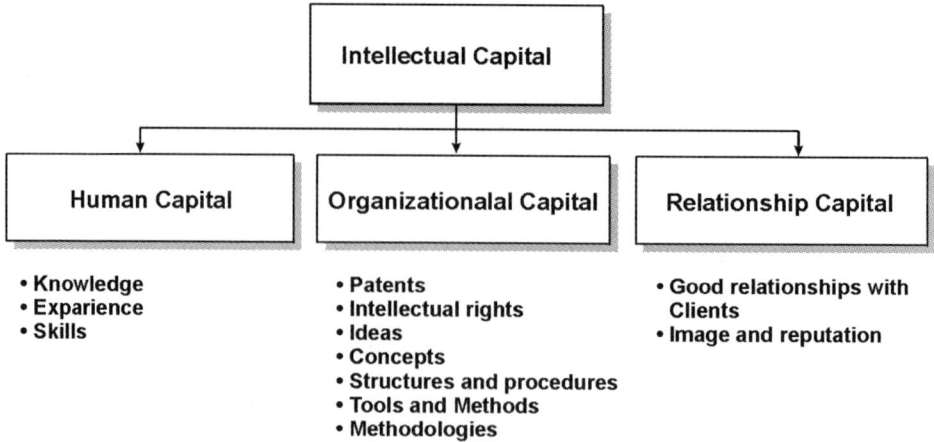

```
                    ┌─────────────────────────┐
                    │   Intellectual Capital  │
                    └─────────────────────────┘
            ┌────────────────┼──────────────────┐
            ▼                ▼                   ▼
┌────────────────────┐ ┌──────────────────────┐ ┌────────────────────┐
│   Human Capital    │ │ Organizationalal     │ │ Relationship       │
│                    │ │ Capital              │ │ Capital            │
└────────────────────┘ └──────────────────────┘ └────────────────────┘
```

Human Capital	Organizationalal Capital	Relationship Capital
• Knowledge • Experience • Skills	• Patents • Intellectual rights • Ideas • Concepts • Structures and procedures • Tools and Methods • Methodologies	• Good relationships with Clients • Image and reputation

Source: Based on IC models developed by Karl-Erik Sveiby and Leif Edvinsson in Sweden. For more details see: Karl-Erik Sveiby, The New Organizational Wealth. Managing & Measuring Knowledge-Based Assets, Berrett-Koehler Publishers, Inc., San Francisco 1997 or Leif Edvinsson, Michael S. Malone, Intellectual Capital. Proven Way to Establish Your Company's Real Value by Measuring Its Hidden Brainpower, Piatkus Ltd, London 1997.

All consultancies involved in KM want to make sure that their clients in any place in the world and at any time receive the best solution based on the knowledge and experience of the whole company not only a particular team working on a client's problem. Knowledge management more than creating knowledge for its own, should be focused on turning it into value. Rene Tissen a managing director for KPMG Knowledge Management practice and Professor at Nijenrode University in Netherlands wrote an excellent book on this subject: "Value-based Knowledge Management" and KPMG KM Team in Netherlands created KM assessment tool called "Value Enhancer". Although, KPMG is a knowledge-intensive and knowledge-creating company (and so other big consultancies), this does not give them a competitive advantage any longer. In fact, consultancies do not need more knowledge – they have plenty of it. What they need, however, is to learn how to become the "Value-adding, Knowledge-based Company".

KPMG was among the first firm that distinguished two different levels of knowledge management: operational and strategic. While **Operational Knowledge Management** focuses on information technology to facilitate organization and distribution of information from and to employees, **Strategic Knowledge Management** links the company's knowledge with its business strategy, and is about designing knowledge-supportive organizational structures that breed Knowledge Professionals.

We can, therefore, define Knowledge Management System at both Strategic and Operational Level. KM at Strategic Level is: **the art of creating the knowledge-based, value-oriented company integrated around business strategy, organizational culture, people, technology and measurement system**. At the operational level KM is: **a set of processes enabling organization to create, codify and apply knowledge (both tacit and explicit) to achieve its goals.** KM definitions used by other consultancies are listed in Table 1.

Table 1. Selected definitions of knowledge management by consulting firms

Knowledge Management is the systematic process of managing knowledge to maximize business results. It is about ensuring that every employee has the knowledge he needs, when and where he needs it, to maximize his contribution to the firm's overall success. <div align="right">**Holland & Davis, Inc.**</div>
Knowledge Management is the systematic management, use, and reuse of information, experience, and expertise to achieve a specific business benefit, goal, or objective. Put simply, it is leveraging knowledge to do things you do well, even better. <div align="right">**Cambridge Technology Partners**</div>
Knowledge Management is a set of the policies, procedures and systems associated with the creation, collection, safeguarding and dissemination of the firm's intellectual capital. <div align="right">**KPMG**</div>

Table 1. Selected definitions of knowledge management by consulting firms (cont.)

Knowledge management is the process of finding, acquiring and using knowledge that leads to the improvement of the firm's competitiveness. **Arthur Andersen**
Knowledge management is a system designed to help companies capture, analyze and use knowledge to make better decisions and achieve competitive advantage. **Ernst & Young**
Knowledge management is the art of turning information and other intangible assets into lasting value for the benefit of organization, clients and its people. **PricewaterhouseCoopers**
Knowledge Management is a business process for the management of an enterprise's intellectual assets. It is a discipline that promotes an integrated and collaborative approach to the creation, capture, organization, access and use of information assets. These assets include structured databases, textual information such as policy and procedure documents, and most importantly , the tacit knowledge and expertise resident in the heads of individual employees. **GartnerGroup**
Knowledge Management is about connecting people to people and people to information to create competitive advantage. **HOYT Consulting**

KNOWLEDGE MANAGEMENT SYSTEM

Companies already aware of the need to distribute information throughout the organization are making use of a variety of operational KM techniques. Their main concern is to connect people to the system being used for the distribution and transfer of knowledge. While this may be a good starting point, companies have found that this tends to become costly, ineffective, and non-productive. Strategic KM gives the right balance by linking knowledge management with the business strategy, organizational culture and organizational structure as well as technology, processes and systems within the firm[13]. KPMG knowledge management approach covers both these dimensions (see Figure 2).

Figure 2. Knowledge Management System at KPMG Polska

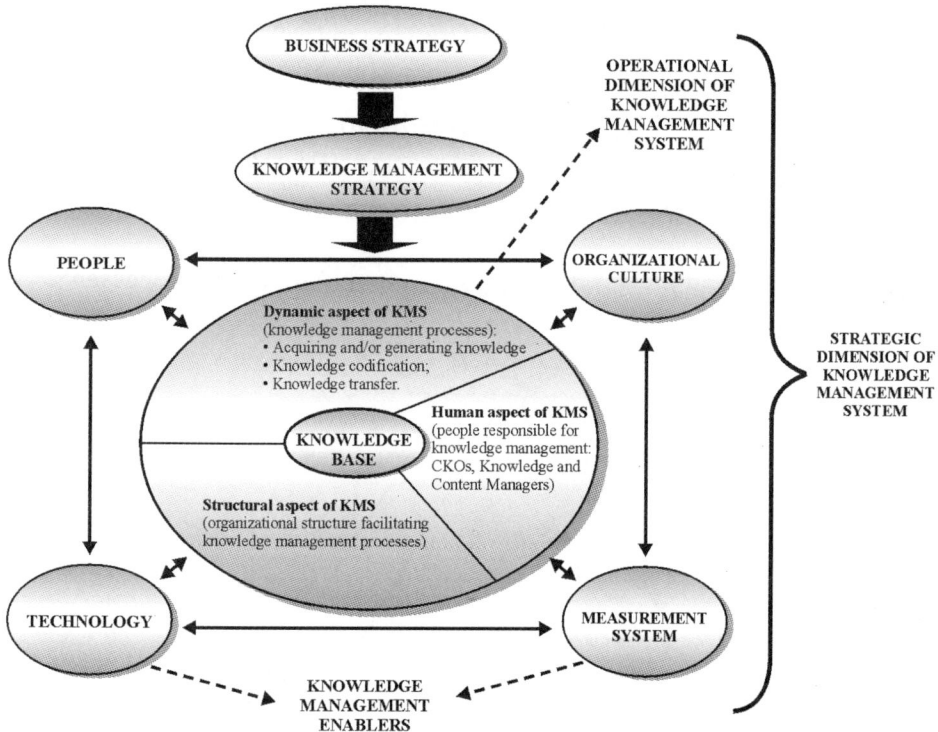

Source: Developed and presented for the first time by Mariusz Strojny at the 7th International Conference „Knowledge Management and Re-structuring and Development Processes in Enterprises" in Krynica – Czarny Potok, October 26–28, 2000.

Operational Dimension of the Knowledge Management System relates to the following three aspects:

* **Knowledge management processes** – this presents the dynamic aspect of KMS and is about creating knowledge in-

---

[13] Rene Tissen, Daniel Andriessen, Frank L. Deprez, Value-Based Knowledge Management. Creating the 21st Century Company: Knowledge Intensive, People Rich, Addison Wesley Longman, Amsterdam 1998.

side the company or acquiring it from the outside, then codifying knowledge and finally transferring it. Three general categories of KM processes mentioned above (creation, codification and transfer) were first introduced by two American consultants: Thomas Davenport (currently with Accenture) and Laurance Prusak (IBM Consulting). They can be divided further into sub-processes[14]. Many argue that this represents linear approach to knowledge management and should be exchanged for non-linear one, in which interdependence and interaction between the elements in the system is one of the most important characteristics.[15].

Figure 3. Non-linear model of knowledge management processes

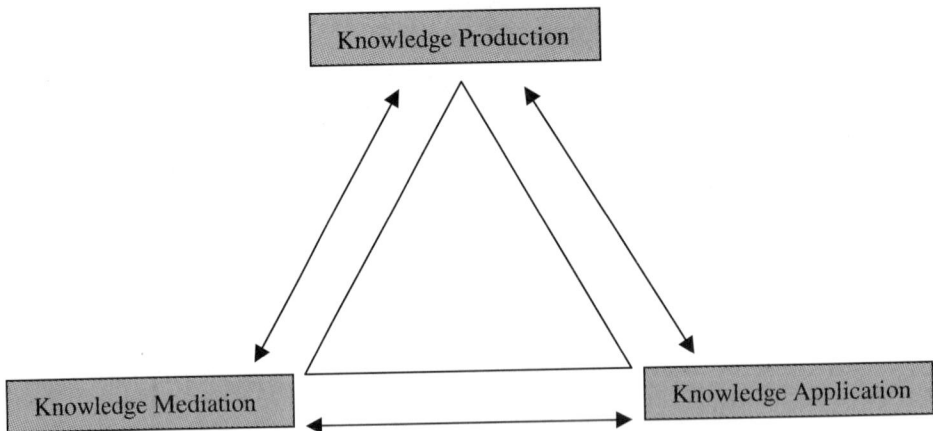

Source: OECD, Knowledge Management in the Learning Society, Paris 2000.

* **KM Team** – in KPMG, KM Team is composed of International CKO (currently Rod McKay), National CKOs, International and National CKO Coordinators, Knowledge Managers, Subject Matter Experts and Content Managers. Each function with its specific duties, rights and responsi-

---

[14] Thomas Davenport, Laurence Prusak, Working Knowledge, Harvard Business School Press, Boston 1998.
[15] OECD, Knowledge Management in the Learning Society, Paris 2000.

bilities. As suggested by different researches, CKO should perform the following tasks:

o Actively promoting the KM project, its adoption and use
o Educating staff on KM role and importance for the organization
o Educating the management team to gain its support
o Building the knowledge sharing organizational culture
o Establishing a KM strategy and systems
o Measuring the impact of knowledge management on the company's performance

* **KM Structures** – organizational structure, systems, technological and technical infrastructure etc. KM structure depends on the size, budget and characteristic of the particular company.

Strategic dimension of KMS encompasses **knowledge management strategy** (based on research by Hansen, Nohria and Tierney, consultancies follow either codification or personalization strategy[16]) and the following four KM enablers[17]:

❑ **People**

❑ **Organizational culture**

❑ **Technology**

❑ **Measurement system.**

Similar to KPMG's KMS, although, more operational and process-oriented model called KMAT – Knowledge Manage-

---

[16] For more details on differences between KM codification and personalization strategies see: Morten T. Hansen, Nitin Nohria, Thomas Tierney, What is Your Strategy for Managing Knowledge, Harvard Business Review, March-April 1999.

[17] Knowledge Management System (an its different components) within KPMG Polska was analyzed in Mariusz Strojny, Turning Knowledge into Value: KPMG Approach to Knowledge Management, (in:) Ryszard Borowiecki, Alessandro Anastasi (Editors), Enterprises in the Face of Contemporary Changes, Cracow University of Economics and University of Messina, Cracow 2000.

ment Assessment Tool was developed jointly by Arthur Andersen and American Productivity & Quality Center (Figure 4)[18].

**Figure 4. Arthur Andersen's Knowledge Management Assesment Tool
(KMAT)**

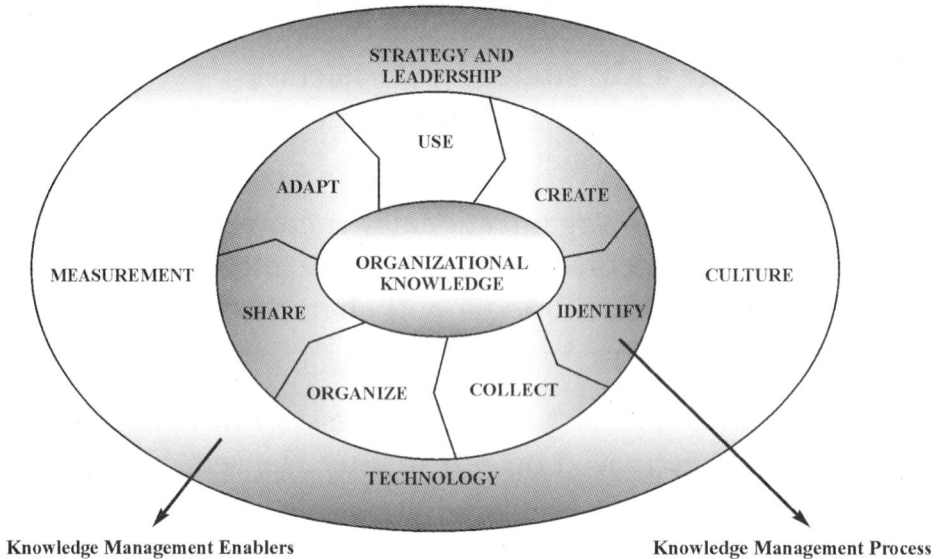

Knowledge Management Enablers   Knowledge Management Process

Source: Carla O'Dell, C. Jackson Grayson, If We Only Knew What We
Know: Identification and Transfer of Internal Best Practices, American
Productivity& Quality Center, Houston 1997.

Central to KMAT is the process itself. The dynamic
knowledge management process often starts with finding and
collecting internal knowledge and best practices Arthur Andersen is so proud of. Second is sharing and understanding
those practices so they can be used. Finally, the process includes adapting and applying those practices to new situations
and bringing them up to best practice performance levels.
Surrounding the process are so called "knowledge manage-

---

[18] Arthur Andersen uses KMAT in the form of a 24-question survey to run
two weeks assessment for a fee of approximately $ 10 000 to $ 50 000 (depending
on the company's size).

ment enablers": technology, culture, strategy and leadership and measures. These aspects of an organization's environment and infrastructure must be addressed in order for the transfer process to have a chance of working. It is worth to notice that both consultancies KPMG and AA indicate almost the same KM enablers.

Miklos Sarvary research, published recently in California Management Review, shows that literally all leading consultancies had such KM systems up and running at the end of 1997. The few exceptions were among smaller, specialist consultancies, 70% of which claimed to be still in the process of building a KM system.[19]

Knowledge Management System forms an intellectual environment facilitating knowledge generation and knowledge sharing that turns intellectual assets of the company into value and, as the result, transform knowledge into hard profits visible in the company's financial statements. But the question is how to link so many different components of KMS into one "smoothly working machine" having the ability to transform knowledge into value? Consultancies know the answer. Almost each of them has developed the unique KM tool: **Knowledge Space** (Arthur Andersen), **KWorld** (KPMG), **KnowledgeWeb** and **Ernie** (Ernst & Young), **Knowledge Curve** (PricewaterhouseCoopers), **PDNet** and **Knowledge Resource Directory** (McKinsey & Co), **Knowledge On-Line** (Booz Allen & Hamilton), **Knowledge Exchange** (Andersen Consulting) to mention just a few.

---

[19] Miklos Sarvary, Knowledge Management and Competition in the Consulting Industry, California Management Review, Winter 1999.

KWORLD – KPMG KNOWLEDGE MANAGE-MENT ENVIRONMENT

To serve global clients, KPMG and other big consultancies need to become truly global and dissolve its own internal barrier – both conceptual and regional. Clients now expect consultancies to support them with globally coordinated teams and integrated products. This means partners and staff sharing knowledge across countries and practices. To succeed in this demanding environment consultancies developed advanced knowledge management tools. Among them, probably the most powerful is KPMG's KWorld - global messaging, knowledge sharing and collaboration environment. As described by Paul Raily, KPMG International CEO – KWorld is: *"the largest global investment KPMG has ever made"*.

KWorld provides KPMG's professionals with an unprecedented means of communicating and collaborating across borders. It is being described as a "digital nervous system to the firm". KWorld is composed of the following three elements:

- **Knowledge Sharing**: providing internal end external information categorized into News, Overviews, Clients & Targets, Engagements, People, Discussions, Library, KPMG Services and Inside KPMG.

- **Communication**: enabling contact with everybody within the firm and accessing constantly updated AddressBook and CV database.

- **Collaboration**: allowing KPMG client and project team members to work together on particular assignment through the Internet

KWorld was designed and developed jointly by KPMG, Cisco Systems and Microsoft Consulting Services and is based entirely on Microsoft platform. Initially KWorld was rolled out across international networks to 25,000 users in the firm's 4 largest countries: the United States, the United Kingdom, the Netherlands and Germany. KWorld incorporated information relevant for the four charter countries, with nationally relevant content to expand as each additional country is added to KWorld. The goal for the project – which was begun in May of 1998 – was to be able to demonstrate the system to an international audience within 3 months and begin implementation of the system within 6-8 months. However, the long-term vision for KWorld is to implement it throughout the entire firm globally. Today KWorld is up and running in twenty countries worldwide and will be deployed in all remaining KPMG practices soon.

Figure 5. KWorld Homepage

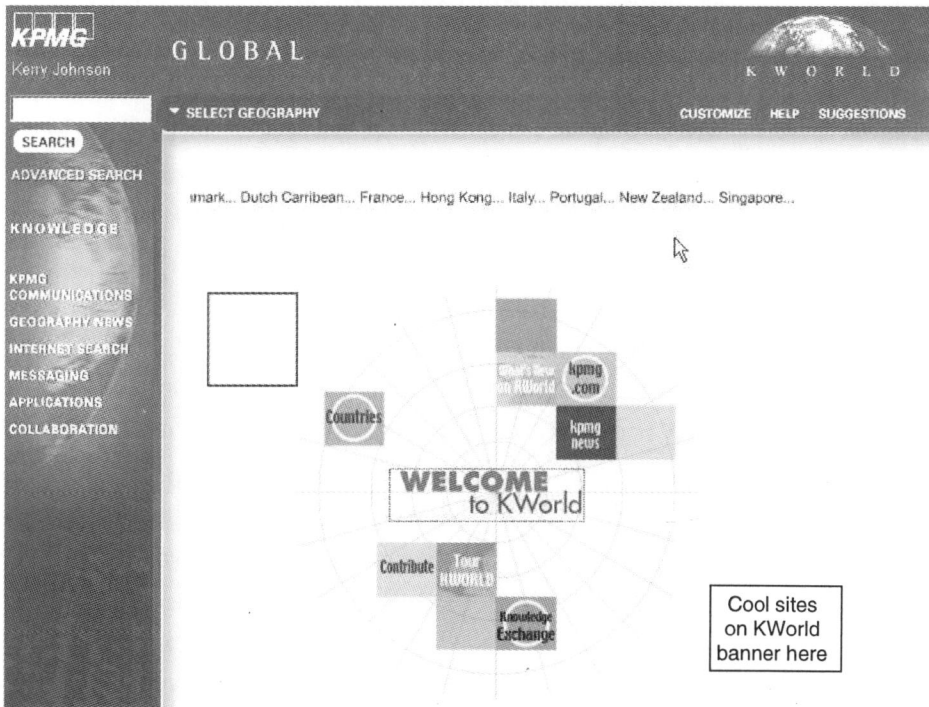

There are three business objectives behind the KWorld:

▶ **Increase Revenue**, by increasing the win rate of business development activities through providing partners and staff with shared client contact information from a common source

- ▶ **Improve Margins**, by reducing service cycle time and improving client risk management

- ▶ **Increase Employee Retention**, by reducing the amount of time needed to integrate new people, and making the life of KPMG's professionals more intellectually robust, productive, and technically sophisticated.

In order to accomplish these objectives KWorld needs to capture the vast value of the firm's knowledge assets and enable those assets to expand and grow in value through reuse. KWorld also needs to reflect and reinforce the values and business objectives of the whole organization; provide a common infrastructure to contextualize, publish and collect information across the organization; and finally be easy to use in order to foster collaboration, accelerate time to market and improve service delivery. This would not be possible without the extensive use of the enabling web-based technologies – groupware, messaging technologies, search and filtering technologies, HTML and graphical technologies. However, KWorld and knowledge management is not simply a technological fix: it is more about winning people's hearts and minds to a brand new way of working.

The driving concept behind KWorld is that it provides information content to the user in context. This is famous KPMG's **content in context approach**. The prototype demonstrated a 3-dimensional navigation model (using geography/industry segment/product and service offering as the three parameters) by which to navigate to relevant content. For example, a user can create a context defined by the 3 parameters US/Banking and Finance/Systems Integration, and will then see an array of content relevant to that context. Throughout the system, users encounter a consistent set of content selections, including both internal and external. KWorld offers access to news, overviews, information about KPMG's existing and potential clients, information on particular engagements, CVs and contact information to all KPMG staff worldwide, and finally the company huge library that contains methodologies, technical literature, white papers, templates, and tools. Knowledge Sharing part of KWorld also enables users to participate in different discussion forums and therefore supports communities of practice existing within the firm. KWorld is accessible via corporate Intranet and available on the desktop with a standard browser.

KWorld has illustrated successfully that knowledge management systems can serve as catalysts to achieving organizational change. It helped KPMG to:

▶ link globally distributed professionals to a common corporate knowledge base,

▶ establish cross-functional collaboration irrespective of geographical or organizational boundaries,

▶ provide a consistent work environment across the organization,

▶ use standard business tools widespread and therefore avoid reinventing the wheel , and

▶ replenish information resources with what is continuously learned during the course of doing business.

▶ In addition, every single professional within KPMG can use KWorld to:

▶ access to information about the firm's products worldwide

▶ receive in-depth analyses of the markets those products serve

▶ share best practices – proposals, methodologies, solutions – from anywhere in KPMG

▶ access updated analyses of the competitors' products

▶ tape into information on existing and potential clients from around the globe

▶ communicate simply and easily with others throughout KPMG, including real-time conferences

► develop professionally and individually through access to the firm's thought leaders, information and knowledge tailored to given specialty

A fully functional knowledge management tool (regardless is it KPMG's KWorld or AA's KnowledgeSpace) is enabled through dynamic **technologies** that allow any individual to "browse" the company's knowledge resources in a number of different ways, **content** or knowledge to be shared within the firm, and **infrastructure** including organizational processes and programs dedicated to support knowledge and content management. Table 2 presents leading KM tools (KWorld, Knowledge Space and KWeb) with these three perspectives.

Table 2. The leading knowledge management tools/ three perspectives

Consultancy	Knowledge Management Tool	Enabling Technologies	Content Management	Infrastructure
KPMG	KWorld	When designing KWorld KPMG entered into a strategic partnership with Microsoft, building its KM platform from a suite of integrated products: Explorer, Outlook, Office, Exchange, and NT. KPMG spends $ 100 million on KM each year.	Divided into: Internal and External News, Overviews, Clients & Targets, Engagements, Library, Infrastructure and Internal Communication	International Knowledge Management organization is composed of: Global Knowledge Exchange (leveraging knowledge within the company), Knowledge Collaboration organization, Intellectual Capital organzation (creating new knowledge), Knowledge Innovation Center (supports KWorld deployment) and GNOC (IT support).

Table 2. The leading knowledge management tools/ three perspectives (cont.)

Consul-tancy	Know-ledge Mana-gement Tool	Enabling Technologies	Content Management	Infrastructure
Arthur Ander-sen	Knowled-geSpace	AA invested $30 million in the de-velopment of GBP database and spent another $10 mil-lion on Knowle-dgeSpace during its first 18 months of operation. KnowledgeSpace is based on web and LotusNotes technologies.	In 1998 GBP con-tained over 30 000 pages describing 100 business pro-cesses. Business Link Da-tabase – with over 400 recommended internet resources, External News re-levant to the user, Discussion Grou-ps	The capturing, screening and se-lection of best practices invol-ves 3 levels of consultants: Knowledge Spon-sor, Knowledge Integrator, Know-ledge Developers. Responsible for le-veraging know-ledge within the company is AA Knowledge En-terprise and for IT support AA Technology So-lutions
Ernst & Young	KWeb	Every employee laptop comes with Lotus Notes, Microsoft Office and an Internet browser. The KWeb Search En-gine currently re-ceives roughly 20 000 hits a day	Leading practices, war stories, bench-marks, per-sonal profiles, a data-base of "Power Packs", which con-tains continuously reviewed specific collection of pre-sentations, out-standing propo-sals, competitive information, mo-dels and speciali-zed tools.	Center for Busi-ness Innovations (creates new knowledge); Cen-ter for Business Technology (stru-ctures knowledge into methods and automated tools); Center for Busi-ness Knowledge (gathers and sto-res both the firm's acquired know-ledge and exter-nal knowledge)

Andrzej Blikle

PROCESS ORGANISATION OF A COMPANY[1]
(Illustrated by the Example of "A. Blikle Ltd")

===================================== *Abstract* =====================================

The described model has been created as a joint effort of all senior managers of A.Blikle Ltd. and implemented there in June 1999. A.Blikle Ltd is a luxury-pastry company owned and run by Blikle family since 1869. The author represents the fourth generation of the family in the company. After over thirty years of his professorship in mathematics and computer science in the Polish Academy of Sciences he took over the company in 1991. In 1995 he came over the ideas of Edwards Deming and his followers and since then he is building a quality-driven learning organization. One of the management tools are seminars with managers and quality circles at all levels.

---

[1] An earlier version of this paper was published (in Polish and English) under the title *"Proces based organization of the company"* in the proceedings of the International Quality School, Warsaw, 13–14 April 2000.

INTRODUCTION

The traditional model of a company organisation – based on a feudal hierarchy as shown in Fig.1 – was developed during the early days of capitalism, in the 19th century. The basic management method at that time was to give orders and control performance. Decisions were made by a group of decision makers positioned at the top of the hierarchy. Orders were handed down to the bottom of the hierarchy while performance reports traveled to the top.

Such an organisation, created to a large extent by Frederick Winslow Taylor (1856–1915), the pioneer of the American productivity revolution, was justified by the conditions of the American industry at that time. The vast majority of workers were illiterate. Many did not speak English, since they were first generation immigrants. Therefore, production procedures covered very simple activities and it was not allowed to make any changes or to question them. It was the management job to make innovations and improvements. Workers' job was to do mechanically what they were told. Today, Taylor's idea is fiercely criticised but at that time it played an important role. Over the period of 80 years the productivity of the American industry increased 50 times.[2]

Hierarchies are typical for centralised management, based on command-and-control scheme. Such a structure is still quite common in American and European (including Polish) companies, where more emphasis is placed on manual control of people, while processes and procedures are considered less important. In most cases this involves a remuneration-by-incentives system, all kinds of sticks and carrots, "performance" based compensation scheme, in other words everything which according to the contemporary management method-

---

[2] Peter F. Drucker, Post Capitalist Society, Oxford 1993, str. 34.

ologists destroys our natural, intrinsic motivation to good and efficient work.

Taylor's productivity revolution was followed by Deming's organisation revolution. The latter occurred at the moment when the rate of market share growth became more important than the rate of production growth. It was developed at the time when it became obvious that survival and success of the company depends on its market position rather than on its productivity.

Deming's revolution destroyed the hierarchical structure of the company, which divided people into decision makers and doers, thinkers and performers. It was based on the firm belief that each company has unused creative potential in the form of knowledge, expertise, and innovative skills of yesterday's per-formers. It had led Peter Drucker to his concept of the *knowledge society*, and Peter Senge to the idea of the *learning organisation*.

A contemporary alternative to Taylor's centrally controlled company is the learning organisation, which is often referred to as a *knowledge creating organisation*. Arie de Geus, responsible for planning at Royal Dutch/Shell in the 1990's, pointed out that *"the ability to learn faster than your competitors may be the only sustainable competitive advantage"*. Peter Senge, the author of the best-selling The Fifth Discipline Fieldbook, claimed that *"the organisations that will truly excel in the future will be the organisations that discover how to tap people's commitment and capacity to learn at all levels in the organisation"*.

Thus, the role of a contemporary manager is less about allocating tasks and checking performance and more about coaching and creating procedures together with those who will use them. The question arises who should be made responsible for learning and procedure improvement processes. The traditional function of the team manager, located in the hierarchy showed in Fig.1, is not suitable, since each company has a number of knowledge areas that require continuous training. It cannot be expected that each team will have only one coach to play this role.

Figure 1 Traditional hierarchical structure

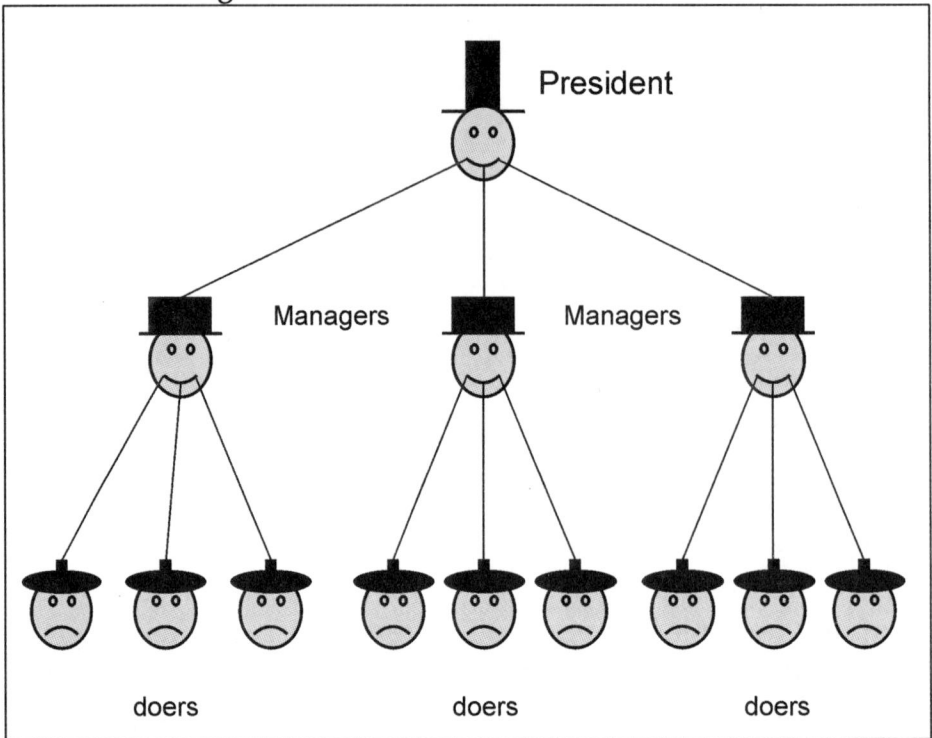

What can be done, then? First, we need to classify the scope of knowledge and expertise used in a given company. We do it by identifying key processes, treated as pools of activities relating to the same area of knowledge. A typical company has the following processes:
► production
► sales
► finance
► personnel
► maintenance
► marketing
► etc.

Processes correspond to skills, which company employees should master to various degrees depending on the specifics of their jobs. Innovations and quality improvements should be part of the processes.

Once we split the existing pool of knowledge and expertise into processes, next logical step is to appoint a group of managers responsible for individual processes. We call them *process owners*. The responsibility of these managers is to expand the employees' knowledge within the scope of each process and to ensure that relevant procedures are created and later become the objects of continuous improvement.

Obviously, the nomination of process owners does not eliminate team managers. They are needed in order to perform two critical functions:

A Develop and ensure proper interpersonal relations within the team.

B Organise work, i.e. decide who and when is going to do what.

Process completion is the responsibility of process owners, while team managers are responsible for deciding who does what and when. It should be emphasised that the "who" carries much more content than it may appear. It is not only about designating specific individuals to perform specific jobs. In the first place it is about making sure that these individuals have positive intrinsic motivation to do their job, that they get satisfaction from the proper completion of their jobs, that they feel comfortable in their teams, understand that their job is meaningful and important to the entire operation of the company, and feel that the company needs them and their work.

If we paraphrase after Peter Senge the Chinese thinker, Lao-tsu – the bad leader is he who the people despise, the good leader is he who the people praise, but the great leader is he who the people say, "We did it ourselves". Team managers should strive to be great leaders in that sense. They should focus on their primary responsibility. If they are successful in their primary job, if they do it with passion, and understand their mission, they will not have much to do with their secondary job, since people under their charge will do it for them.

In process-based model, instead of one hierarchical management group, there are two groups: process owners who take care of the operational performance of processes and team managers who are responsible for organising a conducive work environment. Processes create a non-hierarchical horizontal structure – called the *weft*, while teams build a hierarchical vertical structure – called the *plot*. Fig. 2 illustrates this model.

Fig.2 The warp-weft structure: allocations of processes to teams at A. Blikle Ltd

PROCESSES / TEAMS	THE COMPANY TEAM (RS)																					
	RETAIL DIVISION										GASTRONOMY				FIN	SUPPORT DIVISION						
	SALES DEPARTMENT									MARKETING	CAFE			CHIEF DESIGNER C.PLASTY	ACCOUNTING	PROD DPTM		ADMINISTRATION		CHIEF ENGINEER	CHIEF TECHNOL.	CHIEF IT
	SHOP 1	SHOP 2	SHOP 3	SHOP 4	SHOP 5	SHOP 6	SHOP 7	warehouse	DISTRIB		Kitchen	room	café II			PRODUCTION HIFTS	warehouse	PERSONEL	OFFICE			
marketing																						
stores sales																						
gastronomic sales																						
basic production	▓	▓	▓																			
gastronomic production																						
finance																						
personnel																						
communication																						
hardware maintenance																						
information technology																						
production technology																						
styling and ergonomics																						

THE QUALITY DOCTRINE

Process based management is a technique stemming from the general management methodology, referred to as *the quality doctrine* (see [1]), which is in turn, one of the versions of Total Quality Management as developed by E.Deming, P.Drucker and W.Shewhard. The quality doctrine is based on three principles (see: Fig. 3):

Continuous improvement, which means that everything is being improved in the company, everyone is working on improvements (not only the "Quality Department"), and improvement is a continuous effort. Continuous improvement is implemented through quality circles and training programs.

Fig.3 The quality doctrine

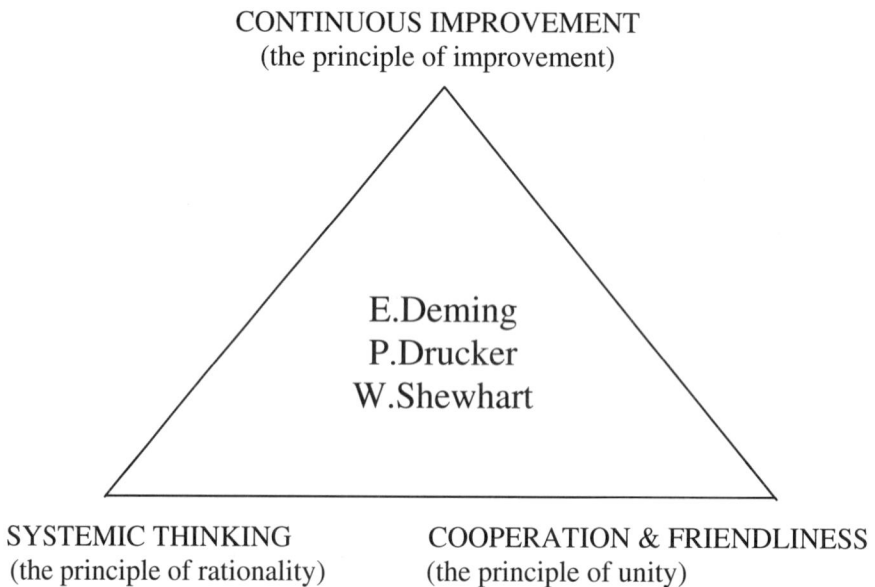

CONTINUOUS IMPROVEMENT
(the principle of improvement)

E.Deming
P.Drucker
W.Shewhart

SYSTEMIC THINKING   COOPERATION & FRIENDLINESS
(the principle of rationality)   (the principle of unity)

Cooperation and friendliness, which means that we play on the same team built on the principle of cooperation, where everyone can openly talk about the mistakes made, and where a continuous education is treated as a basic management method. It also means that all of us work to accomplish the clear and acceptable mission, which we share together.

Systemic thinking, which means that prior to taking a decision of how to perform a certain task we make an effort to understand thoroughly the mechanisms of the environment (the system) where the task is going to be performed. E.g. if subsequent marketing efforts do not trigger bigger sales, we do not neceserily increase the marketing budget but identify and analyse the causes of declining sales (e.g. deteriorated quality; untimely deliveries), and try to prevent them. If sales increase steadily for a period of three months, we do not immediately plan new investment projects but analyse the Shewhart control card of sales and make the judgement whether it is a growth trend or just statistically incidental occurrence, which does not justify any conclusions.

To be able to introduce process based management in a company one has to prepare all employees for it, change the mind frame of many people, and take a different view of the relations between supervisors and subordinates.

PROCESSES

For the purpose of this paper, the word, *process*, means any complex activity (a group of simpler activities) performed by one person or a team, and relating to certain common knowledge of the same nature[3]

Literature offers a number of different definitions of a process depending on the purpose for which it is used. A sequence of events or activities is often related to as a process.

---

[3] The world "activity" would be a better term for what we are going to call a "process". However, we shal adhere to "process", since this term has been already accepted in the literature.

In this paper, the process is not related to sequencing, since it is used only to identify a subject based classification of jobs (activities) performed by company employees and to allocate these jobs to individual teams. In order to define the time order in which activities are performed within the processes the term *procedures* shall be used.

Two groups of processes can be identified in each company. The first group includes *continuous processes*, which are continuously (repeatedly) performed, e.g. production, sales, and bookkeeping. The second group consists of *temporary processes*, for instance, the implementation of a new production line or the construction of a new workshop. This paper deals with continuous processes only. They constitute fixed elements of each management structure.

Below we list basic continuous processes identified at "A. Blikle Ltd." These are called *key processes* since they are not subprocesses of other processes. Key processes should be identified in such a way that they cover all operational activities performed within the company, i.e. the activities that are not reserved for the Management Board or Shareholders Meeting. Non-operational activities (executive management) are not included within key processes. They constitute processes of a higher logical level, since they manipulate (create and change) key processes regarded as objects.

KEY PROCESSES
1. Marketing (including external PR)
2. Store sales (all products sold to take-away)
3. Gastronomy sales (all products served to customers at a table)
4. Basic production (sweet and salty)
5. Gastronomic production (dishes and desserts)
6. Finance (the circulation of financial documents and cash)

7. Personnel (including training and internal PR)
8. Communication (the information flow and circulation of documents)
9. Machine maintenance (excluding IT)
10. Styling and ergonomics (inside and outside of the company premises)
11. Production technology (research and development)
12. Information Technology (hardware and software)

Each of these processes is a highly complex action relating to many areas and types of activities. The key processes are also called the *first level processes*. Their subprocesses are *second level processes*, while the subprocesses of these subprocesses – *third level processes*, etc. Below are two examples of process hierarchies:

Basic production (*first level process*)
  Doughnut production (second level *process*)
  Kneading dough (*third level process*)
  Forming doughnuts
  Doughnut rising (fermenting)
  Frying
  ...
Layer-cake production
  Producing the base (cake)
  Producing custards (layers)
  ...

PROCESS OWNERS

The owners of key processes decide HOW all the operational activities of the company are performed. Each key process should have an owner. Processes of lower levels may also have their owners. Each process (or subprocess) owner has the following responsibilities:

1. Define the process. Identify activities, which belong to that process. To do that the owner will have to negotiate with the owners of neighboring processes which activity belongs where.
2. Identify process suppliers and inform them about the expected quality of deliverables.
3. Identify process customers and their quality expectations.
4. Be responsible for the end result of the process.
5. Split the process into subprocesses.
6. Identify operational procedures within the process.
7. Describe jobs involved in process realisation, from the following perspectives
   • performed activities,
   • necessary knowledge and skills,
   • neccessery equipment and tools,
8. Specify labor intensity of activities and subprocesses, i.e. identify which and how many job units are necessary to complete the process and how many people should be involved in process implementation[4].
9. Specify quality standards and measurement methods, i.e. define what the quality of each product mean and specify how it is measured.
10. Develop and provide a training program for doers.
11. Encourage staff and help them implement Deming's management cycle: Plan – Do – Check – Act.
12. Ensure communication with other process owners, especially in the situation when changes occur to the process, i.e. there are new products or procedures.
13. Inform the manager of the team whenever the process is not properly performed by the team.

---

[4] It should be emphasized that the measurements of labor intensity should be made by employees who normally perform the activities. Otherwis, the results may be quite inadequate.

14. Provide technical assistance to all doers involved in the process.

Unlike traditional team managers, process owners have a global perspective of the company. Their management activities and optimisation efforts target all vertical structures through which a given process runs. As a result, the undesirable effect of the local optimisation — the typical syndrome of hierarchical management structures — is diminished.

It should also be emphasised that process owners should teach and help employees whom they do not supervise in the traditional sense of this word. For instance, in the case of a cafeteria staff, the instructions on handling financial documents will be provided to them by the owner of the *finance* process, while the instructions on coffee making will be offered by the owner of the *gastronomic production* process.

The situation described above is a new quality in management (Fig. 4). It should be noted that in the hierarchical model, each employee has only one supervisor from whom he accepts all instructions. This practice was developed at the time when the term "procedure" was unknown to management. As a result, the manual control of each employee was necessary. When process implementation is described with procedures, instructions of "what to do?" given to the employees by traditional managers, are replaced by two types of questions:

1. how to do it?
2. what to do?

Process owners come up with answers to the first question, while team managers handle the second. In the case of the traditional model, each employee has only one **supervisor** (to know whom he should listen to), while in process based model, he has a number of **advisors** specialised in different areas.

Figure 4 Two communication models: orders (hierarchy) and questions (procedures)

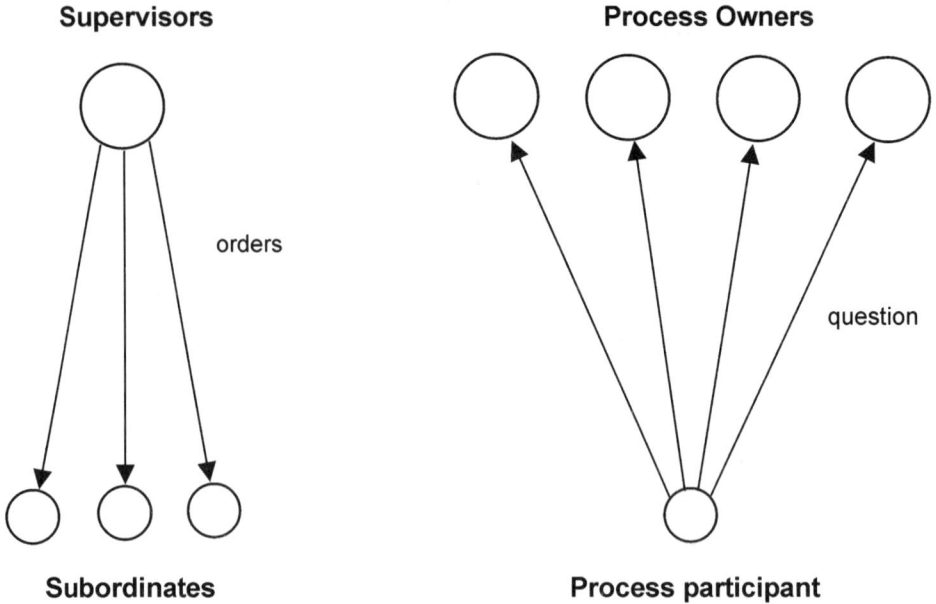

Supervisors

Process Owners

orders

question

Subordinates

Process participant

Process owners are the individuals who are given the responsibility to ensure continuous improvement of all processes performed in the company from the standpoint of organisation, technology, and equipment. In particular, they are expected to take under their charge and professional guidance, employees involved in the implementation of their process.

TEAM LEADERS

The same principle that governs processes, where each operational activity performed in the company should be allocated to exactly one process, applies also to the organisation of a team of employees, where each employee should be allocated to only one team. It should be noted, however, that whereas the allocation *activity* • *process* virtually does not change, the allocation *employee* • *team* is subject to frequent modifications because of substitutions, change of positions, and personnel movements.

The partition of the company into teams forms the following hierarchy:

❑ All employees — the whole of the company

❑ First level teams • divisions

❑ Second level teams • departments

❑ Third level teams • e.g. shops in sales department; shifts in production departments

❑ Fourth level teams • e.g. the teams in shifts

Each team should have its *team leader*, who has the following management responsibilities:

❑ Create a friendly work environment, friendly and sincere interpersonal relations, and the teamwork ethos.

❑ Educate employees, coordinate training programs.

❑ Identify the type and number of jobs in the team (based on data obtained from process owners).

❑ Provide assistance to employees to help them solve their professional, social, and personal problems. Solve conflicts between team members.

❑ Make sure that workstations are properly equipped (based on data obtained from process owners).

- Allocate jobs to team members.
- Evaluate and coordinate processes implemented by the team.
- Develop work and holiday schedules, substitutions, etc.
- Deal with recruitment[5], job descriptions, promotion, rotation of jobs, ...
- Fill in for absent employees in an emergency situations where another substitution is not possible or available.

Besides management activities, the leaders — especially those managing small teams at the basic level — perform all routine activities typical of the team. For instance, a store leader will perform the function of a salesman and kitchen leader will prepare meals.

Team leaders do not decide what tools and instruments their teams should use. This decision is made by process owner. However, it is his responsibility to equip his team with the tools. In some cases, he is able to do it on his own, while on other occasions he may approach his supervisor or the technical department with a request for help. The rule of the thumb is that the leader performs by himself all the activities falling within the scope of his job, which he is able to carry out using his own resources. He is also expected to continuously broaden the scope of his self-reliance. While evaluating the performance of team leaders, first, we look at their self-reliance and willingness to take on initiatives.

---

[5] Team managers should not have the power to fire their employees, since this leads to the substantial dependence in the employee-manager relationship, which in turn limits the sincerity of such relations. Only the Management Board should have the power to terminante the employment. Naturally, the termination proposal is filed by the department manager working with the immediate supervisor of the employee in question. The proposal should detail the reasons for the termination of employment and take into account the regulations of the Labor Law.

Team leader does not decide how many and what kind of employees should become part of the team, though they make the head count. This decision is based on the (previously measured) labour intensity of the processes, which are defined by process owners. However, he allocates jobs to people under his charge, taking into account their expertise and skills. He may approach the process owner to evaluate an employee's expertise and skills. For instance, the store manager may request help to assess which sales assistant mastered the coffee making technique, and which one knows how to operate the cash register. In order to facilitate and systemise the procedures used to evaluate skills, it may be a good idea to introduce individual skills assessment books, in which records would be made to certify that the employees acquired certain skills.

Of course, there is no reason why the team leader could not own one of the processes (or subprocesses) implemented by his team. However, in this case, he should perform both of his functions separately, and he should have a thorough understanding that they must be kept separate. All team leaders are involved in the implementation of the *personnel* process, since they carry it out within their own team. Therefore, they own this subprocess.

Team managers are entrusted with the creative function to improve continuously their teams, interpersonal relations and the overall work environment. Team managers also coordinate the work of their employees, and allocate jobs and processes to individuals.

THE OFFICER ON DUTY

In some teams, especially those positioned at the lower level of the hierarchy, there is a need of a person who would perform some organisational activities such as handling emergency cases, filling jobs that are vacant due to the absence of their holders, preparing daily reports, or attending to a customer who wants to lodge a complaint with the manager.

In the traditional team model, all such activities are performed by the team manager. However, it requires that he is present all the time, which practically means that he needs one or two deputies. In the process based model, the function of the *officer on duty* is established with the following responsibilities:

▶ Assigning jobs to employees for a period of one shift, especially in the case of emergency situations due to absences.

▶ Handling technical failures, i.e. make phone calls, call service crew, etc.

▶ Allocating other unexpected activities to employees, on an emergency basis, or doing them by himself.

▶ Performing tasks specific for a given team, e.g. in production team — writing daily production specification, in shops — cashiers reports, etc

In addition to these duties, each duty officer performs all routine functions and activities of his regular job.

The function of the duty officer is not a permanent position. It is allocated to an employee for a specific period of time, for instance, for the duration of one shift or for a couple of days. It is also recorded on the work schedule. To be able to perform this function, an employee must have certain skills, which are usually related to certain jobs. For instance, in a pastry shop, a senior sales assistant may qualify for the function of a duty officer.

Each team should have several individuals who are able to perform this function. It ensures the continuity of work within the team and eliminates the requirement of the continuous presence of the leader.

Of course, each team leader should be equipped with all the skills necessary to perform the duty function.

The team leader together with the owners of processes implemented by the team decides what skills are necessary to qualify for the duty officer. The function is set up only in the teams where it is needed. This is usually the case with the lower level teams. For instance, the function of the duty officer is necessary in shops, cafés, and production shifts but it is usually not needed at the department or higher levels.

DECISION MAKING POLICY

Managing bodies	Decision	Comments
Shareholders Meeting	Goals	Mission, strategic goals, strategic decisions, including financial decisions E.g. to become a market leader, to assume a given corporate culture, to increase capital,...
Supervisory Board	Opinions	Advisory body; review of the Management Board performance presented to the Shareholders Meeting
President of the Management Board	Objectives and tactics	The special case (majority shareholder); positioned between the Shareholders Meeting and Management Board Identify the company image and decide what is and what is not consistent with it. Identify market positioning of the company. Select the management methodology (Deming). Appoint members to the Management Board. Accept the appointed department managers and owners of key processes.

cont. page 316

cont.

Management Board	Tactics	What shall we do to accomplish these objectives? E.g. new production plant, transformation of an existing shop, new lines of traditional products; frozen goods; and Appoint process owners and team managers. Review the performance of processes and teams, ...
Process Owners	Methods	How are we going to do it and what do we need to do (workshop) See: Section 2
Team Managers	Who & what	Who is going to do it? How to organise his work environment? See: Section 3
Duty Officers	Who & what	Who and what during a given shift

If we decide to introduce the process based model in our company we shall have seven bodies participating in the decision making process (Fig. 5). Each of them makes a decision at a different level of generality and within a different scope.

In order to make and enforce decisions, the decision making bodies have to communicate (see figure 6). Their communication and final decision making policies determine the management model adopted by the company. To identify this model, we need to divide decisions into two groups:

➢ Strategic decisions • made by the Shareholders Meeting, Management Board, and the President

➢ Operational decisions • made by the Management Board, President, and other decision making bodies.

Figure 5 Information flow during strategic decision making process

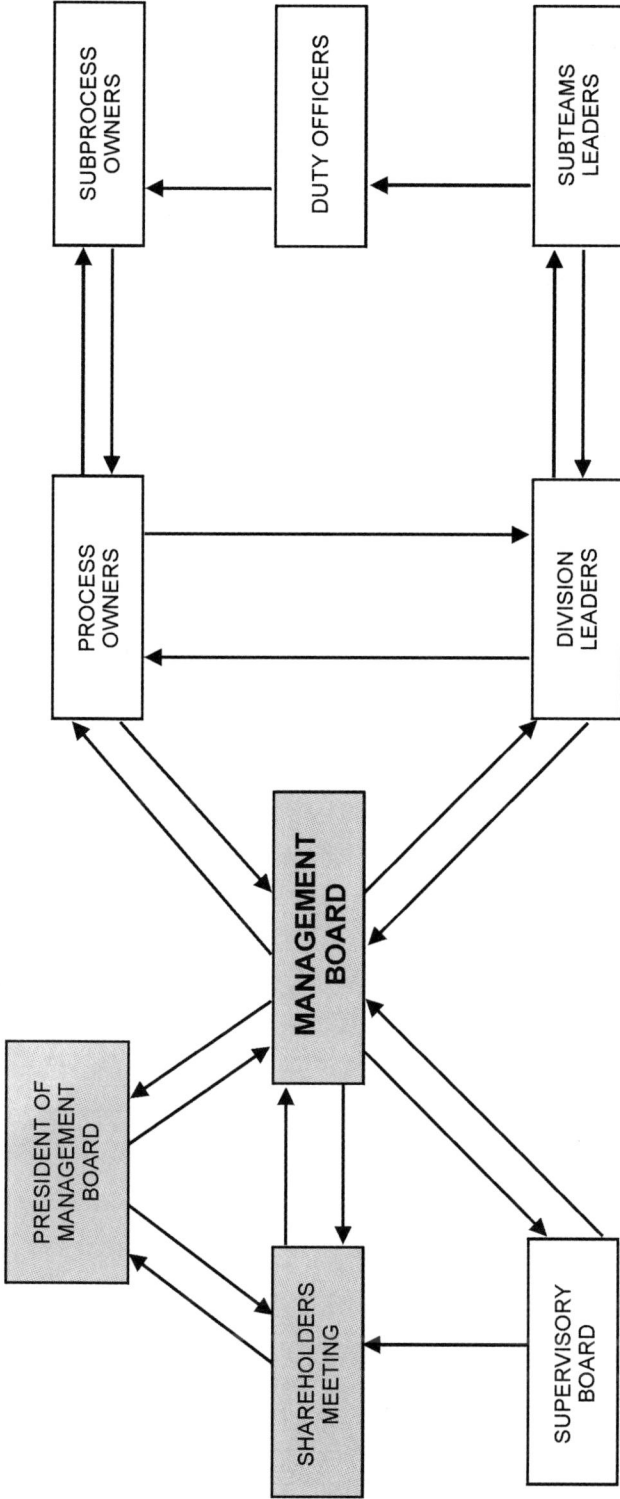

REFERENCES

[1] Andrzej Blikle, *Quality Doctrine*, International Quality School II Session, Umbrella Project, Warsaw April 12–14, 2000

[2] Peter F. Drucker, *Post Capitalist Society*, Butterworth-Heinemann, Oxford 1993, ISBN 0 7506 0921 4

[3] P.M.Senge, A.Kleiner, Ch.Roberts, B.J.Smith, *The Fifth Discipline Fieldbook — Strategies and Tools for Building a Learning Organisation*, Doubleday 1994, ISBN 0-385-47256-0

Irina Sennikova

INTELLECTUAL ENTREPRENEURSHIP IN LATVIA

Abstract

Intellectual entrepreneurship is an emerging type of entrepreneurship in Latvia. Intellectuals engaged in business usually succeed regardless of the sphere or the product they are dealing with. If the environment changes they can adopt to it, they can see opportunities where other people would not see them, having engaged in business they can create extraordinary ventures in an ordinary sphere. Therefore the author believes that intellectual entrepreneurship has its place in Latvia and can become a subject of research into the necessity of creating favourable environment for intellectual entrepreneurship and developing methods of cultivating it.

INTRODUCTION

It has been ten years now since Latvia began its transition from command to market economy. Within a relatively short time the foundations for a market economy have been laid and macroeconomic preconditions for economic growth created. Latvia has achieved political and economic stability which is assured by the country's balanced budget, strict monetary policy, and the most liberal currency exchange regime in the Baltic countries. A mass privatisation program adopted in 1994 is now nearing completion - only the privatisation of a few large enterprises still remains to be finished. The share of the private sector in agriculture, manufacturing, construction and trade now exceeds 90 per cent.

Adoption of the Law on Entrepreneurship in 1990 laid the foundation for enterprise development in Latvia and during the last ten years entrepreneurship became an integral part of business environment. However, although everybody understands that formation and development of entrepreneurship is one of the major factors for creating viable market environment, there has been no serious attempt to analyse the role and place of the entrepreneurship in the social and economic life of the country.

Unlike Western countries where the entrepreneurial traditions have been well established the post-Soviet countries, and Latvia, in particular, are still struggling with developing a comprehensive model of enterprise development. There is no system of training entrepreneurs, the courses taught at different business schools, although often bear the name of entrepreneurship, in most cases give the functional business knowledge but do not develop entrepreneurial ability of a person undergoing the study.

Until recently there has been no systematic research into the issue of entrepreneurship in Latvia. The attempts to attract the public attention to the problems of entrepreneurship development in Latvia take a form rather of a campaign then a systematic activity. The publications that have recently appeared mainly touch upon current practical issues.

This is the reason why Riga International College of Economics and Business Administration (RICEBA) has chosen entrepreneurship as one of its major research areas. But as the phenomenon of entrepreneurship is multifaceted it is a too challenging task to cover all aspects of it in one study. Therefore, in this paper I try to draw attention to the aspect of entrepreneurship that has received so far the least attention, and the mere existence of which is still under question. – the newly emerging concept of intellectual entrepreneurship.

According to the recent research into social and economic aspects of entreprenersip in Latvia in the transition period, intellectual level of Latvian entrepreneurs is rather high: 46,6% of entrepreneurs when started their business had higher education; 6,2% – academic degrees. 31,1% of entrepreneurs increased the level of their education after they started their business. This fact encouraged me to make an assumption that phenomenon of intellectual entrepreneurship, which is currently being developed and studied by prominent scholars in other countries has its place in Latvia as well, and can be studied as a specific type of entrepreneurship.

Experience and examples from business practice show that entrepreneurship is not directly related to the education level but depends mostly on entrepreneur's personal features and abilities to reach goals. But the main factor in achieving business success can be attributed to the ability to see the business process as a whole, the process which appears in the form of a complete image. And here the initial assumption was made that 1) intellectuals might have more developed ability to get the complete image of the business and thus become more successful and 2) as intellectuals are considered to be fascinated by the new and unknown they would always try to create something unique. Because of their critical mind and ability to see flaws in what already exists they would try to overcome deficiencies by introducing new concepts to old ideas.

If this assumption proves to be right, it will then give a reason to a further research into the necessity of creating favourable environment for intellectual entrepreneurship and development of the methods cultivating it (via appropriate education and training programmes, consulting centres, etc.).

A starting point in this research was to identify individual entrepreneurs who might be considered to be intellectuals. Another idea was that they all had to share at least two characteristics:

❑ activity in a standard area but using non-standard solutions in founding and running their businesses;

❑ having created something new and achieved significant results, thus setting rather high standards in their industry.

Ten people who were selected represented different types of business: education, retail, catering, manufacturing, real estate, music and all had different backgrounds. They were:

♦ A biologist, doctor of biophysics, who after collapse of the research institute he was working at, started his business career as a general manager of the newly established retail chain and who later established his own businesses – one in real estate and another in a service industry, opening a dry cleaner's.

♦ A mathematician and physicist, doctor of physics, who is now the owner and president of the biggest household and cosmetics retail chain, as well as of some other companies, and who is also known as financial entrepreneur buying companies, which are going into liquidation, and reselling them.

- A university professor, doctor of economics, but also a former sportsman, who for a long time was engaged in pharmaceutical business and then was invited by the shareholders of a newly established private university for the position of the Rector, which he still holds, and where during the course of time he became the major owner.

- A university professor, doctor of philosophy who established another private university where he is the Rector.

- A biologist, who previously worked at the immunology research institute as a research fellow and saw her future career as a scientist and who is now engaged in real estate business.

- A chemist, holding doctoral degree in chemistry who worked at the Latvian Academy of Science as a research fellow and who started his business career by commercialising his knowledge, but later became engaged in retail and manufacturing business.

- A former university professor, doctor of economics who inherited denationalised family property and a registered trademark which he then used to establish a very successful bookstore chain.

- A famous Latvian composer who established the musical centre containing a concert hall, a disco and a restaurant and where he is the owner and art director, and who is also engaged in promoting young talented singers and musicians.

- An actor, a director of Latvian National Opera, who also owns several upmarket restaurants in Riga and who is calling business his hobby.

- A Latvian-American investor, president of Latvian-American Chamber of Commerce, president of a big diversified company and owner of several other businesses.

By the time this paper was written five of these people had been interviewed. The interviews consisted of two parts and included both structured and unstructured elements. In the unstructured part the interviewees were talking generally about themselves, about their businesses, about dramatic turns in their careers, contemplated on the issues of intellectual entrepreneurship. However, to ensure the consistency with the research done in Poland the structured part also included approximately the same set of questions used by Professor Stefan Kwiatkowski.[*] Each interview lasted for about two hours and it was agreed that once initial interviews are held with all identified entrepreneurs, the workshop will be held to discuss the findings and draw conclusions.

In this paper I will not present complete interviews but will briefly introduce the five interviewed people, whose stories will be taken for further analysis and developed into cases.

INTELLECTUAL ENTREPRENEURS – WHO ARE THEY?

Mark – a biologist by education. In 1973 graduated from the Latvian State University. Worked in Kaunas research institute of cardiology and pathology of cardio-vascular system. In late 70ies defended PhD thesis in biophysics, the title of which was 'Energetic Profile of the Open Calcium Channel'. Continued working as a full-time researcher in the filed of biophysics. Later when coming back to Riga extended the interests into the area of ecology.

After collapse of the Soviet Union, which also resulted in the collapse of the research institutions the obstacles made him go into business. He started his business career in Ko-

---

[*] Stefan Kwiatkowski, 1999, The Intellectual Entrepreneur (initial study), in: knowledge café for Intellectual Entrepreneurship, Warsaw, page 48

blenz, a diversified company dealing with retailing, whole-sale, construction and development. Then due to certain tensions with the owners (he did not specify what the tensions were) he left the company and established his own business.

At the moment he has three companies: one dealing with real estate, one dentist clinics (established for the wife, as he says) and a recent venture, registered in March 2000 – the company IMA Service, providing dry cleaning and washing services. The company employs about 30 people and is growing.

Being well educated Mark still felt the necessity to get a systemised knowledge of business and in 1999 completed an MBA programme. His final dissertation was devoted to the analysis of the Latvian market in terms of investment opportunities and IMA Service was born as a result of the research.

Mark has very conceptualised way of thinking and develops models for his business ideas.

He has some regrets that he is not a scientist any more as those were the best days in his life, he was happier working with his oscillograph than operating in business. He had to withdraw from the research into non-equilibrium (disbalanced) territories in which he was involved and was very interested in. He says that it were the obstacles, which forced him to business.

Rafail – a mathematician and physicist by education, in 1984 graduated from Riga Polytechnics (now Riga Technical University) majoring in applied mathematics, then completed his postgraduate studies and obtained a doctoral degree. Taught mathematics at the polytechnics and worked as a junior research assistant at the Light Industry Research institute.

Got actively involved in business at the time of Gorbachev's reforms, when he participated in the so-called co-operative movement. Now Rafail is a well-known businessman – he is a president of Koblenz Co, President of Koblenz &Partners Co, President and owner of 'Drogas' – the major retail cosmetics and household goods chain, President of Koblenz Drosiba (Security Company). Has recently moved into financial business – buys companies going into liquidation and then resells them. Rafail has a non-standard way of thinking, combines abstract thinking with rationality. Is very aggressive, non-sentimental businessman.

Boris – a university professor. Until the age of 26 was actively engaged in sports (fencing) and achieved quite good results – for many times was the champion of Latvia , participated in the World Cup twice. Having finished his sports career went into the academia. For many years worked at the University of Latvia, from which he previously graduated and obtained PhD in Economics.

During Gorbachev reform period he got actively involved in enterprising activity – established a business school at the Riga Town Hall, which dealt with adult education and provided various training programmes for emerging business activities. Then established another venture – Association of Business Co-operation, the main activity of which was establishing contacts between various businesses, exchange of information, as well as business tourism. Then later, when Latvia gained her independence, founded a pharmaceutical company. The company was importing pharmaceutical products (mainly from Poland) and distributing them in the Latvian market. Approximately at the same time he was offered a position of rector of Riga International College of Economics and Business Administration (RICEBA) that had been in existence for a year by that time. Therefore he was not a founder of RICEBA initially, but an appointed rector. However, due to very high entrepreneurial abilities on one hand and relative indifference of the shareholders to the development of the college, the school very quickly became associated with his name. He is now one of the major shareholders of the school and all major achievements of the college can be attributed to him.

Sergey – in 1973 graduated from Riga Polytechnics chemical faculty. Then did his postgraduate studies at Moscow State University where he defended his PhD thesis, the title of which was 'Behaviour of Nonstehiometric Complexes in Water – Salt Solutions". For a long time worked at the Academy of Science of Latvia in the Wood Chemistry institute as a research fellow.

The first enterprising attempt was made in 1991 when Sergey with two other young scientists established a company called Scientific Shop. As the Academy was very conservative, young scientists felt rebellious against the stagnation of the old tradition and formed a team of young talented people who wished to see their research being applied, which in its turn would lead to both financial reward and satisfaction of scientific thought. Therefore, the activity of the company was based on securing technical-research contracts for various manufacturing enterprises all over the Soviet Union.

The collapse of the Soviet Union and disintegration of economic links between the republics eventually led to the collapse of the company. However, it is worth mentioning that in 1992, when Latvia was an independent state already, Scientific Shop had a very successful project in the Russian town Velikie Luki with the factory of electro-technical porcelain. The research laboratory of the factory and the Scientific Shop worked jointly on introducing a new side product, a cleansing paste. In terms of financial reward, thanks to the Scientific Shop the researchers of the laboratory for a month work gained the amount of their average annual salary.

The second stage of Sergey's entrepreneurship activity started in 1992 when he established a company 'FIL UN KO', which stood for photoinitiators and lacquers. The idea of the company was to develop polymers and photoinitiators and produce optic recording media (CDs). This idea did not work well, although pilot batches were produced. Sergey explains it by the fact that there were too many people involved and everybody wanted money. He says that it was greediness that ruined the idea.

But some of the company's projects were very successful. Thus 'FIL UN KO' had a manufacturing line at the Latvian factory BIOLAR for producing lacquers, of their own invention, that were sold to furniture industry. The lacquers were of very good quality and were successfully competing with the famous German 'Merk' lacquer manufacturer products because a product of the same quality was offered for much lower price. But again because of the collapse of the industry the demand for the product had declined and the company had to think of something else.

Now 'FIL UN KO' specialises in producing parts for industrial equipment to customer specifications on a one-off basis and mainly, exports to former Soviet Union countries. The company is also now looking to the West for new markets and is undertaking promotional activities in Germany (where its products are much cheaper than German counterparts due to lower labour costs). The firm also tried to export to markets such as Britain, but there are problems with miss perception that Central and Eastern European companies are not quality producers. The company in fact imports raw materials from Germany, Sweden and Finland for finishing.

In addition to the manufacturing facility 'FIL UN KO' also has two shops, one selling auto spare parts and another selling food products.

Vija – a biologist by education, specialising in immunology. In 1986 graduated from Latvian State University, faculty of biology. While still being a student she was thinking of pursuing scientific career. Straight after graduating, started working at the Latvian Academy of Science at the Institute of Microbiology as a junior research fellow and was very eager to undertake doctoral studies. In fact her doctoral theses was almost ready when she realised that the Academy was absolutely stagnant. People of older generation were dictating 'the rule of the game' and any initiative on the juniors' part was discouraged. There were times when the laboratory had absolutely nothing to do. And Vija says that was the most terrible thing, as for her the main thing is the result. Therefore one day in 1990 she said that she had had enough and quitted.

Therefore in 1990 Vija's business career started. From 1992 to 1995 she worked in two totally different companies, holding absolutely different positions – at the Latvian Collective Fishers Union first as foreign relations department manager and later as the general manager's counsellor for foreign and local trade, and afterwards at them car dealer company 'Musu Motors' as procurator.

In 1995 she became a director of the company 'R.Gaila Birojs' which deals with real estate management. Initially, when selecting potential candidates for the research I chose Vija as she definitely fits into the category of intellectuals. But later, when interviewing her, I had a slight dilemma – I discovered that she was a manager, but not the owner or the founder of the company. This fact raised some doubt as to her suitability for the category of intellectual **entrepreneur**. However, having considered her situation and especially the fact that the owner of the company is located in another country and, in fact, the company is in Vija's entrepreneurial hands, I decided that she should not be eliminated as a possible 'subject of the research'. On the other hand, she can bring another perspective to the issue.

THE SUMMARISED VIEW OF INTELLECTUALS ON ENTREPRENEURSHIP

As I mentioned earlier the interviews included a structural element, when everybody were asked the same set of questions. This was done in order to see whether there is a simlarity in understanding the issues.

a) How would you describe an intellectual?

When discussing the definition of an intellectual all interviewed stressed the ability to communicate, think in the abstract, ability to reflect, to see the picture as a whole (e.g. to see not the church but religion), to understand the versatility of the concept and naturalness of diversity. Solid educational background was also attributed to the feature of an intellectual, however, on itself, it does not guarantee belonging to the category. It was also stressed that an intellectual would have an ability to use intellectual capacity in everyday life, but would do things differently. There was also an opinion that an intellectual deals mostly with theories and concepts.

b) How would you describe an entrepreneur?

A collective image of the entrepreneur drawn from the interviews looks as follows: It is a person capable of perceiving a complete image of an efficient project, risk-taking and goal oriented, *'resultaholic instead of workaholic'*, a person looking for new ideas, the one who is able to make profit from any potential source and also the one who bears full responsibility for the business.

c) Are there possible linkages between the world of entrepreneur and the one of an intellectual?

Everybody gave a positive answer. They said that there is an obvious link – the urge to see behind the horizon. An intellectual can reconcieve what is known to non – intellectuals thus being able to implement an old idea from an absolutely new angle. These are two harmonious worlds where there are no limits to perception of the world.

d) What made you go into business?

The common feature is that none of the interviewed said that going to business was planned or foreseen decision. Coming from different backgrounds everybody agreed that mostly these were the circumstances that made them undertake entrepreneurial initiatives. Things like need for money, striving to self-actualisation, stagnation and consequently collapse of the old system were also mentioned.

e) What did you have to give up as entrepreneur?

One of the entrepreneurs compared it with sport. Like in sport you have to give up free time, some of your previous entertainments and pleasures. Everybody had to give up lots of free time. Those who were engaged in science also mentioned that unfortunately, they had to give up science as well, the thing they liked and were interested in. They all still have a nostalgic feeling about it.

f) What did you gain?

Opportunity to express oneself, self-confidence and self-respect, application of personal abilities. Stability, including financial one, independence. The knowledge of life.

g) Do you have any intellectual challenges?

All interviewed see the entrepreneurship as intellectually rewarding activity especially when introducing new projects or trying to make a major breakthrough in the business. They say that business is about future and it gives an opportunity to predict it. Business is a logical structure where one takes unrelated fragments and builds a finished product, whatever it might be. It can be compared with playing chess when on one hand you have to see the over-all strategy of the game and on the other hand have to follow the sequence of the moves very carefully as wrong sequence can lead to the defeat. 'Playing business chess' is considered to be intellectually rewarding.

h) Your biggest success, your biggest failure?

Everybody said that both their biggest success and their biggest failure are yet to come. But things like people's believe in them, and the fact that they have followers were attributed to the success. Life consists of small successes e.g. to sell 'hopeless' property or return 'hopeless' debt. There are certain failures but none of the interviewed was able to mention them. They all said that if you do fail, you don't dwell upon it, but try to work it for your advantage in future.

i) Your personal goals?

This was the most difficult question to answer. One person said that he wants Latvia to achieve the economic level of an average European country, where all entrepreneurs will have equal opportunities. Another person said that his personal goal is to have a sense of achieved self-actualisation, be independent financially and physically, to be able to provide support for those who could not succeed in this life.

j) Being an intellectual, does it help in business or makes it more complicated?

It works both ways. On one hand it helps as you can build a complete concept or a model of the project, you can reason with people, make them believe in your idea. On the other hand sometimes it makes your life more complicated as you have a tendency to conceptualise judging from ideal circumstances. Therefore you would spend time reflecting, building concepts, assuming that everything will happen according to the model you have built in your head. Often this proves to be wrong as you have to make adjustments to people's dishonesty, will to pursue win-lose policy, unfair practices.

Another opinion was that being an intellectual is an integral part of successful entrepreneur, as cleverness allows to fulfil ones' responsibilities at an adequate level, whereas intellect always strives for development.

k) Should intellectuals go into business?

The unanimous answer was a definite yes as they would make business more civilised, and bring more ethics into it.

INTELLECTUAL VS. NON – INTELLECTUAL ENTREPRENEURSHIP

Although initial candidates for the research were intellectuals engaged in business activities, discussions with them led me to consider the issue of intellectual entrepreneurship from another angle.

If you ask a question about the most successful entrepreneurial venture in Latvia, most of the people would name a chain of fast-food restaurants 'Lido'. When 'my' intellectuals were asked whether the 'Lido' chain can be considered as a case of intellectual entrepreneurship, most of them, having reflected on that, gave the positive answer and I tend to agree with them.

For the reader to understand what we are talking about I will try to give an idea of the place. There is nothing new in the concept of 'Lido', which is based on providing high quality national food. But whenever a person enters it for the first time the first reaction is 'Wow!', as you can see there is something special beginning with the design, and finishing with the food itself, The place is stylised into traditional Latvian countryside, but you get a sense of absolute naturalness, you see that everything is real there. You perceive it as a flawless, complete piece of art. But at the same time it is a very profitable, economically successful project. 'Lido' restaurants are ideal places for having a quick healthy meal, for business lunches, for entertaining guests or for weekend family outings. Besides the food, the place offers lots of entertaining opportunities both for adults and children, it organises various festivals and celebrations of national folk holidays. Despite the fact that it is made in national Latvian tradition, as Latvia is multy-ethnic community it also organises events on traditional Slavic holidays, e.g. Russian pancake week with national public games, national Russian, Ukraine and Belorussian cuisine. And while politicians are still debating on the issues of integrating the society the 'Lido' owner is practically implementing it.

Originally when selecting potential candidates for the research I did not have any intention to consider the owner of 'Lido' Mr. Kirsons as a possible subject for the reserch for a very trivial reason - he did not fit traditional understanding of an intellectual as he is a former barman who started his business ten years ago with a small restaurant in the centre of Riga. But on the other hand he certainly fits into the six descriptions of intellectual entrepreneurship suggested by B. Johannisson, S.Kwiatkowski and T. Dandridge in their article 'Intellectual Entrepreneurship Emerging Identity in a Learning Perspective'.**

** knowledge café for Intellectual Entrepreneurship, op. cit., pp. 29–46

Descriptor 1: The person draws on many different constituencies, which forms the base for influence.

'Lido' case: Mr. Kirsons, the founder and the manager, although keeping rather low profile, is a very influential person in Latvia. His opinion is valued, his advice asked for by different groups of people.

Descriptor 2: With a diverse knowledge base the person can combine information-screening and absorption capacity.

'Lido' case: Mr. Kirsons is knowledgeable in more then one professional area. Having started from a small restaurant, his business developed into a very diversified venture, which includes own brewery, food processing facility, food shops, entertainment. He is now engaged in a new project – building a big entertainment park next to the biggest 'Lido' place, which envisages construction and management of a five – star hotel.

Desctiptor 3: The person epitomises the concept of 'glocal'

'Lido' case: Having a local, Latvian idea in the core of the concept, he conducts his business locally, but maintains global awareness and international contacts. His managers are offered lots of study and exchange opportunities abroad and he is currently investigating the options for going international.

Descriptor 4: Serendipity replaces luck as environment becomes enactable.

'Lido' case: All new projects are based on thorough and controlled preparation, the ability to see the newly born idea as a whole and vast tacit knowledge allows to make moves into right direction, allowing to be ahead of competition.

Descriptor 5: The person experiences entrepreneurial challenges as intellectually rewarding.

'Lido' case: Expanding the business, and reaching new horizons became an obsession for Mr. Kirsons. He says that he is doing it because he cannot not to do it. He sets ambitious goals and having reached them is eager to see what is beyond.

Descriptor 6: The person has a concern for ethical and hu-
manitarian issues.

'Lido' case: He consistently follows the policy of purchasing food only from local farmers. His business employs hundreds of people and although the demands towards the personnel are very strict in meeting the quality standards, he runs his operations on a win-win basis. He offers very competitive salaries to his staff, invests a lot into personnel training and development believing that it will benefit the business in the long run.

Unexpected involvement of the enterprise like 'Lido' into the study made me look at the problem of Intellectual Entre-prenurship from a broader angle. What is it that makes en-trepeneurship intellectual? Is it only encyclopaedic general knowledge or can broad professional knowledge contribute to it as well? Or is it an ability of intellect to understand the entrepreneurial mechanism, the functional principles of which can be followed in various settings?

One of the interviewed intellectuals, Mark, said that he as a researcher has always been fascinated by the beauty of the idea, which is prerogative of science. But he also became fas-cinated by the beauty of achieving the result, which, in his opinion, is prerogative of entrepreneurship. However, I be-lieve that these two things -the beauty of the idea and the beauty of the result are connecting the two worlds – the one of an intellectual and the one of an entrepreneur.

Trying to prove this idea I will try to draw a parallel between 'Lido' and another venture, which was established by a person with the similar background, also a barman (there should be something in the profession that develops entrepreneurial mind!), who founded a wide - scale retail business in Latvia, 'Gerkens un Ko', a kind of alternative to Western 'C&A' chain. These two businesses were founded approximately at the same time i.e. ten years ago. Both chose to compete on volume offering reasonable prices. But whereas 'Lido' while offering low prices never sacrificed quality, but made it possible because of very efficient operational processes and logistics, which built the company's competitive advantage, 'Gerkens' was offering low prices, because of offering poor quality products, bordering with second-hand clothes. Among the people 'bought from Gerkens' became the synonym of poor quality. Another distinctive feature of two businesses is that while Kirsons was investing into development of the idea he was pursuing, Gerkens was investing into his personal wealth. With appearance of new supermarkets his position of a market leader turned out to be unsustainable. As a result 'Lido' is generally recognised as a very successful entrepreneurial venture, which is still growing, and Gerkens experiencing its decline phase.

One can argue that Kirson's success can be attributed to the fact that he was dealing with the familiar area as he spent many years in the catering business, but Gerkens became involved in the new industry, which was new to him. But what are the reasons of success of the intellectuals in business I was referring to earlier: Mark and Rafail having established a very successful retail chain and Mark then founding a dry cleaning business? Did they study these issues in their doctoral dissertations? Or Sergey, the chemist, becoming successful businessman dealing with metalwork manufacturing and managing two shops? Or a Biologist being a smart property dealer? In my opinion, the answer here is that all of them due to their intellectual abilities reconcile the beauty of the idea with the beauty of the result, thus becoming the drive for the economic development of the country. Where then does Gerkens belong? And Kirsons? Well, my research has only started...

CONCLUSIONS

Looking at the enterprise development in Latvia, we can identify three branches of business development:

➤ The one which is based on the exploitation of the old, existing business. These are mostly former state owned enterprises that underwent privatisation. Some of them are more, some less successful, but they are not entrepreneurial ventures in its true sense. In most cases, those who privatised them had a privilege 'to be at the right place at the right time' or to know right people. In fact, in some way it is similar to the success of those who were successful in Soviet times because of being close to distribution, when deficit was ruling the game.

➤ Standard, craftsman type business, which offers goods and services for the local market and is either not interested in or not capable of growing. These are mostly small businesses established by professionals in certain areas. The paradox here is that there are lots of examples when people having all the knowledge of the industry they are in, have high potential to succeed, but due to various reasons they fail.

➤ Intellectaul business or intellectual entrepreneurship - a new, at least for Latvia, type of business when people of various backgrounds having engaged into business can create extraordinary ventures in an ordinary sphere. The idea can be repeated, but you still get a sense of uniqueness. People engaged in this type of business usually succeed regardless of the sphere or the product they are dealing with. If the environment changes they can adopt to it, they can see opportunities where other people would not see them. Due to their ability to embrace the process as a whole they follow a universal method. Intellectual entrepreneurs bring stability to the economics, they are survival guarantors, they surround themselves with specialists and ensure employment opportunities for a big number of people.

Therefore the main conclusion of this paper is that phenomenon of intellectual entrepreneurship has its place in Latvia and can become a subject of research with the ultimate purpose of developing economic potential of the country. But the question which still remains, is whether it is a universal phenomenon or it is relevant only to the post Soviet countries where the collapse of the system made people change their profession, leave jobs they liked, forget their research aspirations and undertake the unknown. Yes, they have become successful entrepreneurs, but are we sure that the Government has not made a mistake by pushing these people out of the system. Couldn't they contribute more to the development of the country by working with their oscillographs or microscopes, didn't we miss any major scientific breakthroughs?

Renata Gut

COMMERCIAL RAMIFICATIONS OF THE BRAIN

„Manage Yourself
and Then Your Company: set an Example"

Peter Drucker

━━━━━━━━━━━━━ *Abstract* ━━━━━━━━━━━━━

Research on the brain and how it learns, develops, functions, and controls human activity is growing. A review of Nobel price winning research on the brain shows that the subject has attracted serious attention throughout the century. For inventors, scientists and entrepreneurs, our knowledge of creativity suggests that relaxation promotes the association of new ideas to old problems. In Poland, the whole topic of mental productivity and its enhancement has been constrained by long delays in the publication of research on the subject. However, recent market demands for self-improvement books has resulted in a shorter lead time between original publication and translation into Polish. The brain can be trained to enhance physical performance. Individuals can prolong their mental keenness through continued mental activity. These and other insights suggest that the potential for commercialization of the brain's output is limitless.

The structure and structuring of the brain are fascinating subjects. During the past ten years, my passion for learning about the brain has contributed to my professional and private life. As I acquired new information about the brain and how it works, I have attempted to apply this information to improve my own decision making. This paper explores how knowledge of the brain can have useful implications for business and society.

BEGINNINGS OF SYSTEMATIC RESEARCH ON THE BRAIN

The human brain combines billions of cells which incessantly exchange information with one another. The brain controls both mechanical functions of our body as well as our emotions, the ability to think, memory, and our consciousness. Research on the mind has repeatedly earned the Nobel prize as is revealed below.

The past ten years of the twentieth century were named the decade of the knowledge on brain. This is an appropriate designation since all human knowledge is developed and processed throug this wonderfully complex instrument. Researchers and scientists have been working in such areas as neurology, physics, pharmacology, psychology, sociology, biology, cybernetics, linguistics, immunology, surgery, mathematics and many others. These scientists have paved the way to new disciplines of science. As new disciplines emerge, the next ten years may be devoted to defining the relationships and connections between them. Through investigation of the brain, new disciplines came into being, such as neurophysiology, neuropharmacology, biocybernetics and psycholinguistics. Sciences are interrelated. It is no wonder that towards the turn of the century the scientists decided, with courage and determination, to join their efforts to synthesize the output for the first time in the history of mankind and to such a large extent. At the beginning of this process probably very few people realized that developing knowledge on how the brain works would prove to be a multi-level, mysterious, significant and fascinating field.

NOBEL PRIZE RESEARCH ON THE BRAIN

That enormous value of research on the brain is reflected by the number of Nobel prizes awarded:

1902 Ivan Pavlov (Russia) introduces the concept of the **conditioned reflex.** By means of this concept he explained more complex neural activities, especially learning.

1906 is the year of **cortex functions**. Charles Scott Sherrington (British) issues the book *Integrative Actions of the Nervous System* where he presents the results on the experiments with stimulating and excluding certain areas of the cortex in animals. The same year Camillo Golgi from Italy and Santiago Ramony Cajal from Spain are awarded the Nobel prize for their research on the **structure of the nervous system.**

1929 The first EEG. Johannes Berger (German) publishes the results of his research on electric activity of the brain in *On the Electroencephalogram of Man*. It is the first description of an EEG where the electrodes were placed to the neurocranium and thus the potentials of brain biocurrent were measured. The picture of brain impulses is affected by age and the state of consciousness (daily activity, relaxation, sleep, wakefulness) and reveals lesions typical of neurological illnesses. Although not rewarded with the Nobel prize, this achievement marks a significant breaktrough in the understanding how the brain works.

1932 Studies on neurons. The Nobel prize for Charles Scott Sherrington and Edgar Douglas Adrian from Great Britain for their discoveries of neuron actions.

1936 Nobel prize for impulses. Another Nobel prize for neurobiologists, Henry Hallett Dale, British and Otto Loewi,

Austrian, for their description of chemical compounds responsible for transmitting neural impulses.

1955 'transportation' of impulses – American neurobiologist Julius Axelrod contributes to the explanation of transmission mechanisms of nervous impulses in the nerve terminals (synapses).

1970 contacts and signals. Bernard Katz (British), Ulf Svante von Euller-Chelpin (Sweden) and Julius Axelrod (American) receive the Nobel prize for discoveries concerning the humoral transmitters released in the nerve terminals.

1977 hypothalamus. The Americans Roger Guillemin and Andrew Shally are awarded the Nobel prize for discoveries and research on hypothalamus, one of the most important portions of the brain.

1979 computer tomography. Allan H. Cormac (American) and Godfrey N. Hounsfield (British) are given the Nobel prize for inventing computer tomography, now a basic diagnostic method in neurology.

1981 differences in brain hemispheres. Roger W. Sperry (American) discovers fuctional specialization of brain hemispheres. Receives the Nobel prize. The same year the Americans David H. Hubel and Torsen N. Wiesel win the Nobel prize for their discoveries in information processing in the sight enter.

1986 how nerves grow. The American neurobiologists, Rita Monatalcini and Stanley Cohen become Nobel-prize winners in medicine for discovering the nerve growth factor.

1991 plasticity of the brain. Bert Sackmann and Erwin Neher, Germans, are rewarded for their discovery and study of the ionic canals in cell membrane of the neuron. Through these canals neurotransmitters are transmitted. Sackmann joined the studies on brain plasticity carried out by other scientists since the 1960s.

1998 regeneration of brain tissue. Martin Schwab from Zurich University regenerates neurons and spinal cord in ats.

Nitrogen and emotions. The Americans Robert F. Furchgott, Luis J. Ignerro and Ferid Murad are awarded the Nobel prize for discoveries concerning the brain. Their study focused on nitrogen oxide, a signalling substance which, permeating cell membranes can activate transmitters. It has also a significant role in activating emotions.

1999 learning generates neurons. Elizabeth Gould from Princeton University publishes papers on generating neural cells. She finds out that the more intensely the hippocampus works the more effectively new neurons are created.

Numerous methods are used for close observations of brain processes. The earliest investigatory tool was the EEG which provided only the data on electrical activity of the brain. Current methods enable us to 'peek in' the body of a living human. EEG, NMR, or PET map the construction of the brain. Lately the world has admired colour photograps of an impulse running between synapses. Another dream has come true – 'we have seen the flight of human thought'. Isn't it fantastic?

Research on the brain helps us to explore the following issues: 'What made our species the dominating one? What enables us to leave the Earth and go to the space, explore submarine depths, create unique pieces of art, and examine the interior of our bodies? How are we able to receive signals from the surrounding world, collect and process that data?

How are we able to create, experience and inspire progress and be aware of our existence?'

Human achievements are attributable to the most mysterious organ of the human body – the BRAIN. Considering the eons of the evolutionary process of our species, the 'certainly' has been possible for a very short time. There are many questions concerning the brain. Among them are questions about the structure of the brain, reasons for its smooth functioning, its 'diet', mechanisms determining human cognitive processes, the nature of thinking, the features of a creative state of the brain, the nature of genius, the direct or indirect determination by the brain of our self, emotions, behavior, communications, relationships with others, our self perceptions, consciousness, the existence of the subconscious, and the unconscious processes of control.

Scientists have collected their present knowledge on the brain mainly over the past twenty years. Some scientists believe that as much as 99% of the whole data has been gathered within the last decade. Many scientists claim that there is still more that we do not know about the brain than we do know. What is known, however, has tremendous implications for individuals and society.

PACKAGING NEW KNOWLEDGE INTO NEW PRODUCTS

Since the past ten years, knowledge on the brain has been perceived as good worth packiging as product. During the past five years, there has been a boom in selling knowledge. 'The world' uses it daily without much boasting. Why? This knowledge and the way it is applied to business, and to entrepreneurship in particular (where intellectual entrepreneurship plays a leading role), and to education which aims at educating and 'producing' pro-entrepreneurial attitudes, becomes the trump card in the market. Understanding how to inject intellectual content into products and services creates a competitive advantage.

Whether we talk about big corporations or one-person organizations, it is equally important to know how to manage oneself, and the knowledge of how the brain operates becomes a valuable asset. Even the largest companies seek employees who are effective, creative, dynamically developing their knowledge and skills, healthy, and ebullient. Where are they?

How do some people manage to keep that emotional, physical and mental balance? These who maintain a healthy balance sell their services to companies for a high price. Can one learn that? What should be done with career weariness when it comes? How should one cope with depression? How should one organize himself within his time and what for? You cannot organize time itself, can you?

Everybody has his own timing, independent of objective time in which we function (the knowledge on the brain emphasizes that fact). How should one find himself between the „objective" and „subjective" time? How should one find the balance between body-mind-emotions? Is there harmony? How about synergy? Does summimg up simple elements of the human system produce a result of the sort of 2 and 2 equals four, or will we obtain something more.? Intellectual entrepreneurs, creating intellectual products use this knowledge more or less consciously every day. Why? Because they realize that their exceptional perception of the reality results from something, and the knowledge on the brain can elucidate their 'exceptionality'.

The answers to the above questions exist. New information about new possibilities of applying the knowledge to practice is still being developed. If we treat the mind as a tool for creating new products, then an understanding of current research on the brain is extremely valuable. Why not to use that knowledge?

Picture 2

CREATIVITY, IMAGINATION AND REVELATIONS

One of the more interesting aspects of creativity is the role of imagination. For example, Albert Einstein travelled on a sunbeam in his dream. He held that 'imagination is more important than knowledge'. Julius Verne thought that 'everything is brought into life twice, the first time in human imagination.' Salvadore Dali used to fall asleep seated in a big red armchair and holding an iron key in his hand. When the key slipped from his hand, it hit a metal bowl by the armchair, and the din woke him up. Inspired by his dream visions, Dali began to paint another masterpiece. Ernest Hemingway took long walks along the beach, stimulating all his senses. Leonardo da Vinci's life often made people think 'Are there any key elements in his method of learning and shaping intelligence?' 'Can they inspire us and show us the way to realization of our utmost possibilities?' The answer is YES. The basic elements of Leonardo's attitude to learning and developing intelligence (in its broad meaning – left and right brain) are obvious and can be studied, followed and introduced into practice. The creative processes can be explained and analyzed with the contemporary knowledge on the brain and states of brain activities. Mendeleyev is said to have seen in a dream the proper arrangement of the periodic table from which some chemical elements were still missing (yet undiscovered).

One afternoon 1860, August Friedrich Kekule von Stradonitz, a chemist, dozing by the fireplace, could see atoms dancing before the eyes of his imagination. The particles were arranging themselves into 'long sequences', as he wrote in his diary – 'sometimes clinging close to each other, entwining with one another and winding like snakes. Suddenly, one of the snakes bit its own tail and danced derisively before my eyes.' It danced to announce to the world the ring structure of benzene, that is the form which was taken by the dancing snake.

All of us have revelations. They show some common features: they usually follow a frustrating impasse and occur when we are not involved in the problem. Making an invention, therefore, is mostly an automatic and unconscious process, exploding with a novel solution at the last stage.

It is obvious that synergic work of brain hemispheres, especially in creative processes, surpasses the domination of either of them in their respective processes they specialize in. In my opinion, it is improper not to know which hemisphere dominates in one's daily activities, when the brain generates mostly beta waves. It is worth pondering which senses prevail in cognitive processes and what it means for the picture of myself and my surroundings. Why is it improper? Well, sounds too strict, but not in the situation when I make up my mind whether to feature a proactive or reactive attitude towards the future. If I am not making decisions today, at least I want to know where these attitudes are going to bring me.

ENTREPRENEURS AND CREATIVITY

Intellectual entrepreneurs use their energy on discerning opportunities. Hence their 'obsession' of making new contacts, seeing 'new worlds', continuous physical, emotional and intellectual activity. They act in line with their brains. They are slow or off like a shot. Sometimes consciously, sometimes unconsciously, they make decisions based on their intuition. They always add new data to the existing database. The analysis and synthesis of the 'digested' problems and phenomena are simultaneous. All of a sudden, they reveal new ideas, solutions and products, dumbfounding the market.

New data is flowing in. Medicine has recently discovered that new brain cells do grow in adult human brain. Still recently it was falsely believed that the brain and its cells is the only organ of the body which does not regenerate. Once it lost its cells, they are gone forever, and daily four thousand cells die. The new knowledge contradicts the most popular myth that our learning capabilities and intellectual potential deteriorate with age. Other research reveals that the 100 billion of nervous cells make a tremendous supply, but the heart of the matter is not the number of lost or preserved cells, but the possibility of creating new neural connections among them.

With a brain that is replenishing itself and with regular mental training, we can be at peace and should not be afraid that the potential with which we have been endowed by nature will ever disappear. One of the greatest limitations entrapping people is the awareness or its lack that it is possible. Many books explain the notion of self-imposed psychological limitations and their effect on cognitive processes. Many people remain ignorant of this research.

Another interesting issue is how people have remained creative for many years? They are creative in their old age (old age traditionally understood as the number of years lived by the body). Spectacular examples in business are timeless and unique: Peter Drucker, Tony Buzan or Edward de Bono. They lay the foundations of knowledge – effective learning, business theories, theories of effective thinking and solving problems. Their experience and ideas collected in books provide welcome advice on how to cope with the adaptation on the market under the ever changing economic, social and cultural conditions. Being illiterate in these matters is a serious drawback considerably increasing our metacognitive deficiency.

There is a growing need and necessity of continuous learning. At one time, an academic diploma was a proof of knowledge valid for about 30 years. Now, technological progress, changing environment and demand for new information make such knowledge expire after 5 years! Everyday life offers professional and personal improvement. Being an entrepreneur requires learning: how to make new products, manage the company, people and oneself. The market undergoes changes, so do we, and the only constant is change. The art of selection and searching for new tools is a valuable skill. Methods of effective learning help gain this knowledge in line with the brain activity. We can apply memory techniques, speed reading, Mind Mapping, to enhance learning. Our brain, spoils when not used.

POLAND BEHIND IN PUBLISHING SELF – IMPROVEMENT BOOKS ON THE BRAIN!

Knowledge on the brain's functionning results in goods which one can buy. How are the products packaged? There is a high variety. Books definitely are such goods. In 1995, books on the knowledge on the brain hardly existed, they passed unnoticed in sale. This knowledge was discussed in medical, psychological and business books but in an entirely different way than now. New experts in this field were gradually introduced onto the market: Tony Buzan – *Use Your Head* – as one of the first books written on the brain was published in 1974. A Polish publisher, RAVI reprinted it in 1997, only 23 years after its appearance in the USA.

Edward de Bono and his *Six Thinking Hats* appeared on the Polish market in 1996, while the world had been enjoying the theory of lateral thinking for over 20 years. The famous *Superlearning 2000* by Sheila Ostrander and Lynn Schroeder (1994), a book on methods and techniques of accelerated learning and teaching from the '80s and '90s, was translated and published in Poland in 1997. Now Poland is finally up to date!

Polish bookshops are inundated now with such books proving that there are experts on mental self-improvement. More and more teachers, their students and their parents, are hungry for more knowledge of how we learn. They demand effective teaching. In higher education and in Business Schools particularly the first graduates discovered that their knowledge did not match reality. So, they became the potential market for trade books on self improvement, self-awareness and books on the brain. Books on mechanisms and styles of thinking, cognitive processes, describing consciousness, subconsciousness and other states of mind proliferate the market. The latest bestseller by Ole Vedfelt „Bevidsthed.Bevidsthedens Niveauer"?, was first published in 1986. However, it was not published in Poland until 2001! In 1999, Buzan's famed *Brain-Sell* (1995) was published in Poland. The author has co-writers, because the knowledge grows and ideas for applying it mushroom, too. One must write, write quickly, because when you have acquired the knowledge on the brain you can also sell it better. Another top expert on human thinking, the author of 58 books translated into 34 languages, Edward de Bono, also responds to the market requirements with his book *New Thinking for the New Millenium* (1999) which appeared in Poland in 2001. In 2000, Stefan Kwiatkowski's book *Przedsiębiorczość Intelektualna* was published. The book is the first synthesis of the phenomenon of entrepreneurship.

With regular training of mind we can be at peace and we may not be afraid that the potential with which we have been endowed by nature will ever disappear. One of the greatest limitations entrapping people is the awareness or its lack. Books on the market discussing psychological limitations and ways of thinking and their effect on cognitive processes explain precisely those mechanisms and phenomena. Many of us remain immune even to facts. How do some people remain creative well into old age?

The most spectacular thing happened some days ago. It is March 2001. In December 2000 bookshops start selling *The Learning Revolution* by Gordon Dryden and Jeannette Vos. Attention! The completely revised and updated international edition of that book (first issued in 1994) was on the Polish market in 1999. At last the rate of translation is meeting market needs of Polish readers!

The March issue of *Charaktery* has an advertisement: „Revolution in learning. Can we learn faster and more effectively? Under the slogan, 'Learning revolution is on,' Dr. J. Vos, world-famous expert on learning, a psychologist from the USA, conducts a workshop for business people, psychologists, personal managers, instructors, students and anybody interested in new methods of learning." Note the order in which the people are invited. The notice continues: „Dr Vos elaborated rules of accelerated and integrated learning which use the natural mechanism of brain receiving information." A list of clients of Dr. Vos include: American Army, Apple Computer, Cambridge College and many others. These are organizations which deal with information, create it, invent the ways of circulating and understanding it. The book sold in ten million copies. How many seminars and new intellectual products will it inspire? Who knows?

The process of introducing the new knowledge on the brain onto the Polish market is interesting. 'New' in terms of Poland still means from the '80s and '90s. First, it was related practical applications to education and self-development, then business was the hot topic. In Poland we first learned the techniques, now we know why and how they work. The knowledge on the brain will propel new intellectual products. There will be new books for new generations of intellectual entrepreneurs which will spur them to gain knowledge about themselves and learning 'over the loops' as it is called by Stefan Kwiatkowski.

There are two categories of books or products: (1) those created to fill the immediate needs of the market, and (2) those that are not offered until the market is mature. We may discover other categories. How will we classify them? What else will be invented by the human mind? The way is open.

MENTAL STRATEGIES FOR WINNING IN SPORTS!

The knowledge on the brain helps people in **life** (self-knowledge, communication), **learning** (techniques of effective learning), **work** (efficient managing oneself, organization, and other people), **inventing** (creative states, techniques of body and mind work), and **play** (The World Memory Championships). There are two more areas to mention – sports and health.

The world observes a breathtaking success of the Polish long-fly skier, Adam Malysz. Another record of Poland – 218,5 m. Another world record in the number of season victories. It is one more victory of the knowledge on the brain and potential one can use without limits. One only needs some learning on how to employ it. For years remarkable coaches, sportsmen and scientists have been collaborating towards reaching the level of master sport. Their key was the knowledge on the brain and how to leverage 'all parts of the system' (body, emotions and mind). Psychological training focuses more and more on attaining a specific state, called the state of FLOW or peak performance. Adam Malysz credits the role of Dr. Blecharz, psychologist, calling him co-creator of his success. Combining automatic control over physiological stimulation with simultaneous concentration on the goal unites the body and mind. Successful athletes experience a state of full concentration. Mental training is very useful in this respect. It is a combination of methods and psychological tasks which by regular and long-term practising lead to a higher control of behaviour and emotions thus enhancing many psychological traits (eg. concentration) and higher resistance to stress.

Malysz explains that the first stage is learning to relax and concentrate. Athletes use biofeedback. Perhaps now nobody will laugh at me saying 'relaxation to learn concentration?' Those who use these techniques gain serious advantages in heightening their ability to perform, to learn and to create. Intellectual entrepreneurs also use these techniques and they do not allow others to deter them. When nothing disturbs them, the goal can be reached before they set off. Malysz has overcome the firmest barrier in his mind – he already knows that one may and can.

Many corporate trainers are now using Feldenkreis's method of heightening mental performance. Feldenkreis is a British astronomer and physicist, and keen rugby player. The method is based on psychoneurological attitude which is the brain mechanism that controls body movement. According to the author, it is the brain that 'decides', to a large extent, about the movement capabilities of man, and not only his muscles. In the brain are recorded psychoneurological patterns of movement which sometimes can be restraining. Fortunately, brain is a keen learner. The identification of that phenomenon allows it to record new movements which subsequently lead to another success, be it in sports or some other field.

The capabilities of the human brain astonish scientists time and again. The brain activity surprises physicists at a tennis court. From a mathematical and physical point of view, sending a tennis ball precisely to a place at the court is a very complex task. Small errors entail next ones and theoretically the ball can land anywhere. Yet tennis players manage excellently without superfast computers. The 'tennis equation' reveals a peculiar way of hitting the ball, which is nearly free of any disturbances. Such a set of circumstances in which a desired operation is always successful is called 'an attractor' in the jargon of mathematics. American physicists, after laborious calculations found out that if the racket slows down at the moment of hitting the ball, then it is easier to control its route. Therefore a group of tennis players were examined and to the surprise of the researchers, all of them were reducing the speed of the racket just before hitting the ball. Their choice of the attractor parameters was instinctive, without solving equations and comparing the results. In addition, the attempts at hitting the ball blindfold and with a special racket moved by a lever, showed that the key sense while hitting was not the sight, but the feeling of the racket and body position.

The results of 'the tennis experiment' can be inspiring for inventors of moving robots, which, so far, have been funtioning only due to a certain programme and endless revisions introduced into it along with changes in conditions.

INTELLECTUAL ENTREPRENUERS AND THE BRAIN

While describing intellectual entrepreneurs and their products, we are always struck by the dynamics of their personality, multi-faceted treatment of the subject, and associations (sometimes worlds apart from the subject). Their products are created in a given environment. Their products end up living their own life. The intellectual products and companies actually change their creators, clients, environment and market. The entrepreneurs receive signals on the occurring changes. Another flow of information, followed byanother synthesis and analysis, parallel, lateral, multi-level and ... Therefore, anyone attempting to describe them and their products in a linear way, will fail. Such analyses have been out of use for a long time. Lecturers, students or inventors, who think in a linear way and repeat worn-out patterns show no sparkle or inspiration. They have already come to a standstill.

As for health, research on the brain rises hopes for curing dangerous diseases. Polish scientists from Centrum Medycyny Doświadczalnej i Klinicznej in Warsaw succeeded, as the first in the world, in growing three main kinds of brain cells adopting the genetic method to human parent cells. Surprising characteristics of parent cells may give the opportunity to cure diseases of the nervous system like Parkinson's and Alzheimer's diseases, lesions of brain through injuries or a stroke. First results, expected by the end of this year, will answer the question whether the vaccine prepared by Dale Schenk, will help the ill retain normal brain functions permenantly. Will the new vaccine improve the capability of learning and memorising impaired by the disease? Who knows? Maybe man will win the battle over his own brain and recorded memories?

Everyday care of the brain is worth the effort. Feed it well and 'caress' it. Here come next ideas for next products. Breathing techniques, body and mind relaxation. How do the entrepreneur's heart and the condition of his nervous system affect the effectiveness of his work? How can one bring three systems - emotional, physical and intellectual - work? How can one make the body cooperate?

Since the mind is the tool, it is wise to care for our brain. We are systems and we function as a system. Elements of a system are involved in mutual relationships. Any change in any element of the system always results in the change of work of the whole system. There is no doubt that the way we breathe (oxygen), our heart beats (blood) and nourishment delivered to the brain (monosaccharide) may improve or impair our thinking. This knowledge germinates at new trainings, new products and packages come out. Participating in such trainings resembles stages of life experience rather than following a specially paved route. New brains continue to build intellectual capital. The data in our brains become information which, in turn, develops into knowledge and, following, into the process of understanding and so on to infinity.

CONCLUSIONS

There used to be 'The Day of the Brain'. Now, while I am writing this paper, 'The World Week of the Knowledge on the Brain' is being held. A day was not enough! Since the inception of 'The Dana Alliance for Brain Initiatives' in the USA in 1992, the Brain has also made an appearance at SCIENCE Festivals. A similar institution was founded in Europe – European Dana Alliance for the Brain. The declaration of this institution was signed by 60 outstanding European neurobiologists, neurologists, and psychiatrists. Poland is represented by Malgorzata Kossut from the Warsaw Institute of Experimental Biology. When the US Congress declared the 1990s 'The Decade of the Knowledge on the Brain', who would have expected that the 21st century could be the first age when the knowledge on the brain would result in popular products in so many branches?

Certainly, new products are spread. We may see new schools with a subject 'The knowledge on the brain.' We may discover new mental and managerial techniques to improve thinking and functioning. Perhaps the theory of organization as a structure will have its revival of the metaphor of the brain? An entrepreneur probably does not need the metaphor, he needs precise knowledge. Technology is progressing, and so are the prospects of researching the human brain – ad infinitum. Researchers will find better ways of interpreting their discoveries. They will find new applications for their discoveries. New entrepreneurs will create new products and will package them and sell more and more of them in still new ways.

Lech W. Zacher

INTELLECTUAL CAPITAL AND THE COMMERCIALIZATION OF THE MIND

Abstract

Another way of expressing the notion of Intellectual Capital is to use the expression the 'Commercialization of mind.' While the expression is poetic and may be treated as a metaphor, it has pragmatic implications for management. The 'commercialization of the mind' is explored here in order to develop insight into the complexity of mental thoughts, and resulting tangible and intangible ideas which have commercial value.

Commercialization is presented as a general process connected with market system and rather practical orientation of human activities. Not all our actions are commercially-driven. The public-oriented mind seems useful and necessary for a sound society. There are various rationalities not only economic ones.

For what will be intellectual entrepreneurship in the perspective of knowledge society and globalization. Answers may vary since there are several convictions, interpretations and evaluations.

THE COMMERCIALIZATION OF MENTAL ACTIVITY

Intellectual capital comes from the mind or brain. However, not all of the mind's products are intellectual. The brain produces not only thoughts, but feelings and emotions also. Feelings and emotions include not only poetry, music, art (i.e. symbolic culture), but other phenomena such as advice, consulting, expertise, and innovation. Such products, services or activities were always rewarded by society and have economic value. Thus process of commercialization and *marketization* started centuries ago. *Intellectual entrpreneurship* (IE) in modern form is connected mostly with techno-economic and organizational activities. Quite recently a new model of production of knowledge – *mode 2* – was proposed (Gibbons et al.) based on commercialization of formerly "missionary" activity in the R+D sphere. Intellectual entrepreneurship is to some extent an intermediary activity. Intellectual entrepreneurs may resemble Schumpeterian type of innovators penetrating the border area between science and technology sector and economic sector. They bridge the gap between research activities and business activities.

The commercialization of mind's products has always had a connection with *practical applications*. This is also true for politics, media, culture, religion – as well. That is why there are such expressions like the *market* of ideas, of innovations, of ideologies or even of religions. The market of ideas, innovations and ideologies have their practical applications. As concepts or ideas progress to the market, they pass through appropriate filters – cultural, ideological, economic which are reflected in media messages.

Apart from the above interpretation, there is the classic one maintaining that mental activity should serve the pursuit of truth. The classic view is that mental activity should be like a free art or a religious prayer. The human mind is multifunctional and can serve many activities. However, implicit in mental activity is the involvement of a person's value system. Depending on an individual's *values* and *interests,* a mind can be *commercially-driven* or can be used to help an individual achieve self-realization. In practical life these two types of activities may be somehow separated by time and dedication. But in the *mental processing* they may interfere, overlap, stimulate each other etc. There is a relationship between mental activities that are commercial in nature and those that are strictly internally oriented.

The commercialization of mental activity is connected with *instrumental values* while non-commercial uses of mind serve *non-instrumental* values. It is not easy to draw a distinction since even commercial-oriented thinking may resemble art-like activity (the case of all innovations). Some reasonable proportion of these value-orientations are probably desirable. It would be not good – at least from the point of view of the protection of diversity – to limit all activities to commercial ones. Money then would be the <u>universal</u> measure of all human achievements. In today's society, the activities of science and technology have drifted toward privatization (Y. Ezrahi).

In addition to individual mental activity, there are also collective examples of mental activities. Examples of such collective mental activity include: collective research, team work, groupware, network activities and the like. Some authors even talk about the *collective mind* of the Net. Mental capacity, agility and intelligence vary significantly among individuals, teams, groups, organizations, communities, companies, and societies.

COMMERCIAL VERSUS NON-COMMERCIAL MENTAL ACTIVITY

Human skills vary considerably as well. For non-commercial use of mind human skills represent a talent which counts towards and indicates a propensity to produce knowledge. But for commercial achievements, the power of brain to process information is not sufficient to realize commercial success. Other skills are needed such as marketing, advertising, and selling to name a few. Traditional scientific think-tanks (e.g. RAND, Brookings Institution, Worldwatch Institute), working for governments or public, were not interested in these skills. Their employees expect rewards not only in the form of reaching excellence, career, fame, influence, but they also expect to earn a decent income. They operate on a quasi-market of ideas. For-profit think-tanks that work for business or governments are more interested in producing competitive advantage for companies than in publishing reports, books and articles. Commercial consultant firms' contribution to society can be at best indirect and often not publicized.

Intellectual entrepreneurship may also be present in non-technological and non-economic area. Consulting firms were organized in the post-communist countries when it became legal and profitable. However they were often not fully commercial since many of them have a foundation status. The ideas and socio-political expertise market is different than the technological or economic one. Those individuals who created and controlled the demand for such consultants are mostly politicians and administrators of national and local level government agencies. Ideally, those individuals in government using the services of consultants should be not autocratic, but well educated, willing to listen and learn, and not overwhelmed by their power and the "political game." In Poland (and surely in the other CEE countries) these conditions have not been fully met, to put it in a delicate way.

For some, a *public-oriented mind* (non-commercial mind) seems to be morally superior to those interested in commercial gain. This is not necessarily a valid position. Non-commercial activity and products can be of bad quality for many reasons, including lack of sources, poor rewards, haste, or due to political expediency. There is a trade-off between possible negative impacts of usually under-financed and bureaucratized public-oriented units and competitive, well-financed and advertised commercial products. There is no evidence that important values are sacrificed when choosing commercial mind's product, provided that professionalism and trust is assured. Trust – according to F. Fukuyama – is valid not only in social relations but is also required in the new electronic or high technology societies. The grand ideas and goals of humankind, civilization, development, reforms will not be necessarily neglected in a free market economy. In a free market system where competition reigns, both types of perspectives should remain on stage and compete in proper proportions, so as not to lead to a monopoly or to "one right truth".

A NEED FOR NATIONAL INNOVATION POLICIES

There is a vast array of issues to be explored. Let us mention some of them as exemplary cases.

In the market system the commercialization is usually tied up with entrepreneurship. Intellectual entrepreneurship makes sense if there is a market for intellectual products. Intellectual products may include services such as giving advice, expertise, training, or innovating methods of production or distribution, or providing technological, or organizational innovations. However, the situation in LDCs and in the transition economies in Eastern and Central Europe is different. In the case of transition economies, research and development funding is marginalized and there is a lack of understanding of the investment needed to innovate.

In the advanced countries, business and government encourage research, and innovation, especially high technology. A good example is the Advanced Technology Program conducted by the US Department of Commerce – Technology Administration and the National Institute of Standards and Technology. They are looking for better *partnerships* among sectors of the economy. Etzkowitz et. al. provide an example of the concept of Triple Helix – a series of conferences involving government, university, industry. It is useful to explore the role of the intellectual enterpreneurship in such partnerships. The countries in transition should explore other examples of *national innovation systems* which started first time in the early 70s.

More research is necessary to analyze and assess the proportion of intellectual products resulted just from a production, and such ones which resulted from thinking and experiencing. Research is needed on why some intellectual products are successfully marketed and some products fail even when they are innovative and technologically sound.

FUTURE ROLE OF INTELLECTUAL ENTREPRENEURS IN THE EMERGING KNOWLEDGE SOCIETY

There are three additional perspectives that should be considered while discussing the IE or commercial mind as the symbols of free market, informational capitalism and human entrepreneurship. One perspective can be tied to *knowledge society* which has to follow the presently emerging information society (or e-society). Certainly the knowledge society ought to deal predominantly with knowledge production and its use. Intellectual production and consequently the intellectual entrepreneur can constitute a significant part of the knowledge society. In future, there will be probably more knowledge producers than now exist. R. Reich labels these knowledge producers as *symbolic analysts*. The optimistic vision debated recently within the OECD is the vision of a *creative society*. Intellectual Entrepreneurs will certainly contribute to its realization, it is beyond doubts.

The other perspective is a *postmodernistic* one. There are important authors who have written much, also referring to scientific and global problematique (e.g. J.-F. Lyotard, A. Giddens, Z. Bauman). Their considerations seem rather inconclusive or controversial for non-believers (in postmodernism). However, they touch upon many serious issues of which some can be somewhat connected with intellectual entrepreneurship – uncertainty, changing roles and contexts, and pluralism. In the other words – the future will bring more diversification, decentralization, and more uncertainty. This situation leads to a rising demand for the services of intellectual entrepreneurs.

And the third perspective is even more *futuristic*. The future is approaching. There are two issues to be addressed here: the further development of artificial intelligence (AI) and mass use of multimedia and virtual reality (VR). Will people escape from "hard" reality to illusory world of multimedia (which will determine what reality is) and will they become addicted to VR worlds? Will humankind be then divided into intellectual and power elites and masses of manipulated idiots? This danger is known today in the form of advancing McDonaldization (Ritzer). Are we headed toward a *new world* which is called post-biologic and characterized by a post-human mind? For the time being, it looks like science-fiction (Gibson's "Neuromancer"), but perhaps the question can be formulated as follows: Will cyborgs need intellectual entrepreneurs or will they condemn them to other living or rather existing objects? Who will operate storehouses of knowledge, located probably mostly in cyberspace? Will it be some place left for intellectual entrepreneurs? And will *mind, reason, intelligence, intellect, brain, head* have any meaning in the new world?

COMMERCIALIZATION AND GLOBALIZATION – PERMANENT TRENDS?

Commercialization can be connected with various sectors of human activity either intellectual or not (like for example paid sex services). What is usually observed is that commercialization of some sectors can have a *negative* result. For example, *commercialization of media* – means more and more advertisements, less and less ambitious programs, tendency to so called infotainment etc. Commercialization of culture and art leads to mass-culture production (e.g. paintings) and is subjected to more primitive tastes of mass not-refined audience. One can say that the Copernicus-Gresham law works here. It is evident that the pressure of market (demand) is vital here. Some can argue, however, that without commercializing of some cultural – in broad sense – activities many of them could not be possible at all, or for a significant scale (e.g. in TV). And, one can argue that mass culture is really a democratization of culture as compared with societies where only the wealthiest elites enjoyed art, music and entertainment.

The *Commercialization of science and technology* is not a new phenomenon. However earlier the commercialization was not as much widespread. Many inventors and innovators were private entrepreneurs or at least they functioned in a private sector. They sold their patents or licensed them. Today, the industrial and research institutions restrict their innovators from conducting personal research and they require their employees to share any rights in innovations they may develop on their own.

Of course, commercialization is the proper approach for a business firm and for society, at least in market economy. The commercialization of ideas is related to the corresponding *economic rationality*.

The question is whether economic rationality can be useful (and eventually to what extent) in non-economic activities. A provisional answer is that most human activities encompass both economic and non-economic outcomes. Most human activities involve the use of different rationalities at the same time (e.g. technological, social, political, household, individual) in different proportions and often without a possibility of their reasonable separation. There are good reasons to think that more and more *complex* systems will require the use of different rationalities of technological, social, political character. New complex systems labeled as e-economy, e-society, networked society, all demand mental activity that merge different rationalities. Having access to information through advanced communication technologies (ICTs) will make it possible to conduct various commercial and non-commercial activities not only by companies but by individuals as well. The integrated communications technologies provide a vehicle that may increase the possibilities for intellectual entrepreneurship.

It is still uncertain how the ongoing processes of *globalization* and of making societies *informational* will finally shape society. The present advancement of *neoliberal* project of globalization is based on certain assumptions. These assumptions include the concepts of economic rationality, market, competition, global fluidity of capital, commercialization of everything, individualism, concept of *homo economicus* and the like. The trend toward a global economy will become an even more serious subject for debate by intellectuals and those involved in environmental, social and protest movements that are critical of the spread of global materialism and consumption. Culturally and politically the globalization of economies may not be fully accepted by less developed countries. The debate has started on postcapitalist society, postcorporate future, postmaterialism and the like. The "final" shape of future societies and their characteristics remains undetermined.

THE ROLE OF THE INTELLECTUAL ENTREPRENEUR

Commercialization can be viewed as a process of gaining *economic* (money) *rewards* for some activity; but market rules constitute another condition. The latter rules make the difference in comparison with the non-commercial, though financially rewarded, activity like e.g. research (the Nobel prize is not a commercial reward). The more complicated case for classification is the research position in a commercial organization (e.g. consulting company, e-incubator). Commercialization may be connected either with a *goal of activity* or with a *type of organization*. Of course, there are more fuzzy cases that are difficult to separate in two opposite categories – commercial and non-commercial (e.g. the case of scientists working at state universities or laboratories and at the same time in private, commercial sector, or if their university conducts extra some commercial activity – for industry, military etc.). Scientists working at universities who are also involved in some commercial or military research reflect the freedom of the market system. These scientists have intellectual abilities aided by entrepreneurial skills.

Intellectual entrepreneurship – types and characteristics

Type (orientation)	Degree of commercialization	Basic goals	Expected effects
– economic (market), – scientific & technological, – political, – social, – cultural, etc.	declining order	– profit, – competitive advantage, – seeking resources, – building structures, – political support seeking, – creating institutions and laws, – social activism movements, – projects, – laws imposing new ideas, – performances, popularization, – bigger audience, – funds raising	sellable goods and services, financial support, grants, projects, programs, new structures, winning elections, implementing programs, protests, public hearings, local and global events, new regulations, artistic ideas, events, exhibitions, public interest

For all these entrepreneurship types, their basic goals and expected results can be local, regional, national, and international.

There are various sorts of markets for products of entrepreneurship, appropriate to their type. In the case of economic market – it is the real market. Converting research and development results to commercial markets is more difficult because it requires *practical* results involving integration of innovation, improvements, technologies, organization, transferred solutions, etc.

In the coming *knowledge society* (or knowledge-based society) it is especially important to have a source of knowledge as the intellectual entrepreneurship. If this kind of activity will gain a critical mass it may become a significant resource for society. Such a positive impact activity is found at the applied or practical level. Some commentators may still question whether some human resources (e.g. scientists, engineers) are not *redirected* from – at least of the same significance - cognitive, fundamental spheres of intellectual efforts of man. It seems to be rather an academic question, however, since the processes of intellectual entrepreneurship are already widespread and advancing. Intellectual entrepreneurship should perhaps be countered in a country's innovation policy to promote its growth and development and not to hinder them.

MOTIVATIONS AND CONTRIBUTIONS OF INTELLECTUAL ENTREPRENEURS

There are a number of motives of those who seek to commercialize their expertise. For some, the motivation is greed, for others the propensity to "produce and sell" in order to see products' practicality, and others have a materialistic orientation. Some want to exercise their ability to sell the mental effort and have a mindset that everything should be measured in money terms and be a subject to marketization. There are in reality many different motivations, aspirations, views, assumptions for choices and for undertaking actions.

Historically, selling one's mental products or services was less widespread than it is today. Examples from the past include astrologers and advisors. Kings and princes competed to get them from the "advisory" market. Some names are famous like for example Seneca, Machiavelli, Francis Bacon. In the area of science and technology "intellectual entrepreneurs" usually were not interested in commercialization of their work and achievements (e.g. Copernicus, Maria Curie, Einstein). Guided by cognitive interests with a conviction of mission, they were not appreciated nor rewarded enough in monetary terms though they certainly earned honors and awards.

Intellectual producers are rarely well-remunerated with the exception of Nobel prize laureates and perhaps those who work in military research or industry sectors. They are usually underestimated by market, by business people, by politicians and by public. This is in spite of the fact that they are *agents of progress* – technological, economic, organizational, political, social etc. This is especially true in the case of the less developed countries and the post-Communist countries undergoing transition. The lack of a reward system results in migration or what is called the brain drain phenomenon. Intellectual entrepreneurship diminishes possible outflow of minds by giving them chances to meet their financial aspirations and needs (money, respect, position, good conditions of research). Mind producers are agents of change, sometimes only instrumental, sometimes fundamental. Mind producers should be rewarded at least as highly skilled and creative managers.

Commercialization of mind or rather of mind's products should be investigated in a broader context in connection with profit and non-profit activities and organizations, or with a role of state and public sphere (vs. private sphere).

Commercialization can have many subjects, objects, faces and focuses. It can be conducted by the state. An example is

Poland's privatization of banks. Commercialization might include parts of economic sectors like higher education in Poland which is partly commercial and partly governmental. Such partial commercialization looks somewhat incoherent. Such commercialization involves some specialization of the undertaken efforts - for money, for prestige, for better hierarchical or bargaining position. Such "schizophrenia" serves the mind's owners. Examples include G. Soros who is an international "financial shark," but is also a critical thinker and a man of philanthropy. Another example is Bill Gates, a businessman, innovator and missionary author. There are similar cases in the sphere of politics where some business people have become active. Berlusconi in Italy, Perot and Forbes in the US, are examples. Moreover, such situations happen almost daily in the life of individuals in the post-industrial societies. Imaginary visions of intellectual entreprepreneurs turned philanthropic entrepreneurs were given a long time ago by A. Toffler in his "Future shock" and "Third Wave." Nowadays the postmodernist thinkers, like Z. Bauman, try to describe such human situations in which there are – thanks to networking – many interactive contacts, many social assignments, many roles and loyalties and many opportunities. One of them seems to be intellectual entrpreneurship which can appear in a more generalized form of the commercialization of mind. From the other point of view it may be described as an opportunity – in its content and form – connected with the *informational capitalism*. Entrepreneurship, networks, and multiroles are responsible for these new and perhaps long lasting situations.

Evaluation is not easy. From the point of view of rationality it sharply varies. For the research and development sphere, the results of the intellectual entrepreneurship may be controversial since some talented researchers and organizers go to intellectual business not to academia. On the other side, they contribute to practically-oriented research and development constituting often the "missing link" in chain of innovation creation and diffusion. Moreover, intellectual entrepreneurs will not migrate to richer countries, though *via* telework their minds' products can cross all borders (what can be called a new form of brain drain if it goes just one way).

From the standpoint of economy (especially e-economy) and society in general the intellectual entrepreneurship looks *only beneficial*. From the point of view of interests of all spheres and individuals in particular (i.e. commercial minds owners) it seems beneficial and advantageous as well. What can be problematic to some extent is the difficulty of controlling it in the cases of military affairs, espionage and terrorism. For example, drug producers use advanced chemistry.

Another point of concern is related to the *proportion* of the commercial and non-commercial minds' products. It can be taken for granted that both types of activities cannot fully substitute for each other. So it is socially wise to keep them both. It will constitute a challenge for coming knowledge societies to find for these types proper proportions and forms of *coherence* to gain *synergetic effects*. These effects can have form of a kind of multiplier because of multiroles, plentitude of contacts and interactions, new opportunities, and diffusions. Inappropriate proportions (i.e. disproportions) could be treated as *market failures* and should be corrected by deliberate government, corporate or social actions. Of course, the assessment and choice of policies are not easy either in real space or in cyberspace.

SELECTED BIBLIOGRAPHY

Etzkowitz H., Leydesdorff L. (1997), Universities and the Global Knowledge Economy – A Triple Helix of University – Industry – Government Relations, Pinter, London and Washington

Etzkowitz H., Gulbrandsen M., Public entrepreneur: the trajectory of United States science, technology and industrial policy, "Science and Public Policy", Vol. 26, No. 1, February 1999

Ezrahi Y. (1990), The Descent of Issues – Science and the Transformation of Contemporary Democracy, Harvard University Press., Cambridge, Mass.-London

Gibbons M. et al. (19940 The New Production of Knowledge, Sage, London

Grunwald A. (2000) Technik für die Gesellschaft von morgen, Campus Verlag, Frankfurt – New York

Halbert D. J. (1999) Intellectual Property in the Information Age: The Politics of Expanding Ownership Rights, Quorum Books, Westport, Conn.

Kukliński A., Orłowski W. M. (eds.) (2000), The Knowledge-Based Economy – The Global Challenges of the 21st Century, KBN, Warsaw

Kukliński A. (ed.) (2000) The Knowledge-Based Economy – The European Challenges of the 21st Century, KBN, Warsaw

Kwiatkowski S., Edvinsson L. (eds.) (1999) Knowledge Café for Intellectual Entrepreneurship, LKAEM, Warsaw

Raffensperger C. et al., Definig Public – Interest Research, LOKA INSTITUTE <loka@amherst.edu> July 9, 1999

Rifkin J. (2000) The Age of Access, Tarcher/Putnam, New York

Ritzer G. (1996) The Mc Donaldization of Society, Sage, London

Rowe G., Frewer L. J., Public Participation Methods: A Framework for Evaluation, "Science, Technology & Human Values", Vol. 25, No. 1, Winter 2000

Special issue on public participation in science and technology – "Science and Public Policy", Vol. 26, No. 5, October 1999

The Creative Society of the 21st Century (2000), OECD, Paris

Walsh V. (1995) Social Criteria in the Commercialisation of Human Reproductive Technology, in: Rip A., Misath J., Schot J. (eds.), Managing Technology in Society – The Approach of Constructive Technology Assessment, Pinter, London – New York

Webster F., Information, capitalism and uncertainty, "Information, Communication & Society", Vol. 3, No. 1, 2000

Zacher L. W., Towards an Information Society and Beyond, "Dialogue and Universalism", vol. 8, No. 7–8, 1998 (Polish Academy of Sciences)

Zacher L. W., The Way Towards a Knowledge Society – Some Barriers not only for Countries in Transition, "Véda, Technika, Spole nost", 1-2/1999 (Prague)

Zacher L. W., The Emerging Information Society (Some questions on theory and practice), "Dialogue and Universalism", vol. x, No. 9-10, 2000 (Polish Academy of Sciences)

Krzysztof Pawłowski

THE VIEW FROM THE MOUNTAINS: A GLOBAL APPROACH TO ACHIEVING EXCELLENCE IN HIGHER EDUCATION*

Abstract

Against the changes presently occurring in higher education which are taking the university from an elitist, isolated institution to an institution providing mass education.

The author presents the most important features of Wyższa Szkoła Biznesu -National-Louis University, an institution of higher education he founded, that distinguish it in the Polish education market. The characteristic features of the School are its nationwide orientation and achievements of its students and alumni.

The article also presents the School's influence on the regional development of Nowy Sącz, emphasizing the fact that the school employs over 200 people and provides additional income for several hundred families. A substantial increase in the number of Nowy Sącz residents holding a university diploma, and a gradual creation of a local innovation center on the basis of the School, are of fundamental importance to the town's development.

---

* Illustrated by Andrzej Szarek, Ph.D

FROM THE UNIVERSITY AS REMOTE ISLAND TO THE UNIVERSITY AS GLOBALLY CONNECTED ENTERPRISE

The 21st century will be a century of change in the academic world. Ever-quickening changes in wider society, the continuing spread of higher education, and transformations brought about by globalization may result in the disappearance of not only numerous corporations – giants of the 20th century - but also of numerous universities. These universities, for centuries unique symbols of excellence, progress and knowledge, have been at the same time symbolic of an unchanging constancy. Now, however, they are forced to recognize the signs of the coming times and prepare themselves for new challenges. The coming turbulent times will see only the most adaptable and reactive educational institutions surviving and thriving.

For centuries, European universities were virtually isolated organizations, ivory towers accessible only to an elite (the most talented, most persistent, best prepared and usually also the wealthiest), that stored available knowledge, created new disciplines of science, and often protected and hid it from the wider population. So, higher education was accessible only to a very small percentage of the population even into the 20th century, and using 'exalted' knowledge for mundane, utilitarian purposes (for instance, to create new products, or using applied science) was considered inferior by scholars. Indeed, the university professor was a true master who often educated only one disciple, who then became his successor during his lifetime. Even today, it is not hard to detect the contempt demonstrated by the most respectable Polish universities towards research into new technological solutions as well as their annoyance at the influx of young people who want to study. Admitting only one candidate out of fifteen to departments where the total number of students in each year is twenty to thirty still gives many a reason to boast.

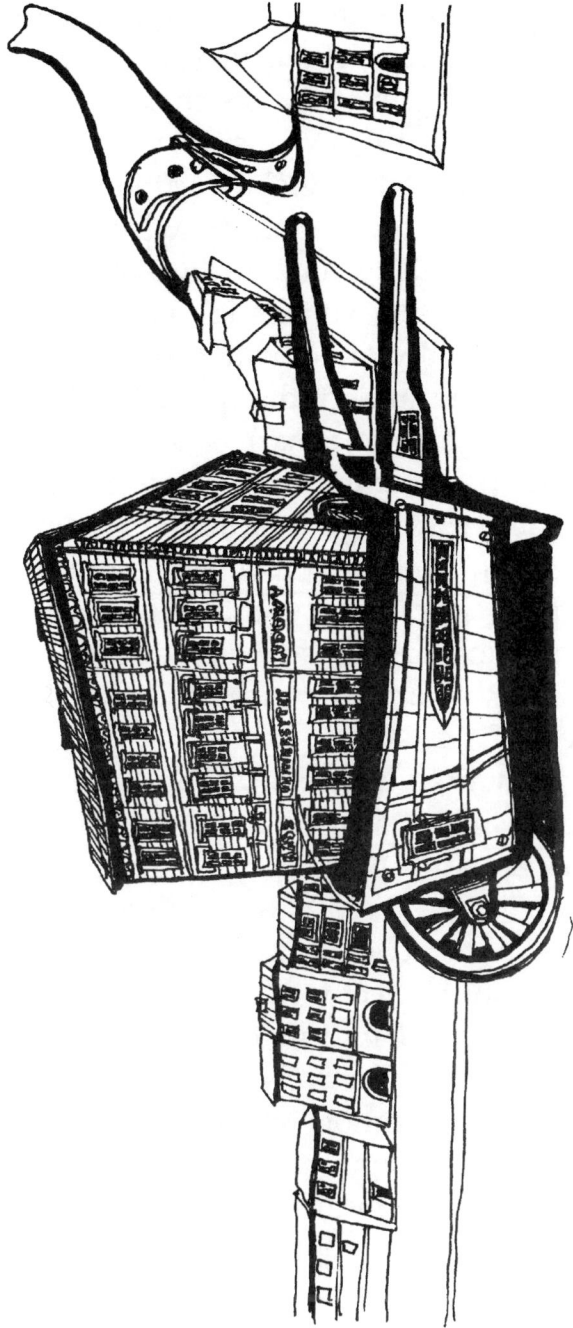

Figure 1

Nowadays, in developed countries approximately 50 % of young people from each age-group decide to study, and education has become one of the biggest 'industries'.

The role of the university has changed and will continue to change following the expansion of higher education and transformations in the global economy. It has become a unique enterprise processing knowledge and providing this knowledge to students and, at the same time, teaching them the skills to use this knowledge and utilize it for practical purposes. An individual relationship between the master-professor and the student-disciple who studies extensively to gain deep insight into a narrow subject area is becoming a thing of the past (apart from a few exceptions of the most expensive universities). What matters now is time and effectiveness – both from the university's and the student's point of view. It is clear that a completely different system is needed, one which targets the mass education of students – and not necessarily or only the exceptionally talented, but also the average ones.

The information revolution, happening in front of our very eyes and the limits of which we cannot even begin to fathom, constitutes an additional agent of change. Suddenly, right in front of our eyes, thanks to the Internet, all contemporary knowledge has become accessible to millions all over the world, not only to elect few. In my opinion, the Internet and the development of information technologies spread democracy much more effectively than any political solutions of the European civilization we are so proud of. At the beginning of the third millennium, all knowledge is global, and it is especially accessible to the younger generation, which has no inhibitions concerning computer use.

The new winners of this period of transition will be those academic institutions that learn the fastest how to transform the available knowledge into the individual intellectual capital of their alumni. The successful university's alumni will be able to process and utilize their knowledge and skills, to demonstrate their dynamism and entrepreneurship, and to continue to develop their knowledge and skills throughout their professional lives. In short, the defining feature of the best universities will be the professional success of their alumni – and not only science graduates, but also those graduating from Arts departments. Talented professionals, who are adaptable, innovative and capable of lifelong learning will be of the highest possible value sought after by the economy and jobs market of the future.

Figure 2

It has become evident in recent years that human resources (in particular, intellectual capital) constitutes the most fundamental asset that makes a country, a multinational corporation, or a small company competitive on the global market. It is these resources, not money or raw materials, which have a decisive role in achieving success on the market today and even more so in the future. This intellectual capital has yet another advantage over other resources: namely, it can be easily renewed and may become self-propagating provided that people using this capital are taught to actively process and constantly update their knowledge. This is not the knowledge hidden inside the dusty pages of unused books, but knowledge that is easily and quickly accessible thanks to new information technologies and supported by a person's proper preparation for its active use. This kind of knowledge has become a determinant of the 21st century.

Figure 3

Transformations we are witnessing force us to review the fundamental mission of the university/ institution of higher education. In the past three centuries, the core of the university were masters – professors engaging in studying science, on whom the prestige and the position of the university depended and whose achievements were the main product of the university. The process of educating students accompanied research, and the most important task was to select the most talented students who would stay at the university after graduation and join its research team.

I am deeply convinced that the coming times will necessitate a clear change of mission, and the main product of the university's activity will be alumnus capable of facing the challenges of the future. This means that the university will have to follow the needs of its students and quickly react to changes occurring externally, not only in its closest environment. Research in fields recognized as relevant to the new economy will be carried out mostly by the research teams of huge multinational corporations or by multi-person teams selected especially to deal with one particular research issue, which will be working outside university rather than at the university. Silicon Valley provides us with the most convincing example. Corporate universities and universities established on the 'for profit' basis, whose only aim is professional education, provide an additional impulse that accelerates the transformation process in the academic world. Managing knowledge available at the university becomes a key to success in the changing education market.

There exists one more essential agent of change which, in my opinion, is often overlooked by organizers and reformers of education systems, namely a change in the relationship between the lecturer and the student. For quite a long time this relationship was rather one-way (except for genius students): the master (professor, lecturer, instructor) presented knowledge taught. Now, often there is more interaction, co-operation: the student, by posing questions and problems, forces the lecturer to process knowledge and present new solutions. This is most apparent in disciplines that develop the fastest e.g., in computer science where the process f change is so rapid that more and more often the skills of the student match those of the teacher and the younger mind absorbs, and processes new solutions faster. The future university will have to achieve apparently mutually unattainable results: on the one hand, it will have to provide effective mass education, on the other, through an active partnership between the lecturer and the individual student, to ensure synergy of intellectual capital of both subjects of this partnership.

LOCAL INITIATIVES, NATIONAL ASPIRATIONS AND AMERICAN FACILITATION

What differentiates the Nowy Sącz School from other traditional institutions of higher education is a clear student-centered approach. This approach is so distinctive that it is at times contested by new lecturers coming to teach at WSB-NLU who so far have operated only at traditional universities. A great problem of educational systems is caused by the fact that the image of alumni and their needs is created from the single perspective of those who teach, but not by the job market (by a businessman or a manager of an institution which hires a new employee). Therefore, it is no wonder that so many graduates complain about the unsuitability of curricula to their particular needs or even about teaching them redundant, useless knowledge.

Figure 4

In case of the Nowy Sącz school, its fundamental curricular issues came from recipients of future graduates, namely, business people. Parallel to organizing WSB-NLU, I created or was actively engaged in establishing organizations that associate business people and managers such as Business Centre Club, National Chamber of Commerce or a regional Nowy Sącz-Podhale Chamber of Commerce. It was my partners from business circles who influenced my views on the curriculum and sometimes they even initiated new programs (e.g., in financial management or computer science). At the beginning of the 1990s, the needs of newly-established or restructured firms were clear-cut: new ideas, openness to change, being active and entrepreneurial and, finally, fluency in one foreign language and high computer literacy. It did not seem much but, from the perspective of graduates of the majority of universities, it was too much. Our curriculum was strengthened by an extensive group of the so-called general studies, required by our American partners. The convergence of the two approaches Polish organizers' leaning towards both the student and the expectations of the recipients of our work (i.e., business people), and managers with the American pragmatic approach and the comprehensive curriculum that offered broad but superficial knowledge produced unexpected results. WSB-NLU alumni became immediately and positively accepted and recognized on the job market in Poland.

Since its beginnings, i.e. since 1992, WSB-NLU has been deeply immersed in American academic reality, which naturally gave this small local school a global character. Our partners from NLU brought to Nowy Sącz not only their business curriculum and active teaching methods, but also their excellent English language curriculum. They also set up a criterion of a good knowledge of English required for admission. In addition, during three years of study, our students received initially over 1,000 hours of language instruction. The effect was dramatic: in the mid 1990s, our graduates had a much better knowledge of English than their competitors. The Americans also brought to WSB-NLU their organizational culture – respect for students, obligatory evaluation of all professors and instructors by their students, and methods of internal communication. After a few years, my local co-workers started to feel like aliens in their own country, we were annoyed with tardiness, lack of immediate response to our letters, and with breaking promises (even spoken ones). During the first, most critical period i.e., in the academic year 1992/93, we were joined by three lecturers from NLU. It was thanks to their persistence and accurate observance of principles set in writing (which was at that time perceived as too rigid by us) that the university became a smoothly running organization oriented to the satisfaction of the student – our client and partner.

In the years 1994–96, a group of professors from CSB-CSU, Fresno, joined NLU professors in Nowy Sącz. Thanks to the USIA grant, as many as 27 full courses were taught by experienced business professors of a renowned Californian university. They set up a high standard of lectures taught in an interactive way with strong emphasis on examples from real business practice. Alumni who studied at that time still remember the lectures of professor T. Wielicki, G. Bryan and Manab Thakur.

For us, the founders and organizers of the School, it was obvious from the very beginning that our success depended mainly on the success of our alumni. Therefore, we strove to inspire our students with openness to the world: we invited to the School politicians, diplomats, managers and entrepreneurs. We also created conditions that enabled the most active students to show their talents. Soon, the richness and variety of student life became a feature of the School. Now students act not only in the Students' Council, local AEISEC Chapter or in various student societies and clubs; they also organize large student conferences, lasting a few days and attended by several hundred people. They are so successful that students from other universities come to these conferences with the single purpose of checking what we do and learn from us. The strong curriculum and active students have brought recognition and success: our students' teams have won several times an international business competition via the internet called MarketPlace, and they have been three-time winners of a national business competition, 'Entrepreneurship', organized by the Entrepreneurial Education Foundation. Students' good morale, the positive attitude of the faculty and administration towards students, and the ease of finding attractive jobs at prestigious companies quickly resulted in high admissions to the School.

Since 1997, WSB-NLU has become a countrywide school, taking into account students' permanent residence. As a rule, private colleges and schools draw their student body from their local area. WSB-NLU is the only Polish college that is an exception to this rule.[1] In the past three years, students coming from beyond Małopolska voivodship have constituted the majority of the WSB-NLU student body (70%) with only 12–20 % of local students.

We have put into use all the mechanisms that enhance students' individual activity and their engagement in studying and acquiring new skills. We send lists of our top graduates to 200 presidents of the biggest and most prestigious firms (the so-called ' Top 50 List'), the best students get scholarships abroad (e.g., to DePaul University in Chicago, thanks to grants from the Kościuszko Foundation), we also offer merit-related grants. We are not complacent about the results achieved, but constantly seek new forms of enhancing and bringing to light in young people qualities that are the most valuable: their creativity, courage in thinking and acting, and entrepreneurial spirit. We strive to add one more new dimension: namely, character-building.

The Nowy Sącz School is an institution that can be considered an organization characterized by constant change. Change and progress have become a permanent feature of our operations. We started with elementary things such as providing a good, efficiently implemented curriculum, and we have created close relationships with business, which has facilitated job-seeking for our graduates. Now, we aim to strengthen the academic dimension of the School in order to develop the

---

[1] See the results of a study carried out by Prof. J. Dietl and presented at the conference 'Experience of and perspectives for non-state universities – the quality of teaching.' Conference proceedings, pp. 27–61 'Business studies at non-state universities from the perspective of empirical research.'

scholarly talents of students and faculty. Therefore, we have increased the number of programs offered at WSB-NLU to enable all talented and ambitious people (even those who do not dream of a career in business) to find their place at WSB-NLU.

Figur 5

The long-term success of the School depends on our continual efforts to build strong and lasting relationships between:

♦ our clients (the students)

♦ the founders and employees of the School (the faculty and its leaders) and

♦ the recipient of our efforts (the job market).

We need a new formula, one adjusted to both the challenges of the new global reality of constant change and to the need to educate individuals whose main resource will be their intellectual capital.

I am convinced that the main mechanism of this new formula should be the partnership occurring in the above student-school-recipient triangle and this partnership needs to be active, the one to which all parties contribute their best resources. Close relations with selected big companies, especially those of bi- or multi- lateral nature, constitute an element of this partnership. Our co-operation with Optimus S.A. sets an example here. On the one hand, WSB-NLU provides an exclusive MBA program for top managers of the firm, on the other, Optimus acts as the Programming Board for the new program in Computer Science and offers internship opportunities and, later, jobs for its graduates. We still need to implement an essential element of full partnership, namely, to provide consulting services to firms and conduct contractual research on demand, as well as employ practitioners: entrepreneurs and managers as professors. We have already taken initial steps: all our assistant lecturers hold internships at the best companies, which familiarizes them with operating in a business reality, and a substantial group of assistant lecturers have substantial experience of working for big companies.

THE INFLUENCE OF THE SCHOOL ON THE LOCAL COMMUNITY

Until the beginnings of the 1990s, one of the tenets of the Polish education system was the belief that an institution of higher education could only function in a city, at best in a metropolis. And truly, the only universities highly respected by the public and considered the best were located in Warsaw, Cracow or Poznan, and universities operating in Rzeszów, Kielce or Zielona Góra were often referred to as 'provincial' with its negative connotations of inferiority. The

Nowy Sącz School became an exception to this rule: it was the first university established in a small town of less than 100,000 inhabitants; moreover, the town is located on the peripheries of the country and far away from the metropolis. As an additional surprise to the public came the fact that the school's founders clearly intended to establish an elite school.

Figure 6

It was obvious to us that the institution built with the participation of foreigners would change both the mind-set and the local culture of Nowy Sącz. For decades, Nowy Sącz was a regional administrative center, a set-off point and supply base for a tourist industry supported, thanks to urban planners, by a few big companies providing a substantial (by local standards) number of jobs for manual workers. The transformation of the economic system that took place at the turn of the

1990s resulted in a substantial reduction of jobs in big companies and, although only two big firms went bankrupt, the unemployment rate quickly reached 15%, despite the fact that a few big private, nationally recognized companies were set up by Nowy Sącz residents. Additionally, the voivodship of Nowy Sącz ceased to exist and local politicians realized that the town's development could not be based on tourism. A new plan of the development of the town was badly needed.

At a time when intellectual capital is becoming more and more important and information technologies (Internet) radically change the notion of distance and allow the creation of virtual enterprises, almost devoid of classical permanent location, WSB-NLU has become a natural center for local development, a development well correlated with global developmental trends:

➢ The School has become a big employer (on a local scale). At present, there are over 200 people directly employed at WSB-NLU and its related institutions. Moreover, the School has become a major source of income for another few hundred residents of Nowy Sącz. Over 1,700 students who come from out of town had to find accommodation and entertainment in Nowy Sącz. There are private dormitories being built for WSB-NLU students. However, a direct influence of the School on the residents' welfare is strongly correlated with its size. We plan to stabilize the number of full-time students (who mainly create opportunities for residents to earn additional money) at 2,000, which will limit such opportunities.

➢ An increase in the level of education among Nowy Sącz residents will be another important factor, though not fully apparent yet, determining the long-term development of the town. WSB-NLU part-time programs attract mainly inhabitants of Nowy Sącz and neighboring towns and villages. The majority of these people are young, working (over 90%), strongly connected with Nowy Sącz by family ties and home/flat ownership. Over the next several years, 200–300 people will be graduating from WSB-NLU part-time programs each year. Most of them will stay in Nowy Sącz. In ten years' time, a group of several thousand people will appear in the town not only armed with a degree and new skills, but also inspired intellectually and convinced of their own new capabilities. These dynamic individuals will influence the economic reality of the town that has now a total of 33,700 jobs and where, until recently, the number of people with a degree reached 10,000. On the one hand, there should be an increase in quality and efficiency of actions on behalf of existing small companies, operating with employees who are aware of their own capabilities and understand the importance of intellectual capital; on the other, some graduates will set up new firms and seek their fortune as individual entrepreneurs.

➢ More and more scientists dealing with issues of regional development are convinced that development will occur through regional or local innovation centers and that the so-called sustained development methods are ineffective and bring few results. One of the essential features of an innovation center is an institution of higher education that influences and co-operates with its environment in a creative and entrepreneurial way. Establishing an innovation center is a long-term and costly venture that requires the active involvement of local and regional authorities. However, for a town with no other perspectives, the only chance is development through building an economy based on knowledge generated and inspired by a local university/business school whose faculty constitute also a group of founders, managers and consultants for local businesses.

Figure 7

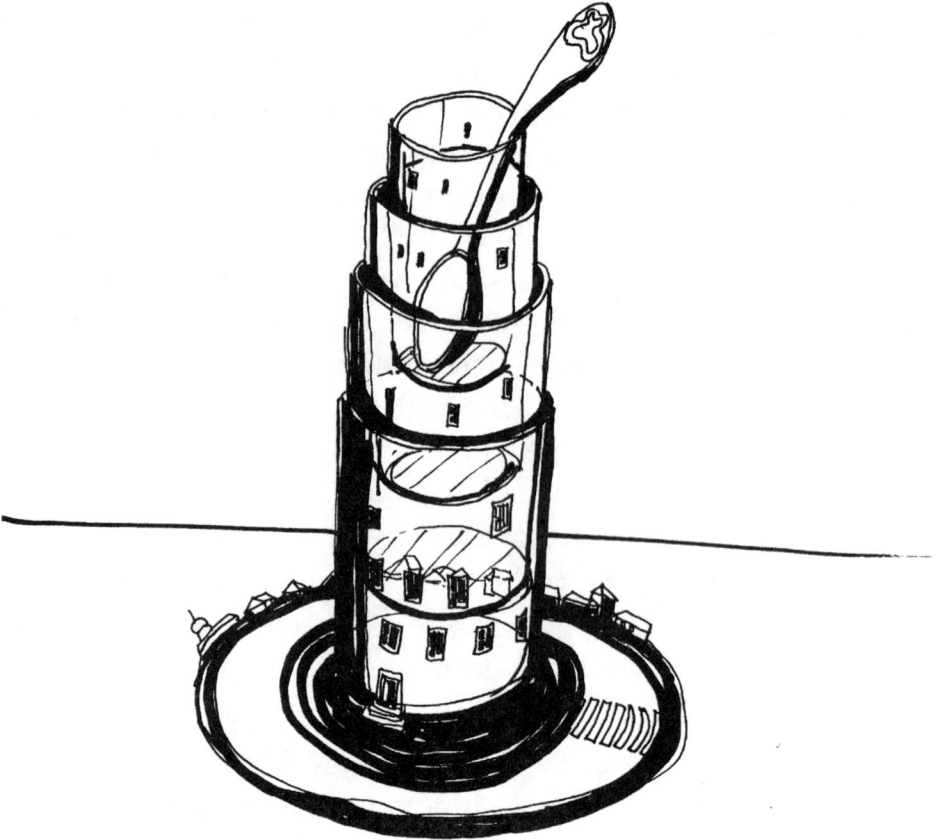

➤ It is obvious to the founders of WSB-NLU that the School cannot become yet one more ivory tower of knowledge. It must become an institution whose mission is to produce intellectual capital and external entrepreneurial activities which propagate the active growth and dissemination of knowledge.

Charles R. B. Stowe

FOUNDAINS FOR INTELLECTUAL CAPITAL – CHALLENGES AND OPPORTUNITIES FOR INSTITUTIONS OF HIGHER EDUCATION

Abstract

The concept of intellectual capital is applied to institutions of higher learning. A theoretical analysis is followed by sampling of new strategies taken from a two year survey of news reports on universities and colleges. Both a theoretical and applied analysis of the ways some institutions are responding to new external and internal pressures imposed by information society is presented. While there are considerable differences in the history of American and European institutions of higher learning, the concept of intellectual capital and the practical application of this concept to the management, organization and teaching strategies of colleges and universities have profound implications for all institutions of higher education throughout the world. Further investigation of the concept of intellectual capital for the entire educational system is advocated.

INTRODUCTION

The concept of intellectual capital is receiving increased prominence in academic and business literature. This concept that the value of organizations in contemporary "information" economy is less measured by bricks and mortar of tangible assets but in the intangibles. Intellectual capital relates to the ability of the organization to "add value" to product or services in a manner that offers extraordinary growth or high profits which may well be more than a firm's intellectual property. This paper explores this relatively new management concept and the implications it holds for higher education. While there are considerable differences in the history of American and European institutions of higher learning, the concept of intellectual capital has profound implications for institutions of higher education on both continents. This chapter provides selected examples of how some institutions are responding to the challenges of the information era. The role of education from early childhood through continuing postgraduate programs in the context of creating intellectual capital deserves a more thorough investigation.

CONFLICTING TRENDS IN HIGHER EDUCATION

In one sense, American institutions of higher education have never been in a better financial position to offer first class education. University endowments – until very recently – were at record levels due to the new highs on the stock market. And, philanthropic giving is also at a new high. On the other hand, costs have risen resulting in a decade of increasing salaries and administrative overhead running an institution. Tuition increases continue to exceed the rate of inflation. But, the picture is uneven. Universities, which receive funding from State governments, are finding that other social needs have resulted in static budgets. State governments must fund prisons, highways, welfare agencies, etc.

While education is very expensive at most private universities, the universities are competing for students and are aggressively offering scholarship to lure new students. Higher education has become like McDonald's hamburgers: fast, quick and convenient – but bland and not very filling. American education has been described as providing excellent access but poor quality control in outcomes. This may be in part because students are now empowered by an entitlement attitude toward education: "I have registered for your course, I am the customer, now you deliver the product!" Students rebel at long reading assignments and institutions that have faculty evaluation systems that really impact faculty pay, find that the range of faculty scores are remarkably within a very narrow range. Obviously many faculty members have learned to cope with the new reality.

The introduction of web based courses has led to active debates over who owns the intellectual property of the "electronic course" or casebook; what constitutes a "quality" courses; and what role is the professor to play – a computer administrator or a mentor. Some administrators gleefully look to technology as lowering the costs of education, but are surprised to find out that really well done courses require up to a million dollars to prepare and that professors have more demands on them when teaching through the web. In a normal lecture class of over 100 students rarely do students interrupt to ask questions. However, many students find it very convenient the write an email to a professor. They have grown up writing to "chat rooms" and feel no hesitancy to participate electronically when they would otherwise sit passively in a class. For the professor, reading through "chat room" discussions can be more time consuming than reading through one set of term papers! Technology has promoted several of these conflicting trends: many students have the expectation of elaborate (and expensive) multi-media, interactive www based courses while at the same time refusing to do the background reading. They do not want to actively participate in class, but fill pages in course chat rooms, and they want "relevant" education but in the shortest and most convenient time possible without interfering with part time employment, social life and other non-university related activities.

The reality in Central Europe reflects new realities of transition from command to market economies and from authoritarian political structure to democratic forms. State university budgets have not kept up with increases in cost of living, resulting in faculties having to teach and pursue other employment to survive. In the field of business, having a faculty that is actively consulting and interacting in business actually contributes to the quality and relevancy of information. However, classes are often huge and economic incentives are not encouraging enough students to pursue an academic career. This could result in serious shortages of faculty. The demand for education is exceeding supply, but the governments are also facing tremendous needs in maintaining a social safety net for the older populations not able to fully participate in the benefits of the new economy. In many countries, private institutions are being formed to fill the gap. Fortunately, organizations like CEEMAN and EQUIS are in place to encourage quality programs through accreditation procedures.

The reality in Western Europe is that the once 'elitist' view that only those who test at the highest levels at high school should move on to higher education is being revisited. There is some recognition that having more of the population gain access to higher education may be beneficial to society. France and Germany still have their vocational or professional schools, but a greater percentage of students are being offered some type of college experience than before.

Throughout Latin America new institutions have been formed over the past twenty years – both public and private. In the Middle East, the tradition was that the elites would send their children to Europe or to the United States for higher education. However, during the past decade millions of dollars have been spent on building the higher education infrastructure. Asia is still exporting students, but even their institutions of higher education have been expanding and new ones have been built during the past ten years. The situation in Africa is mixed due to some countries suffering from constant civil war. In those countries that are not in bitter conflicts, there is evidence to suggest that slightly larger percentages of the population are getting access to higher education. In conclusion, societies around the world have recognized that there is a societal value to higher education. There is recognition that building a country's intellectual capital base is a sound investment. While this paper explores the American and European models of higher education, the lessons may be of some value globally.

DEFINING INTELLECTUAL CAPITAL

The concept of intellectual capital is more than a topic to be covered in a management course. If there is any validity to the concept of intellectual capital as being the framework for creating wealth in the new information economy, then its underlying approaches deserve consideration by those in academia. Edvinsson, former Director of Skandia Financial Services proposes an analogy of a tree whereby current accounting conventions and financial statements only measure the fruit whereas the truer strength of a firm lies in analyzing its root system (Edvinsson, 1997). If the root system is the structure that ultimately feeds and nourishes the tree's ability to produce fruit (profit), then we should look at the role of business or management education as part of that invisible system that creates future wealth. If we apply this analogy to society, then educational institutions are the greenhouses to cultivate plants that will eventually go into society. As in plants, some will not bear fruit but others will create new innovation, wealth and hopefully, human progress.

My basic hypothesis is that the structure, design, curriculum and culture of institutions of higher education should address the challenge of creating intellectual capitalists.

INTELLECTUAL CAPITALISTS – A DEFINITION

The application of the concept of intellectual capital to management suggests that those who lead organizations must be capable and imaginative enough to maximize an entity's intellectual capital. This requires an innovative approach to management not currently widely understood. Intellectual capital is a relatively newly coined concept. Like gravity, however, it has existed even prior to its formal discovery.

The term intellectual capitalist refers to management personnel, scholars and educators capable of creating systems, policies and environments highly conducive to creating or maximizing intellectual capital. To limit the responsibility of creating intellectual capital to management majors or to MBAs, however, misses the essence of the concept of intellectual capital. Intellectual capitalists should be developed from all disciplines. A firm that creates intellectual capital is one that has combined structural capital, human capital, and leaders with a supporting system of values and culture. To continue with the tree analogy, the root system includes all employees.

Looking at the American business curriculum, most American colleges still bear the title Business Administration. Such a title suggests that business is being busy and that the solution is to impose some administration – ordering. Edvinsson notes that the Swedish counterpart is *naringsliv*, which translates as "nourishment for life" (Edvinsson, 1997). But the issues of developing intellectual capitalists – future business leaders capable of creating an intellectually nurturing environment go much deeper than the names institutions bear. The issue is what are the attributes of an intellectual capitalist that a business education should seek to develop among its students? While this is only a preliminary discussion of this issue, I would suggest that the following attributes facilitate an individual's capacity to contribute to the development of intellectual capital:

❑ Highly developed ability to communicate.

❑ Critical thinking skills involving an understanding of different approaches to logic, reasoning and learning.

❑ Well rounded appreciation for technical expertise in each business discipline

❑ Imagination and ability to "think of out of the box".

❑ Humility and child-like curiosity and willingness to question.

❑ Ability to research solutions.

❑ Ability to both work in teams as a worker but also as a leader and sometimes concurrently.

❑ Comprehension and sensitivity toward the legal environment and strategies to protect intellectual capital.

In addition, future intellectual capitalists need to have an understanding of the concept of intellectual capital, the evolving and changing nature of work and the workplace (which suggests an appreciation for business or economic history), and an understanding of human motivations. Those who understand intellectual capital develop certain attributes which may include personal maturity, the ability to engage in constructive self-analysis to bring one's own self-perception clearer in line with how others perceive one, and an understanding that education takes many forms. True intellectual capitalists understand that their intellectual development does not end with graduation or attainment of formal degrees. Some intellectual capitalists may even aspire to create their own organizations in which they would become true "intellectual entrepreneurs." I am defining intellectual entrepreneurs not as intellectuals who start businesses, but entrepreneurs who build businesses based on the philosophy of developing an organization with intellectual capital.

Intellectual capitalists is a concept not limited to business leaders. Society needs individuals who comprehend that the information and creativity aspects of organizations now transcend the bricks and mortar or physical size of organizations. Society needs leaders of governmental agencies who can implement more efficient, responsive and compassionate services. Just as businesses are learning to alter mass production techniques to be able to customize products for individual buyers, governments need to harness intellectual capital to come up with new and more flexible approaches in dealing with societal challenges. For example, President Bush has announced new initiatives whereby government and non-profit charities would explore ways to combine their efforts in dealing with certain societal problems: education, drug abuse, etc.

The issue is whether institutions of higher education can contribute to a more vibrant, intellectually constructive and creative society.

TRADITION ROLE OF UNIVERSITIES

Under the traditional paradigm, universities are residential places of learning. Under this paradigm, the university experience was seen as a rite of passage. Students were essentially a captive audience. Under this traditional paradigm, all programs were designed to fulfill degree programs and the organization of academic disciplines reflected a certain mix of ingredients to achieve a specific degree. The outcome of the traditional paradigm is a degree. Continuing education was seen as an auxiliary program usually under the direction of a non-academic using whatever faculty resources were available. Little or no prestige was seen in participating in or supporting this function. Alumni relations meant keeping in touch with former graduates to build financial support for the institution.

Under the traditional paradigm, faculties are specialists in narrow academic disciplines pursuing academic recognition and prestige through research. Teaching became a necessary part of the "academic" regime as "on the job training" but certainly no coursework in pedagogy was ever offered or required of Ph.Ds (other than those earning an advanced degree in education). Tenure was necessary and probably still is to protect against intellectual arrogance and backstabbing internal politics as opposed to the more publicly cited reasons of "academic freedom".

The problem with the traditional paradigm is that for-profit institutions and angry legislators fed up with decreasing productivity of faculty are beginning to challenge many of the sacred academic traditions. State legislatures have begun to cap tenured positions; demand minimum teaching loads, and have capped funding with the admonition that even publicly funded institutions must develop other sources of support.

A NEW PARADIGM: FOUNTAINS OF INTELLECTUAL CAPITAL

Clearly a new paradigm is needed. The phrase "fountains of intellectual capital" is chosen deliberately. A fountain is often placed in the center of a garden, viewable from all angles and available to all regardless of the route they take. A fountain consists of recycled water, but it is constantly refreshed with new water. A fountain is not visited once, but repeatedly by those who seek its refreshment. The water of the university fountain is intellectual capital. Intellectual capital is not measurable by degrees or programs. Intellectual capital is the sum of knowledge plus creativity or imagination, plus critical learning skills, plus value structure. Seen from the perspective of the emerging knowledge-based economy, intellectual capital is the measure of the individual or society's ability to add value to products and services. The concept of adding value, however, should not be limited to an economic perspective but to a broader perspective to include compassion, integrity, trust and quality – all concepts needed to maintain a civil and democratic society.

This analogy constitutes a new paradigm for universities as they face the challenges of the new millenium. The application of the new paradigm has important implications for the management of universities. First, it forces a new approach toward faculty. In the traditional model, new faculty must earn tenure through adequate teaching and very specific research accomplishments. Tenured senior faculty are often viewed as "burned out" or as "dead wood" so that many universities are trying everything they can to give incentives for early retirement. If, however, we use the fountain paradigm, then we recognize that old and new water is totally indistinguishable and what is important is the mission. This suggests that faculty must be treated as a renewable resource.

While travel for research may be considered an investment in the intellectual nourishment of the faculty, this should be one small element of a new approach to manage intellectual capital. The analogy suggests many other approaches. First, mixing. Most institutions do not consider that intellectual capital gets enhanced through a mixing of ideas and personalities. They tenure administrators for long periods of service. Corporate entities do not, and for that reason respond much more quickly to changes in the external environments. Secondly, while universities talk about life long learning, they expect faculty to engage in life long learning through only one method: research. Corporate entities often send their best to learn from other institutions. Universities rarely encourage professors to take courses. In fact, some universities that offer lower tuition to the children of faculty do not offer any reduction for faculty wanting to take courses! And many universities charge faculty the same price as students for taking a course! Third, intellectual capital is acquired by going out of the routine to gain new experiences. However, traditional universities restrict or even discourage faculty leave of absences. Bringing challenging points of view often excite intellectual inquiry and creativity together. In yet, most traditional universities are unable or unwilling to design courses that permit more than one professor. And when team teaching is used, the worse element of it is brought to bear: one professor turns the class over to another rather than having two professors in the same classroom. While accounting systems and computers make such a task of accountability fairly easy, the traditional management of university is oriented to controlling the institution and not toward stimulating the development of intellectual capital beyond that of research.

Converting institutions of higher education to fountains of learning means that the university must more creativity sell core liberal arts curriculum as relevant, skill-building, intellectual capital building exercises. This is particularly true for the traditional 18–24 year old students. They need to know that history is relevant if we are not to recreate the mistakes of the past. Mathematics and logic are necessary so that they will be able to direct rather than be directed by technology. Literature and art reflect lessons of life that form the groundwork for healthy social and emotional development. Science helps build the mental capacity to cope with experimentation and analysis. American institutions of higher education are pressured to offer "relevant courses". But, intellectual capital for individuals entails a "core" liberal arts curriculum. What makes Bill Gates so phenomenal, even with the recent outcome of the anti-trust litigation, is not his code writing ability but his amazingly broad vision. This is true of other leaders. Truly great artists have the intellectual capacity to appreciate other aspects of life. The knowledge based information society requires specialists in computers and electronics with broad intellectual capacity and vision. Those who study genius suggest that intellectual curiosity is the underlying basis for creativity. Those who aspire to be future leaders in the public sector need to understand economics and business. The point here is that universities have a societal obligation to present a vision of education and intellectual capital that is more than the attainment of a degree.

At the same time, the realities of the modern economy with its large number of individuals who seek and need updating means that universities must break down the artificial wall between continuing education and regular courses. Treating 40 year-old "returning" students as children is not only bad public relations; it is damaging to the potential of creating a truly exciting intellectual experience for faculty and other students. Corporate trainers receive education on how to teach "adult" learners. Most college professors have never taken such a course. The university must break away from the mentality that a semester defines when a course must start and when it must stop. Really innovative universities will offer "topics" or smaller subsets of courses to fit personal and corporate needs, and charge accordingly. Some universities are offering travel with a faculty member serving as a traveling expert. This sort of activity not only benefits the alumni, but refreshes the faculty member as well.

A fountain of intellectual capital paradigm suggests that the university should serve as a creator and generator of intellectual capital. While the issues of academic freedom and intellectual inquiry are very central to the tradition of a university, most professional research organizations assemble teams to do research on a common project. While I am not suggesting involuntary assignment to a research team, some universities actively discourage joint or multiple authored research projects. Such policies are the antipathy to nurturing intellectual creativity and productivity. Individuals who have the imagination and leadership to inspire teams of faculty to combine efforts often lead those institutions that have achieved public recognition. A good example is Somona State University's College of Business. A new Dean looked at the College and saw a traditional departmentalized organization where individuals fought over a smaller and smaller amount of state funding. So, he convinced his colleagues to form an institute to focus their research on the wine industry. The result was the institution received serious funding from local vineyards and a front-page article in the Wall Street Journal recognized this previously un-noteworthy institution. While serendipity often leads to discovery, some leadership in bringing different faculty together for both applied and pure research may heighten the intellectual yield.

To become an institution that creates and nurtures intellectual capital, it may be necessary to involve the faculty in exploring not the issue of pedagogy but the real issue of how the brain actually works. Recent scientific exploration of this issue by those seeking to program computers with "artificial intelligence" has revealed that the mind really learns by making associations or pattern recognition using all senses. And medical research suggests that the basic structure of the brain is similar without regard to race, ethnicity or gender (though there are significant chemical variances by gender from different hormones affecting the brain). These discoveries have profound implications for the university. Instead of trying to teach to meet the "different ways" which students have developed to learn, perhaps we should incorporate some teaching on how to learn properly! Tony Buzan, author of some 84 books, articles and videos on that subject, suggests that studies have shown tremendous increase in intellectual retention, articulation, and analysis when that strategy is used as opposed to teaching in different styles that were developed by those ignorant of how the brain actually works. This would mean that either Ph.D programs need to be changed, or universities should sponsor special orientation programs for new faculty. The mere thought that a university would "invest" in the intellectual development of its faculty (other than by sponsoring independently proposed research) may seem radical, but it has ample precedence in the corporate and even in the military establishments. Obviously any institution that fosters such teamwork among academicians must change its incentive/reward system. Total quality management theories suggest that corporations that have changed their reward systems to funding bonuses based on institutional measures rather than on individual sales patterns foster greater teamwork and organizational efficiency.

Finally, the notion of a university serving as a nurturing agent of intellectual curiosity and excitement has radical implications for the design of the physical facility. Look at a French Café and what do you see? Tables of people conversing. Look in a typical American classroom and what do you see? Bored students nodding off to sleep. Should universities dare explore the efficacy of offering courses over meals? The same is true of university libraries. Look at what Borders Books has done to bookstores. By putting in café's and by inviting customers to take their reading materials into their café's, the modern bookstore has created a learning environment. Why not university libraries?

If all the senses are engaged in learning, why then are typical classrooms so incredibly dull. Why not paint up a simulated mural of a Paris café for use by classes taking French? Why not use artificial lighting and movable chairs to either diffuse or focus lightening depending on the style of the presentation? Why not pump background music into study halls (as some organizations do to promote concentration)?

The environmental design of today's university should be re-evaluated if our mission is to become a center for the nurturing and creation of intellectual capital. This goes beyond merely offering child-care for returning students. It means more comfortable seating, it means more convenient timing of courses, and it means scheduling "study" time with a subject matter expert/proctor as part of the course requirement. It means new approaches to teaching by giving students an experience rather than a passive exposure to subject matter.

More fundamentally, at some point, universities must reconsider their emphasis on making faculty produce "teaching portfolios" which at most institutions has become a major waste of time. This is particularly true for those institutions that have exposed their faculty to new research on the brain and intelligence, Perhaps faculty should be encouraged toward teaching strategies that engage students to "prove" their learning. One such strategy is to require a "student learning portfolio" of short assignments where the student proved their ability to define a problem, obtain data, and develop an analysis outside of the textbook. Too often our methods of evaluation (exams) focus too much on retention of memorized information and not enough on the skills related to intellectual capital.

EXAMPLES OFF INNOVATION IN EDUCATION

A review of the past two years of *Chronicle of Higher Education*, a periodical focusing on news and issues in higher education in the United States, provides some examples of specific strategies that some institutions have adopted in response to their competitive environments. Selected samples of some of the innovative programs, which are likely to foster the creation of intellectual capital, are presented below.

One the difficulties facing universities is obtaining technology to enhance their educational programs. Four universities – University of California at Berkeley's extension program, Pennsylvania State University's World Campus, the University of Washington, and the University of Wisconsin's Learning Innovations program – have formed an alliance to share information and make joint technology purchases (Young, *Chronicle of Higher Education*). Apparently these universities felt they could benefit from a sharing of ideas on new technology and that their joint purchasing power would provide some incentive to vendors to provide information more readily than if they dealt with each university on a one-to-one basis.

At the same time that universities are investing in 'distance education' technologies, the University of Maryland at College Park has built a dormitory designed to be an 'entrepreneurial incubator.' Twenty one student entrepreneurs will be given the chance to learn informally by doing all the things that entrepreneurs do – coming up with ideas for new businesses, working in teams, writing business plans, seeking venture capital, making presentations, and if they are successful, managing the growth of real businesses. The residential learning program not only attracted business and engineering majors but students majoring in architecture, classics, economics, journalism, and life sciences. They are all enrolled in the university's four-semester Entrepreneurship Citation Program. University officials report that there are more student applicants than the high-technology dorm's capacity and there is a long waiting list. The dorm offers special meeting rooms equipped with video transmission equipment. Maryland's program, Hinman Campus Entrepreneurship Opportunities was started with a $1.7 million gift from Brian Hinman a 1982 electrical engineering graduate of the university and now boasts 87 students (Olsen, *Chronicle of Higher Education*). Stimulating ideas by placing prospective student entrepreneurs into a dormitory equipped with lots of computer and communication equipment not only creates intellectual capital but also may result in the creation of financial capital as dreams are realized into companies.

American institutions are not the only ones interested in creating entrepreneurs. Oxford University has announced that Beeson Gregory Bank will pay for one third of a state-of-the-art chemistry building in return for a share of the profits from any spin-off companies in the next 15 years. The bank will receive half the university's share of any spin-offs. Oxford operates a technology transfer company called Issis Innovation that is involved with over 300 continuing projects and it files one patent per week (Birchard, *Chronicle of Higher Education*).

Related to the issue of sharing new research and stimulating academic discussion and additional is the problem of publishing faculty research. Traditional hardcopy publications require quite a bit of time from submission to review to publication. More than a thousand scholars have joined an economist from St. Andrews University, in Scotland, who is launching the Electronic Society for Social Scientists (ELSSS) to produce peer-reviewed journals at half the price of their commercial counterparts. Manfredi La Manna's publication will compete with Elsevier Science which is part of Reed Elsevier, a multinational publishing company and Springer-

Verlag, a subsidiary of Bertelsmann A. G., a German media conglomerate. ELSS will pay authors $500 and referees $200-$250 depending on the journal. The pricing for subscriptions of ELSS electronic publications will be quite a bit less than Elsevier. For example, a college in the US could subscribe to ELSS's *Review of Banking and Finance* for one year for $500 as compared with $1,066 for Elsevier's *Journal of Banking and Finance*. What is interesting about this initiative is that it arose in response to a program between the University of St. Andres and the Scottish Enterprise Fife, a government economic development agency (Payne, *Chronicle of Higher Education*). Here is a case of a grant competition designed to foster both intellectual capital and new ventures.

Many institutions are beginning to offer courses in e-commerce. What makes the graduate diploma course at the Central Institute of Technology, Wellington campus, interesting is that their e-commerce program is built on a foundation of seven courses, which must be completed within a certain period of time. Course controller Armadeep Sandhu is quoted as saying that because of the fluid nature of the subject, content will vary to keep up with current practice (Fraser, NZ Infotech Weekly). Such an admission reflects the challenge facing higher education in terms of breeding intellectual capitalists. The information must be fresh though the foundation of critical thinking, communication skills, logic, etc are timeless skills.

Attacking the problem of providing library services to students has resulted in some competing institutions joining forces. The Association of American Medical Colleges has voted to set up a virtual, electronic library of not only books, but videos of complex operations for medical students, undergraduates in premedical programs, students in other health-related fields, faculty members, practicing physicians. Currently, many universities have developed their own electronic libraries such as Wake Forest University where medical students are required to have laptop computers and much of the instruction is computer-based. Tufts University School of Medicine has a database for its own medical schools where 3,000 faculty members from area universities have access (Mangan, *Chronicle of Higher Education*). Competing organizations realize that the information era requires a leveraging of assets and a sharing of expenses. While traditionally, university libraries have shared resources on a limited basis, the electronic format now permits virtual and immediate sharing among a greater audience. Fostering access to information is critical for institutions to stimulate both effective learning and research on the threshold of knowledge.

Other medical sources have been organized. Researchers at the University of Illinois at Chicago Laboratory for Advanced Computing are working on an Internet protocol that will help scientists share data over super-fast research networks (Olsen, *Chronicle of Higher Education*). The laboratory is part of a Terabyte Challenge 2000 project, a high-speed data-transfer experiment that sends data across several open network connections simultaneously and lets scientists publish their data online. It is conceivable that such technology will permit extremely large data sets perhaps involving human genetics to be shared.

One of the problems with computer-based learning is the lack of human contact. Critics of medical education based on computers complain that bedside manners are not learned from computers (Mangan, *Chronicle of Higher Education*). Social isolation is not exactly the way to foster intellectual capital if human interaction helps to associate and assimilate new information. The University of Illinois requires distance education students to stay in a campus dorm for a two-week summer "boot camp" (Carnevale, *Chronicle of Higher Education*). Another approach to building human networks is to create a multiple-user object-oriented environment (MOO) for distance education students. Professors Cynthia Haynes and Jan Rune Holmevik at University of Texas at Dallas developed a program called enCore Express which is distributed free of charge online, provided that the users agree to share any improvements they make (http://lingua.utdallas.edu/encore). What is interesting is that this high technology solution was developed by professors to teach rhetoric, writing and arts and humanities courses (Young, *Chronicle of Higher Education*). Professor Joel English (no pun intended) used MOO to teach an advanced composition course whereby ten of his students logged on to the class from their homes while the rest sat in a classroom. Mr. English used a video camera to stream his lectures live over the MOO. Students at home typed in their questions or comments (Young, *Chronicle of Higher Education*).

For-profit publishers are active in pushing new joint ventures. The University of Cambridge, the University of Michigan, Regents College and Pearson Company have joined forces. Pearson is also a partner with American Online in an alliance that will add new Web sites packed with material for schools, college students, professors, and adults seeking professional and career education. Pearson, the London based media conglomerate and now the world's largest educational publisher (thanks to the acquisition of Simon and Schuster) has been sending its executives to meet with 13 of the 15 top ranked American business schools to line up partnerships with schools (Blumenstyk, *Chronicle of Higher Education*). And Pearson is not the only publisher seeking to bridge the world of published books and the Internet. Thomson International Publishers, Houghton Mifflin, Harcourt Publishers are all engaged in looking for ways to redesign or refashion the traditional textbook through the web.

Even the United States Army is investing in education partly to help in retaining soldiers, but also to produce a more 'thinking' force. The U.S. Army selected PricewatershouseCoopers, a consulting company, to lead a $453 million project to deliver distance education to soldiers all over the world. The consulting firm set up a team of 10 companies and 29 colleges to work together on the initial offering of courses which will be provided to over 15,000 students. Blackboard and Peoplesoft will provide the administrative system (Carr, *Chronicle of Higher Education*).

These are but a few of the types of innovations or experiments that universities and their partners are engaged in to maintain their competitive position. While only selecting a few of the articles on educational innovations, an analysis of two years of such articles reveals the following: (1) technology is becoming an integral part of learning even for the "classics," (2) the issue of developing opportunities for human interaction is viewed as critical for retention of students in distance learning programs, (3) there seems to be a concern over the relationship of creativity and the use of technology... the more prestigious institutions require some creative report or intellectual outcome from distance education programs, (4) technology is extremely labor intensive and the whole internet-web-based effort almost forces collaboration among competing institutions to amortize the costs, (5) technology is related to the issue of teaching values and morals as new distance education courses and web-assisted courses permit students to observe and interact in simulations that test and challenge their values. Clearly, the American universities reflect the American culture which is enamored with technology. It is not clear, however, that technology is the sole vehicle for inspiring intellectual capital. As previously discussed, there are policy and structural changes to our system of higher education that can foster creativity and intellectual growth.

CHALLENGES

There are clearly challenges that lie ahead for universities. First, the notion that we are the exclusive providers of education is being challenged by commercial organizations offering "education" and un-accredited programs. In the past, un-accredited degrees had little value. However, commercial organizations have found a way around our exclusive franchise by obtaining trademarks on educational attainments. One example is the notation Certified Financial Planner ™. Another is Microsoft Certification TM. Universities must think beyond our medieval traditions to develop alternatives to our degree programs. In addition, for-profit institutions like University of Phoenix have received regional accreditation to offer degrees. And, publishers are moving from traditional textbooks to partnering with institutions to deliver course content electronically.

Secondly, technology will not diminish the importance of human interaction in learning. Rather, technology may be used, as my examples of innovation show, to increase human interaction. The reality is that really quality web-based learning does not reduce labor, it increases it. What universities should resolve is the intellectual property rights issue over web-based courses. One potential resolution would be to treat web-based instruction as copyrighted property of the professor and institution much as a extbook and a publisher. This would give the creator of the web-based course a 15% royalty of an amount equal to the cost of an average textbook in the field. The other 85% would be held by the institution as reimbursement for their overhead in providing computer support. The total additional cost to the student would be a premium amounting to the cost of one textbook over the cost of taking a normal course. In actuality, this would be a reduction of the 30-40% premium that students are now paying to for-profit universities that offer web based courses. Such a policy would give professors an incentive to make their course so good that others would use it – similar to the competition to writing a good textbook.

Third, clearly universities need to do a better job of articulating this new paradigm and mission. This would really change universities from merely serving students to being "shopping mall" of intellectual excitement and personal fulfillment. As a fountain of intellectual capital, people would seek continuous involvement with the university. It may be that for a fee, professors would design specific courses for organizations that wanted their members to have particular skills, or knowledge. This should not imply a sell-out to commercial interests, but a better integration with the society that is funding the institution. Some universities offer "adult" courses or continuing education, but it is too often organized and coordinated as an auxiliary venture rather than as a component of the organization.

The notion of continuous learning means that the entire relationship between alumni and the university should not be directed by an autonomous organization called "Alumni Affairs" or "Development". Rather, it should be moved to the college where communication and individual networks would be created. One of the key foundations of the knowledge-based society is a personal network. In a world in which corporations no longer offer job security, one's true value is in having and utilizing networks. Universities that bring in alumni for a fun weekend every five years are missing the opportunities to help their alumni build networks. By utilizing the computer to track individuals as they progress through stages of life in career and personal aspects, universities can begin to offer truly age-appropriate programs. For example, those in their 30s and newly married, might well sign up and pay for a program on "Ten Great Thinkers Examine Elements of Child Rearing" featuring a psychologist, literature professor, sociologist and child development professor. Maintaining communication by college means that the college might well refresh its own intellectual capital by inviting alumni to come to talk with faculty on major developments outside the university. Unfortunately, at most universities such exchanges do not occur because only the development office tracks alumni.

This paper only traces a few of the major ramifications of adopting a new paradigm for universities. As more individuals attend universities, the institution may well be one of the few commonly held experiences in the diverse American culture. As opposed to being a distant and irrelevant critic of society, the university as a creator and generator of intellectual capital can make a more significant and enduring contribution to society by encouraging those virtues that have been the pillars of intellectual institutions: compassion, tolerance, intellectual curiosity, and integrity.

Finally, it is clear that the process of creating intellectual capitalists starts much earlier in life. Those who have expertise in childhood development should explore the intellectual capital paradigm. There are many questions to explore such as the definition of intellectual capital and how that might differ from training, and simple acquisition of knowledge. The concept of intellectual capital has the potential of profound implications for the entire educational system.

REFERENCES

Birchard, Karen "U. of Oxford Sells a Share in Its Future" *Chronicle of Higher Education*, December 15, 2000, p. A60.

Carr, Sarah "Army Picks Consulting Group to Run Distance-Education Effort" *Chronicle of Higher Education*, January 5, 2001, p. A46.

Carnevale, Dan "Social Bonds Found to Be Crucial in Online Education" *Chronicle of Higher Education*, Vol. XLVII, Number 9, October 27, 2000, p. A48.

Fruin, Mark *Knowledge Works: Managing Intellectual Capital at Toshiba*, Oxford University Press, 1997.

Kwiatkowski, Stefan and Edvinsson, Leif, editors, *Knowledge Café for Intellectual Entrepreneurship,* Warsaw: Leon Kozminski Academy of Entrepreneurship and Management, 1999.

Mangan, Kataherine S. "Medical-School Group Proposes Huge online Library for Students" *Chronicle of Higher Education*, November 17, 2000, p. A 65.

Olsen, Florence "Electronic Dorm Gives Maryland Students an Entrepreneurial Environment" *Chronicle of Higher Education*, Volume VLVII, Number 18, January 12, 2001, p. A32.

Olsen, Florence "New Protocol Helps Researchers Share Large Sets of Data" *Chronicle of Higher Education*, Volume VLVII, Number 4, September 22, 2000, p. A45.

Payne, Doug "A Revolutionary Idea in Publishing" *Chronicle of Higher Education*, March 9, 2001.

Stewart, Thomas A. *Intellectual Capital – Realizing Your Company's True Value by Finding its Hidden Brainpower*, New York: HarperCollins Publishers, 1997.

Stewart, Thomas A. "Brainpower – How Intellectual Capital Is Becoming America's Most Valuable Asset" *Fortune*, June 3, 1991.

Young, Jeffrey R. "Four Universities Create Alliance to Deal with Technology Vendors" *Chronicle of Higher Education*, February 9, 2001, p. A 34.

Young, Jeffrey R. "MOOs, the Old Chatrooms are Updated for Distance Education" *Chronicle of Higher Education*, Vol. XLVII, Number 11, November 10,. 2000, p. A47.

CONTRIBUTORS

ANDRZEJ BLIKLE (ajb@medianet.com.pl), professor in mathematics and computer science at the Polish Academy of Sciences and President of the Board of Directors of A. Blikle Ltd. He is a member of several organisations, eg. Academia Europaea, Polish Information Processing Society (honorary member and past president), Polish Federation of Food Industry (vice president), Warsaw Rotary Club (past president), Mazovian Quality Award Committee (vice president). As a scientist he used to teach at several universities, such as Warsaw University, The University of California at Berkely, Danish Technical University at Lűngby, The University of Copenhagen, Linkőping University (Sweden), Waterloo University (Canada) and others.

BOHDAN BUDZAN (imi@mim.kiev.ua) Ph.D., since January 1997 serves as Director General of the International Management Institute (IMI-Kyiv), where he is also a senior lecturer in management. He is consultant for top management of companies operating in Ukraine. He is also advisor to the Government of Ukraine, and a member of several boards of business and academic institutions. Dr. Budzan completed the International Senior Manager's Program at Harvard University and Certificate Course of Management at London Business School. From April 1993 to December 1996, Dr. Budzan was Executive Director of the International Renaissance Foundation (the Soros Foundation in Ukraine).

DOROTA DOBIJA (dobija@poczta.wspiz.edu.pl) is assistant professor at Leon Koźmiński Academy of Entrepreneuship and Management, Accounting Department. She graduated form Cracow University of Economics where she also obtained her Ph.D. degree. Her doctoral dissertation was entitled "Income statement model under condition of market efficiency". At present she is also Director of International Programs at LKAEM. Her research interest focus on measurement of intangibles and their reporting to stakeholders of an organisation.

MIECZYSŁAW DOBIJA (accountd@ae.krakow.pl) is professor of Accounting and Accounting Theory. He is the Chair of the Accounting Department at Leon Koźmiński Academy of Entrepreneuship and Management and similar department at Cracow University of Economics. His research interest is in general accounting theory, management accounting and human resources costing and accounting. Currently his research is focused on theory of money from the accounting point of view.

AMIR FAZLAGIĆ (fazlagic@novcil.ae.poznan.pl) is the assistant in The Chair of Services at The Poznan University of Economics, Poznan, Poland. He is the author of a number of articles on Knowledge Management, Education and Relationship Marketing.
Other research topics include: the knowledge worker productivity, marketing in tourism.
He has been engaged in extensive research on measuring intellectual capital and knowledge rich products since 1995. His doctorial dissertaion is to be completed in Summer of 2001.

RENATA GUT (rgut@cn.sita.pl) entrepreneur, founder and manager of all-Poland chain of the SITA Learning Centres. NLP Master Practitioner. Since six years trainer in practical applications of brain structure and functioning, stress-relaxation, and techniques of effective personal development in business and education. The hero of "A train named Adventure for Thought" case.

ANDRÉ HELIN (ahelin@bdo.pl), President of BDO Polska, is both Danish State Authorized Public Accountant and a certified auditor in Poland. He graduated from the Graduate School of Commerce in Copenhagen, and holds M.Sc. degree in audit and business administration.

He is the author of two popular handbooks, "Techniques and Methods for the Auditing of Financial Statements" and "Consolidation of Financial Statements: Methods and Techniques", setting standards in the field of accounting and auditing in Poland.

BDO Polska, International Auditors and Consultants, headed by Andre Helin, is ranked six in the industry in Poland.

JAN KOZŁOWSKI (jkozlow@kbn.gov.pl) former researcher at the Institute for the History of Science of the Polish Academy of Sciences, is currently employed at the State Committee for Scientific Research, and at Warsaw University, Center for Science Policy and Higher Education Studies. A member of the Science Studies Committee of the Polish Academy of Sciences. In 1994–1995 performed the function of the National Coordinator of OECD Review of National Science and Technology Policy in Poland. Authored 4 books, and over 40 research articles on history of science, science policy, scientometrics and S&T statistics.

STEFAN KWIATKOWSKI (kwiat@wspiz.edu.pl),
UNESCO/EOLSS Chair in Intellectual Entrepreneurship, Professor of Entrepreneueship at Leon Koźmiński Academy of Entrepreneurship and Management, Professor of Management at Warsaw University, Member of International Academy of Management and of European Academy of Management. Past President of Polish Association of Management Development 'forum'. Past Chairman of Polish Association of

Scientific Management. Consultant of United Nations Organization, UNESCO, UNIDO and other intergovernmental and non-governmental organizations.

ALOJZY Z. NOWAK (anowak@mail.wz.uw.edu.pl), Associate Dean, Professor of Economics, Chair of Department of International Economic Relations, School of Management, Warsaw University; Professor of Finance and Chair of Department of Finance, Leon Koźmiński Academy of Entrepreneurship and Management. Professor and Director of the Centre for European Studies, Warsaw University. Visiting professor at the University of Illinois, University of North Florida, Free University of Berlin. Member of Editorial Board: "Journal of Interdisciplinary Economics", London; Encyclopedia of the Developing World, Chicago; Journal of Economic Research, Greece; Studia Europejskie, Warsaw University.

KRZYSZTOF PAWŁOWSKI (kpawlows@wsb-nlu.edu.pl), Ph.D. in physics, and honorary doctorate from National-Louis University. A Senator of the Republic of Poland from 1989 to 1993, founder and president of Wyższa Szkoła Biznesu – National-Louis University in Nowy Sącz, and of Wyższa Szkoła Biznesu in Tarnów. He has been the president of the Nowy Sącz-Podhale Chamber of Commerce and co-founder of the Business Center Club in Warsaw. Past Chairman of the Conference of Presidents of Non-state universities, member of the National Council of European Integration.

IRINA SENNIKOVA (irina@riceba.lv), vice-rector in charge of international relations of Riga International College of Economics and Business Administration (RICEBA). In 1987 she graduated from the University of Latvia, the faculty of foreign languages. For many years she was teaching English as a foreign language, specialising in Business English.

Then, later in her career she changed the focus into the business area and in 1999 obtained MBA degree at the International Executive Development Centre (IEDC, Bled School of Management).

CHARLES R. B. STOWE (fin_crs@shsu.edu) born Seattle, Washington, raised in Connecticut, earned a BA from Vanderbilt University, in Nashville, Tennessee, an MBA from University of Dallas, a Doctorate of Jurisprudence from University of Houston Law Center, and was the first American to earn Ph.D. from Warsaw University Faculty of Management. He is a retired captain in the United States Naval Reserve. In 1994 he served as U.S. Military Liaison Team Chief in the Ministry of Defense, Republic of Poland. He authored *The Implications of Foreign Financial Institutions on Poland's Entrepreneurial Economy* published by Edwin Mellen Press, contributed chapters to *Knowledge Café – Intellectual Entrepreneurship* and has published several journal articles on jurisprudence and entrepreneurship. He is currently a Professor, College of Business Administration, Sam Houston State University and holds a joint appointment as Professor of Entrepreneurship at the Leon Koźmiński Academy of Entrepreneurship and Management.

MARIUSZ STROJNY (mstrojny@kpmg.pl) – Chief Knowledge Officer Coordinator responsible for knowledge management implementation at *KPMG Polska,* including deployment of KWorld – the firm's global messaging, knowledge sharing and collaboration platform. Co-founder of Knowledge Management Institute, based in Kraków and devoted to research, and promotion of knowledge management and knowledge economy among Polish business community. Author of numerous articles on knowledge and intellectual capital management.

MARTYNA ŚLIWA (martynasliwa@hotmail.com) is teaching and research assistant at Cracow University of Economics. She graduated from Cracow University of Economics and Northumbria University, UK. In her research she focuses on theory of accounting and theory of control.

LECH W. ZACHER (lzacher@wspiz.edu.pl), economist and sociologist, is the Head of Department of Social Sciences at Leon Koźmiński Academy of Entrepreneurship and Management in Warsaw. He also heads the Center for Study of Information Societies at the Department of Radio and TV of the University of Silesia in Katowice, and is advisor to the Chairman of the Government Center for Strategic Studies. He is the founder and president of the Educational Foundation TRANSFORMATIONS, and the editor-in-chief of its interdisciplinary journal TRANSFORMATIONS.